THE COMPLETE **IDIOT'S** GUIDE® TO

Dreamweaver® CS5.5

by Cheryl Brumbaugh-Duncan

ALPHA

A member of Penguin Group (USA) Inc.

To David and Tasmin.

ALPHA BOOKS

Published by the Penguin Group

Penguin Group (USA) Inc., 375 Hudson Street, New York, New York 10014, USA

Penguin Group (Canada), 90 Eglinton Avenue East, Suite 700, Toronto, Ontario M4P 2Y3, Canada (a division of Pearson Penguin Canada Inc.)

Penguin Books Ltd., 80 Strand, London WC2R 0RL, England

Penguin Ireland, 25 St. Stephen's Green, Dublin 2, Ireland (a division of Penguin Books Ltd.)

Penguin Group (Australia), 250 Camberwell Road, Camberwell, Victoria 3124, Australia (a division of Pearson Australia Group Pty. Ltd.)

Penguin Books India Pvt. Ltd., 11 Community Centre, Panchsheel Park, New Delhi—110 017, India

Penguin Group (NZ), 67 Apollo Drive, Rosedale, North Shore, Auckland 1311, New Zealand (a division of Pearson New Zealand Ltd.)

Penguin Books (South Africa) (Pty.) Ltd., 24 Sturdee Avenue, Rosebank, Johannesburg 2196, South Africa

Penguin Books Ltd., Registered Offices: 80 Strand, London WC2R 0RL, England

Copyright © 2011 by Cheryl Brumbaugh-Duncan

THE COMPLETE IDIOT'S GUIDE TO and Design are registered trademarks of Penguin Group (USA) Inc.

International Standard Book Number: 978-1-61564-1-284
Library of Congress Catalog Card Number: 2011908145

13 12 11   8 7 6 5 4 3 2 1

Interpretation of the printing code: The rightmost number of the first series of numbers is the year of the book's printing; the rightmost number of the second series of numbers is the number of the book's printing. For example, a printing code of 11-1 shows that the first printing occurred in 2011.

Printed in the United States of America

Most Alpha books are available at special quantity discounts for bulk purchases for sales promotions, premiums, fund-raising, or educational use. Special books, or book excerpts, can also be created to fit specific needs.

For details, write: Special Markets, Alpha Books, 375 Hudson Street, New York, NY 10014.

Publisher: *Marie Butler-Knight*
Associate Publisher/Acquiring Editor: *Mike Sanders*
Executive Managing Editor: *Billy Fields*
Development Editor: *Jennifer Moore*
Senior Production Editor: *Janette Lynn*
Copy Editor: *Krista Hansing Editorial Services, Inc.*

Cover Designer: *Kurt Owens*
Book Designers: *William Thomas, Rebecca Batchelor*
Indexer: *Brad Herriman*
Layout: *Rebecca Batchelor, Brian Massey*
Proofreader: *John Etchison*

Contents

xii **The Complete Idiot's Guide to Dreamweaver CS5.5**

Appendixes

Introduction

This book is designed to help you learn how to quickly and efficiently build a website using Dreamweaver CS5.5. You'll be delighted by the ease with which you can use Dreamweaver CS5.5 to translate your creativity and ideas into a web page that you can share with the world.

I wrote this book to help you learn how to design and create a website using Dreamweaver. I start with the basics by explaining the Dreamweaver interface and tools, step you through the process of creating your very first web page, and move on to more advanced topics, such as using CSS to enhance the look of your site and integrating other web technologies, such as Spry widgets and extensions, to really ramp up your site.

DREAMWEAVER TIP

Dreamweaver CS5.5 is part of Adobe's Creative Suite 5.5 Web Premium, a package of software products that help you design, create, and communicate. In addition to Dreamweaver, the following software is bundled in the Creative Suite 5.5 Web Premium package:

- Photoshop Extended version
- Illustrator
- InDesign
- Flash Professional and Flash Catalyst
- Fireworks
- Acrobat X Pro
- Bridge
- Device Central

Mobile devices like iPhones and Androids are all the rage, and because of these new devices, mobile applications (or apps, for short) are more popular than ever. Dreamweaver CS5.5 has been revamped to include development tools for the smart phone revolution, and in this book I introduce you to this technology and what it means for web design.

How This Book Is Organized

This book is divided into four parts.

Part 1, Dreamweaver and Web Design, serves as a basic introduction to the World Wide Web, the Internet, and Dreamweaver. You'll learn about the basic Dreamweaver tools and how to navigate the Dreamweaver interface. By the end of this part, you'll have defined your website, which is the first step for creating your first web page.

Part 2, Building Your First Web Page, provides step-by-step instructions for creating your first web page, adding basic content, and creating document structure. This part also introduces you to many features and elements you can use to add pizzazz to your site, including CSS style sheets for formatting your site and adding images, links, and tables.

Part 3, Building a Website, focuses on Dreamweaver tools and features that make the web design process a little easier. You learn how to create page layouts that work with many types of screen window sizes, and you learn how to use the all-powerful <div> tag as well as AP elements to add more structure to your site. You also explore more uses of CSS for page layout and design, create templates for consistent site layout and structure, and test and maintain your site before posting it to the web.

Part 4, Powerful Friends for Interactivity, takes the web design process one step further by introducing other web technologies and walking you through the process of integrating them with Dreamweaver. Among the interactive tools covered are forms for two-way communication on your website; Spry widgets for adding menu bars, panels, and ToolTips; third-party widgets and extensions that expand Dreamweaver's functionality; and Adobe Flash movies and videos.

Extras

Hundreds of figures accompany the instructions included in this book. These are primarily screen captures of the Dreamweaver application that point out the various features and tools being explained.

In addition, you'll find the following boxes that contain insights for harnessing Dreamweaver's power:

DREAMWEAVER TIP

Read these tips for design and development hints. Many of these sidebars provide more insight on correct design techniques or offer shortcuts for various tasks.

DREAMWEAVER DON'T

Follow these warnings to avoid common pitfalls while developing your website.

DEFINITION

The world of web design is fraught with jargon. Turn to these sidebars to find out what unfamiliar terms mean. In addition, Appendix A contains a glossary for easy reference.

The Tutorials

Most chapters conclude with a tutorial that provides hands-on practice applying many of the topics covered in the chapter. The tutorials build on one another; if you work through them progressively, by the end of the book, you will have developed a website for a travel company called Walkabout Adventure Travel. To use the tutorial, you'll need to access the tutorial files at **www.idiotsguides.com/dreamweaver** and download them to your computer.

Acknowledgments

The process of writing a book is wrought with challenges—from getting the gig, to signing contracts, writing the book, meeting deadlines, and going through the many edits and reviews. Throw in being part of an active family and running your own company, and you have a huge amount of work to balance. That's what this project has been—a multitasking balance of work and opportunity. I couldn't have done this without the help of others.

Many thanks to my agent, Carole Jelen of Waterside Productions, for bringing this project to my attention. I look forward to more projects and opportunities with Carole and Waterside. I would also like to thank Mike Sanders of Pearson Education for all his help, support, and advice throughout the development of this book. My technical editor, Terry Toepfer, is a colleague of mine and deserves credit for the many extra hours she put into the book to help make it more accurate. Terry jumped into this project with ease and provided wonderful insight and superb edits that made this book more robust and technically focused for both Macintosh and PC users of Dreamweaver.

The people at Adobe deserve to be recognized, too. They offered a great prerelease program for learning and testing the latest release of Dreamweaver. The creative folks at Adobe put a lot of thought and skill into the CS5.5 release of Dreamweaver. With this release, Adobe has raised the bar in the competitive field of web design.

The website used throughout the tutorials is based on a real website my company created for Walkabout Adventure Travel. While the book's site is a scaled-down version of the public site, I am grateful to Walkabout for letting me use their content for the tutorials of this book. If you'd like to see the full site in its present-day development, visit www.ByWalkabout.com. And while you're at it, check out Walkabout's current tour offerings for informative and fun "soft" adventure tours around the world.

I'd also like to thank the other editors, designers, and reviewers who worked on this book. Their help, ideas, and suggestions have made this book much better than what I could have created on my own. Many eyes, thoughts, and suggestions helped in the development of this book and only made it better.

And finally, I would like to thank my family: my husband, David, and my daughter, Tasmin. David stepped up to the plate and did more of the housework and made—or bought—many of our family's meals while I was working on this book. Tasmin played her part in the household chores, too, and developed an interest in cooking and baking. When a door closes, a window opens. Teamwork is what it's all about. Thank you, and I love you both!

Special Thanks to the Technical Reviewer

The Complete Idiot's Guide to Dreamweaver CS5.5 was reviewed by Terry Toepfer, who double-checked the accuracy of what you'll learn here, to help us ensure that this book gives you everything you need to know about Dreamweaver CS5.5. Special thanks are extended to Terry for all her hard work, great insight and suggestions, and late hours.

Trademarks

All terms mentioned in this book that are known to be or are suspected of being trademarks or service marks have been appropriately capitalized. Alpha Books and Penguin Group (USA) Inc. cannot attest to the accuracy of this information. Use of a term in this book should not be regarded as affecting the validity of any trademark or service mark.

Dreamweaver and Web Design

This part serves as a basic introduction to the World Wide Web, the Internet, and using Dreamweaver to create a website.

The chapters in this part focus on the Dreamweaver interface—what you actually see when you open the program and start creating a site. The program's many panels, buttons, and toolbars can be a bit daunting when you first view them, but there's no need to worry: The chapters in this part introduce you to the Dreamweaver interface and show you how to navigate it like a pro. You also find out how to use basic Dreamweaver tools and techniques to define a website, which is the first step in creating your new site.

Dreamweaver and the World Wide Web

In This Chapter

- Distinguishing between the Internet and the World Wide Web
- Getting acquainted with HTML, CSS, and other web languages
- Understanding how Dreamweaver simplifies the web design process
- Exploring new features of Dreamweaver CS5.5
- Installing Dreamweaver CS5.5 on your computer

To make the most of Dreamweaver CS5.5, it helps to be familiar with some basic concepts related to the World Wide Web (or simply the web, for short) and the Internet. If you already have a good grasp of these topics, then skip ahead to the section titled "Installing Dreamweaver CS5.5," to kick off your foray into website development.

Web 101: The Basics

Understanding the hardware and technology for displaying and supporting a website is essential for web design. This includes understanding what the Internet, the web, domain names, and hosting servers are all about. Here are the basics of these topics.

Although the web and the Internet are related to one another, they're distinct entities. The Internet is a huge infrastructure of connected networks and computers. It entails all the wires, routers, computers, networks, and other hardware needed to support this massive global network. The Internet is the backbone for the web because it connects millions of networks and computers throughout the world.

The web is the compilation of the billions upon billions of documents and files, including entire websites and individual web pages. These files and documents are located on a hosting server, which is a computer connected to the Internet.

To be able to find a website or page on the web, you need a *URL*, or address for its location. Since you are looking on the web, you use the protocol of **http://www. domain-name.com**, as well as shortened versions of this protocol like **www.domain-name.com** or just **domain-name.com**. The *domain name* of your site is part of the URL.

DEFINITION

A **hosting server** is a computer that's set up for displaying websites via the Internet.

URL stands for Uniform Resource Locator and is the address or path for a website or web page on the web.

Domain names are used to establish a connection to one or more IP addresses of a hosting server. It is part of the URL or path to the hosting computer and your website.

An **IP address** is required for any computer on the Internet. IP addresses are unique and associated with a specific computer.

Each domain name must be unique on the web. If you're creating a new website and need a domain name, you can search a registrar site like www.GoDaddy.com to see what domain names are available.

DREAMWEAVER TIP

Many third-party companies offer domain registration services. Prices range from $4 to $20+ per domain name. You can register a domain name for multiple years. Check with your registrar for details on the number of years they allow.

Once you find a domain name, you need to register it so you establish ownership of the domain name. Part of the registration process is designating a hosting server. Just like a domain name is an essential part of the website's address on the web, the *IP address* of the hosting server is an essential for establishing the location of the computer on the Internet. During the registration process, you are required to provide the IP address for the hosting server of your website.

Many companies offering registering services also offer hosting services. They make the registration process simple by automatically establishing their hosting server's IP address for your domain name.

Websites and Web Pages

This discussion brings us to websites and web pages. A website is a collection of web pages. A web page is a document that's written in a web markup language such as *HMTL*. HMTL is short for HyperText Markup Language and is the most popular language for a web page. HTML uses markup tags and attributes to create document structure like paragraphs and headers (see Chapter 6), formatting like bold or italic, and web elements like Div tags (see Chapter 13).

Viewing Your Website on the Web

To make your website visible on the web, you need to *post* or upload it to the hosting server. Once on the hosting server, others can view it through a *web browser*. To access the website, you type its web address or URL in the browser, and the browser processes the request and displays the web page that exists at that address. For example, if you want to visit the website for *The New York Times*, type www.nytimes.com into the web browser's address field. The website for *The New York Times* appears on your screen. The browser interprets and then renders the code into a graphical display of the web page. Popular browser applications include Microsoft Internet Explorer, Mozilla Firefox, Apple Safari, and Google Chrome; they are all available as free downloads at the developing company websites.

DEFINITION

A **web browser** is an application developed to interpret the markup code (typically HTML) and render a graphical display of the information when requested over the Internet.

Post is the process of uploading your website to a hosting server.

How Dreamweaver Fits In

Dreamweaver is a powerful HTML editor with a graphical interface that aids in the process of web design and development. Dreamweaver has a Design view that lets you create a web page through text, images, links, and other media. The program enables you to design your web page graphically, while Dreamweaver generates the supporting HTML code behind the scenes. This enables you to see what you are creating as it will look in a browser. Dreamweaver creates the HTML code required to support all the bells and whistles you might need for a dynamic and entertaining website.

Before Adobe introduced Dreamweaver, most HTML editors were straight code editors. In other words, you needed to know HTML and its many markup tags to create a web page.

With each new release of Dreamweaver, Adobe has made it an even stronger web design and development tool.

Web Development Languages

There are many web development languages used in web design today. HTML is the popular choice for a web page but you can use other languages like PHP, ASP, or Javascript to add advanced functionality like dropdown menus or dynamically changing content. Cascading Style Sheets or CSS is another language that works hand-in-hand with HTML to create document structure and format of your web page. Dreamweaver is an HTML editor, so this book focuses on the HTML markup language and CSS to create websites.

The Many Versions of HTML

As a web designer, you need to know that HTML itself has several different variations. Each new release of HTML introduces new functions, web elements, or advanced format.

DREAMWEAVER TIP

Dreamweaver generates a web page that's based on the World Wide Web Consortium (W3C) conventions for HTML code. The W3C is the governing organization for dictating syntax and markup tags for each release of HTML and CSS. Dreamweaver-generated code adheres to the syntax and programming conventions for each version of HTML and CSS. Visit the W3C website (www.w3c. org) for more information about each version of HTML and supported tags.

Dreamweaver CS5.5 supports the following HTML versions:

- HTML 4.01 Transitional
- HTML 4.01 Strict
- HTML 5
- XHTML 1.0 Transitional
- XHTML 1.0 Strict
- XHTML 1.1
- XHTML Mobile 10

The difference between HTML transitional and strict versions has to do with the HTML tags and properties that are supported. A transitional version supports some of the older tags or properties that have been phased out from earlier versions of HTML, whereas a strict version only supports the properties and tags for that version. XHTML is part of the XML family and supports XML tags in a web page. You can find more information about each version of HTML by visiting www.wikipedia.com.

You might be saying, "Wow, that's a lot of versions of HTML." That's true—and you may run into others that I haven't even mentioned. In an effort to streamline the learning process, I focus on XHTML 1.0 Transitional for this book.

Understanding HTML Structure

HTML stands for HyperText Markup Language, and it's a *plain-text document* that uses "markup" tags to format the text. These tags instruct a browser on how to format and display a web page. Figure 1.1 displays the HTML code of a simple web page.

DEFINITION

A **plain-text document** is any document with a TXT file extension like **page.txt**. TextEdit or NotePad are applications that create plain-text documents. You can use these programs to create HTML code. If you have a strong grasp of HTML you can use these programs to create an entire web page.

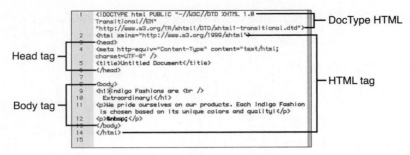

Figure 1.1: HTML code provides the basic building blocks behind all web pages.

A browser's job is to interpret the HTML code and then visually represent the code in a browser window. Figure 1.2 shows a visual representation of the HTML code shown in Figure 1.1.

Indigo Fashions are Extraordinary!

We pride ourselves on our products. Each Indigo Fashion is chosen based on its unique colors and quality!

Figure 1.2: In the paragraph of text, the <strong> tag has been applied to the company name, Indigo Fashion, and it displays in bold format.

All HTML tags are displayed between angled brackets and are structured in pairs. For example, the head tag begins with `<head>` (starting tag) and is closed with `</head>` (ending tag). The starting tag tells a browser where to begin the tag, and the ending tag tells the browser where the tag ends. A web browser interprets all the tags and then renders a display the page content.

For example, in Figure 1.2, in the second paragraph, the company name of Indigo Fashion displays in bold because of the `<strong>` tag. The correct syntax for applying bold format is to surround the text that you want to make bold with a starting tag and then an ending tag, as in `<strong>`Indigo Fashions`</strong>`. This can also be called an inline style rule (see Chapter 7 for information about an inline style rule).

When you create a new web page, Dreamweaver generates the supporting HTML code. Here is this code for an XHTML 1.0 Transitional web page (see Figure 1.3).

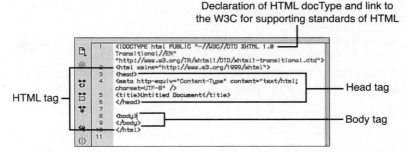

Declaration of HTML docType and link to
the W3C for supporting standards of HTML

HTML tag

Head tag

Body tag

Figure 1.3: Fortunately, when you use Dreamweaver, you don't have to create all this HTML code each time you create a web page. Dreamweaver does this for you automatically when you create your page.

Each line of code has its own line number. Notice that the first line of code is the <!DOCTYPE> tag, which determines the HTML version for the web page and provides a link to the *W3C*.

DEFINITION

W3C stands for the World Wide Web Consortium, which is the governing organization that establishes standards for HTML, CSS, and other web development languages.

Line 2 begins with the <html> tag. Keeping in mind that HTML has both a starting and an ending tag, notice that the <html> tag wraps around both the <head> tag and the <body> tag. These three tags make up the content and area of the web page. The <head> tag wraps around both the <meta> tag (see Chapter 2) and the <title> tag (see Chapter 4). The <head> tag is an HTML tag that isn't visible to the website visitor, but is visible to search engines. The <body> tag is where all the web page content resides and is what a visitor sees when they visit your website. Though the <head> tag is invisible to the visitor, it plays a big part in Search Engine Optimization or SEO, which is covered in Appendix D.

Throughout this book, I point out the supporting HTML code for the design elements of a web page. As a web designer, you should know a little bit about HTML. Even though Dreamweaver does a great job with creating the HTML code, there will be times when you'll need to look at the supporting code to fix certain problems with your web page.

CSS and Web Design

Cascading Style Sheets, or CSS, is a relatively new way to design and format websites. CSS is a style sheet that holds a group of style rules used to format website content. A style rule is a set of formatting properties that you can apply to different elements of your web page. CSS uses its own code, which is distinct from HTML, for these style rules.

Style sheets have been around for a long time in word processing and page layout programs, so you might already be familiar with them. Dreamweaver offers this same functionality through CSS and applies the style rules to HTML tags.

CSS works hand-in-hand with HTML and is the recommended technology for formatting your web page. Through style sheets and style rules you can control the format of web elements like text, images, lists, hyperlinks, and even your web page layout for any and all pages of your site. Using CSS makes it easier to achieve consistent formatting throughout your site.

Using Dreamweaver for Web Design

Dreamweaver uses a visual interface between the actual HTML code and the web page graphical design. This streamlines the web design and development process and makes it more intuitive, letting you focus on the visual aspect of the process while Dreamweaver creates the supporting HTML code. The visual interface lets you focus on being creative without having to get bogged down in the HTML code.

Dreamweaver streamlines the entire web design and development process, enabling you to more easily create pages, format their content, and post and test them. Thanks to the visual interface, you don't need to be an expert programmer of HTML code. You simply select the various options, buttons, or menu choices that you want on your site. Dreamweaver lets your creativity flow while taking care of the code on the back end.

What Dreamweaver Does Well

Dreamweaver is a wonderful tool for designing web pages.

It shines as an HTML editor due to its visual interface for creating web page content, layout, and design.

It automatically generates the HTML code for supporting your page content.

This automatically generated HTML code is very clean in *syntax* and adheres to the HTML standards that the W3C set for each version of HTML.

Also, Dreamweaver CS5.5 now includes a validation feature that checks your web pages for compliance against these W3C standards for HTML code. This validation ensures that you have the correct syntax, HTML tags, and attributes for the HTML code used in your web page.

DEFINITION

Syntax is the arrangement and order required in the construction of a programming language's code.

Dreamweaver also enables you to go "behind the curtain" and edit your page using HTML code. This flexibility to design graphically, or through the HTML code, is probably the most powerful feature of Dreamweaver.

Dreamweaver does a great job of facilitating the creation and integration of CSS with your HTML web pages. As discussed already in this chapter, Cascading Style Sheets are the newest way to format and create page layouts in web design. CSS supports plenty of tags and features for making your web page really stand out. CSS is introduced in Chapter 7 and expanded upon from that point on in this book.

What Dreamweaver Can't Do

As powerful as Dreamweaver is, some things are beyond its control. For instance, Dreamweaver can't guess what fonts visitors to your website have installed on their systems, decipher the resolution of their monitors, or determine the dimensions of their browser window. To complicate this even more, each web browser also has its own interpretation of HTML. Although they're all similar, some differences exist. Dreamweaver only creates the HTML. It's up to you to test your pages in the many different browsers to see how they interpret the code in their display. It is also a good idea to view your site on both a Macintosh and a PC as there are slight color and resolution differences between the two platforms, too.

> **DREAMWEAVER TIP**
>
> BrowserLab is a Dreamweaver feature that facilitates the process of testing your website's appearance in various browsers. It automatically generates a graphic of how your web page looks in each different browser. This feature is covered in Chapter 4.

What's New in Dreamweaver CS5.5

As more people use their cellphones, iPads, and mobile devices to browse, share, and access web content, fewer people are accessing the web the old-fashioned way—from their home computers. To stay current, web designers must create web pages that display well on windows ranging in size from tiny smart phone screens to huge monitors.

With each release, Dreamweaver gets more powerful. The CS5.5 version represents the gold standard for website design software today by offering more functionality for web development for mobile devices like cellphones, iPads, and smart phone applications.

Dreamweaver introduced the Inspect mode in its CS5.5 release (see Chapter 11). Hovering your mouse over an element on your web page when you're in this mode enables you to see the supporting code and the CSS rules and properties that apply to that element. You can also see the CSS box model and it's formatting for that element as shown in Figure 1.4. The CSS box model and Cascading Style Sheets are covered in detail in Chapter 8.

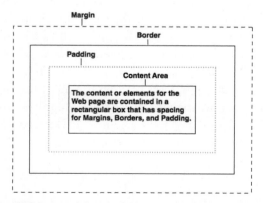

Figure 1.4: The CSS box model is used when applying format and layout to web page elements and content.

DEFINITION

The **CSS box model** is the visual model used for the rectangular boxes that hold or contain web page elements.

Another feature that's greatly enhanced over the CS5 version is better integration of JavaScript and the addition of the jQuery library. JavaScript is a programming language and can be integrated into a web page for advanced functionality and inter- activity. For example, JavaScript can be used to hide or show certain web elements based on the visitor's interaction on the web page. The jQuery library is a JavaScript library of code snippets. These jQuery snippits enable web developers to quickly add advanced functionality from the library directly to their web page.

Dreamweaver CS5.5 also supports more integration with social media sites such as WordPress.

In addition, Dreamweaver's code hinting feature is more accurate and responsive. When you begin to type HTML code, Dreamweaver tries to help you by providing a pop-out menu of code that it thinks you are creating. All you need to do is click the code hint or tag from the pop-out menu.

Finally, Adobe also fixed some bugs and faulty behavior in the CS5 version of Dreamweaver with this release of CS5.5.

Multiscreen Preview

New to CS5.5 is the Multiscreen Preview feature (see Chapter 11). This feature enables you to see a web page as it would display on a mobile device. You find a Multiscreen Preview button in the Document toolbar of the Dreamweaver window. When you click it, a list of standard menu sizes displays as shown in Figure 1.5.

Sample of selected Multiscreen Preview   Menu for Multiscreen Preview

Multiscreen Preview button

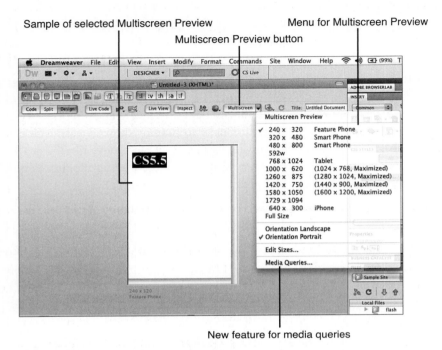

New feature for media queries

Figure 1.5: The Multiscreen Preview feature enables you to set different-size windows based on standard mobile device display dimensions.

Media Queries

To help make web content a little smarter, Adobe added media queries to Dreamweaver CS5.5. Media queries enable you to create code that detects what media is being used to view the web content and then sizes the content window accordingly.

Mobile Application Templates

You can use Dreamweaver's new Mobile Applications templates to create *mobile applications* for the most popular personal devices on the market today (see Appendix C). A mobile application is a program that's accessible through a mobile device like a cell phone, smart phone, or other personal mobile device. This requires a web page interface with some advanced backend programming for the functionality of the mobile application. For instance, the iPhone offers many different applications that enhance the functionality of their phone, like an application that lets you identify a constellation. This mobile application lets you take a picture of the night sky and then identifies that constellation for you. The visual graphical display for the application interface is a web page that is formatted to fit on the iPhone, but the identification process for the constellation is a program that accesses a database of constellations for identification.

DREAMWEAVER TIP

The Apple PhoneGap Framework is the standard for building mobile applications and is now integrated in Dreamweaver CS5.5.

You can quickly create mobile applications from sample pages that come with Dreamweaver CS5.5. These sample pages give you a start for designing mobile applications. See Appendix C for more information about creating mobile applications.

You can find these templates under Page Samples in the New Document window as shown in Figure 1.6.

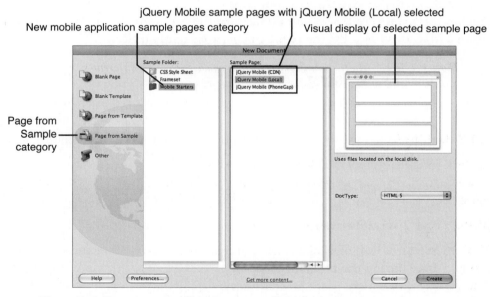

Figure 1.6: Dreamweaver offers three types of Mobile Application sample pages.

You access these sample pages through the **File, New** menu bar command. Click the **Page From Sample** category and then click **Mobile Starters.**

You can also create your own application framework and also build and emulate the application for testing. You can find this new functionality in the menu bar by choosing **Site, Mobile Applications.**

Installing Dreamweaver CS5.5

The process to install Dreamweaver CS5.5 is similar to other applications. Before you even open the package on your new software, you should double-check the system requirements of the software against your computer and operating system. You need a retail copy of Dreamweaver CS5.5 or a 30-day trial version; you can download either from Adobe's website (www.adobe.com).

System Requirements for Dreamweaver CS5.5

The system requirements for Dreamweaver CS5.5 are the same as for any other Adobe CS5.5 software that makes up the Creative Suite. Based on whether you are using a Macintosh or a PC the requirements are slightly different.

DREAMWEAVER DON'T

You cannot install Dreamweaver on any type of a removable flash storage device.

A PC running Windows must meet the following minimum system requirements:

- Intel Pentium 4 or AMD Athlon 64 processor

- Microsoft Windows XP with Service Pack 3, or Windows Vista Home Premium, or Business, Ultimate, or Enterprise with Service Pack 1 (Service Pack 2 is recommended), or Windows 7 with at least 1GB of RAM

- At least 9.3GB of available hard-disk space for installation and additional free space during the actual installation.

- A display of at least 1280 x 800 with a qualified hardware-accelerated OpenGL graphics card, 16-bit color, and 256MB of VRAM.

- 32 bit Java™ Runtime Environment 1.5 or higher

- DVD-ROM drive compatible with dual-layer DVDs
- Adobe Flash Player 10 software
- QuickTime 7.6.2 software
- A broadband Internet connection

> **DREAMWEAVER TIP**
>
> On a PC or Mac, graphics support might be required for Shader Model 3.0 and OpenGL 2.0 of the GPU-accelerated features. Updates to system requirements as well as more detailed information about video hardware compatibility can be found by visiting http://www.adobe.com/products/creativesuite/design/systemreqs/.

To install Dreamweaver CS5.5 on a Macintosh, you need the following minimum system requirements:

- A multicore Intel processor
- Mac OS X v10.5.8 or above
- At least 1GB of RAM
- At least 10.3GB of available hard-disk space for installation and additional free space during the actual installation.
- A display of at least 1280 x 800 resolution with a qualified hardware-accelerated OpenGL graphics card, 16-bit color, and 256MB of VRAM.
- Java Runtime Environment 1.5 or higher
- DVD-ROM drive compatible with dual-layer DVDs
- QuickTime 7.6.2 software or higher
- Adobe Flash Player 10 or higher
- A broadband Internet connection

Access the Software

A copy of the software is required to start the installation process. Adobe makes it easy to access all its applications through direct downloads of the software from their site to your computer (see Figure 1.7). You can download any software in the Adobe Creative Suite by visiting www.adobe.com/downloads.

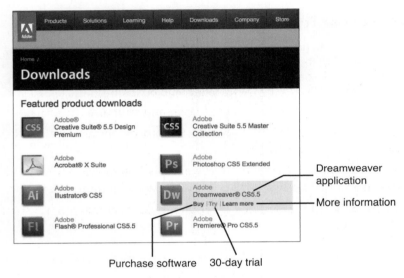

Figure 1.7: Adobe has a trial version for all software in their Creative Suite.

You can choose to try out Dreamweaver through a 30-day trial or purchase the software. Either way, you can download the software directly from their site to your computer. Click **Buy** to purchase the software and **Try** to try it for 30 days and follow the screen prompts. You can also request a hardcopy or DVD of the software when you purchase it.

DREAMWEAVER TIP

The 30-day trial software is fully functional—it's exactly the same as the retail software. This trial is a great way to try out Dreamweaver prior to buying it.

After you've downloaded the software to your computer, you can install it. Double-click the downloaded file (a DMG file on Macs and a Zip file on PCs) and follow the screen-by-screen instructions for installing Dreamweaver CS5.5. The installation process takes about 30 minutes depending on your computer processing speed and Internet connection.

The Least You Need to Know

- The Internet and the World Wide Web are separate entities that work hand-in-hand with each other.
- The most popular web markup language is HTML.
- CSS is the recommended way to format and structure a web page.
- Dreamweaver simplifies the web design process through its interface, tools, buttons, and menu options.
- Adobe introduced many new features in its Dreamweaver CS5.5 release, including new functionality for designing web pages for mobile devices.
- To install Dreamweaver, your computer must meet minimum system requirements.

The Dreamweaver Interface and Workspace

Chapter

2

In This Chapter

- Launching and opening a new web page
- Organizing the Dreamweaver workspace
- Manipulating panels and panel groups
- Making sense of the Files panel
- Setting up the Favorites menu of the Insert panel
- Using the Application bar to set layout views and workspaces
- Switching modes of the Property Inspector

The first step in learning any new software is to get acquainted with its interface and workspace. Dreamweaver uses panels for many of its web design functions and features. It also has toolbars and menu bars, and it employs different views based on the task at hand.

Typical of other applications, Dreamweaver usually offers a few different ways to accomplish the same command. This gives you flexibility for accessing the function or feature that you want based on how you like to work. You can even customize your workspace to increase the efficiency of your workflow.

Launching Dreamweaver

To begin using Dreamweaver, you need to open, or launch, the application. The process for launching Dreamweaver differs based on whether you have a Macintosh or a Windows system. After you have installed your Dreamweaver application (see

Chapter 1), you'll find the application on your computer in the location you specified during installation. By default, the application is in the Applications folder on a Macintosh and the Programs folder on a computer using Microsoft Windows. To launch the application use your systems launch feature, click the name of the application when presented with a list of applications. Dreamweaver launches and then displays the Welcome Screen (see Figure 2.1).

Creates a new HTML document

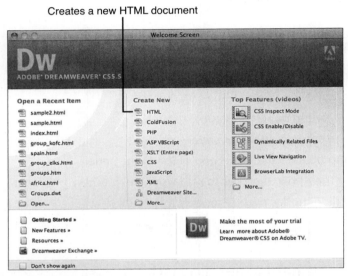

Figure 2.1: The Welcome Screen offers quick access to many features of Dreamweaver, including features for creating an HTML page.

The Welcome Screen is set to display by default when you open Dreamweaver. From this screen, you can quickly select options for creating different types of documents like web pages or CSS style sheet documents. You can also quickly access recently opened documents for editing and revising.

Creating a New HTML Page

The Welcome Screen provides the most direct way to create a new HTML document—a web page—in Dreamweaver.

To create a new web page from the Welcome Screen, click **HTML** under the **Create New** section. Dreamweaver generates a new web page.

> **DREAMWEAVER TIP**
>
> To follow along with the instructions in this chapter, go ahead and create a new web page from the Welcome Screen.

Changing Default Settings in the Preferences Window

When you use the Welcome Screen to create a new web page, Dreamweaver uses the default settings. These default settings are located in Dreamweaver preferences. You can change the default settings in Dreamweaver preferences. To open Dreamweaver preferences, choose **Dreamweaver, Preferences** (Mac) or **Edit, Preferences** (PC) from the menu bar. This opens the Preferences window (see Figure 2.2).

Categories with New
Document selected

New Document
options

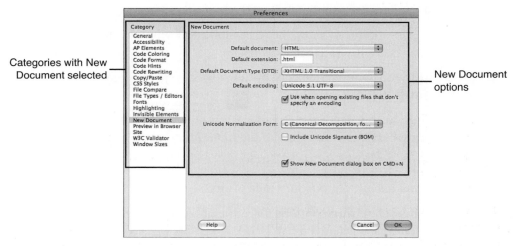

Figure 2.2: Define and modify the default Dreamweaver settings by choosing the appropriate category on the left and then selecting the appropriate setting(s) on the right.

The left side of the preferences window displays all the categories for Dreamweaver preferences. Each category has its own settings and options for different features and functionality of Dreamweaver. To see the default preferences for new documents created through the Welcome Screen, choose the **New Document** category on the left. This displays your default New Document settings.

> **DREAMWEAVER TIP**
>
> Accessing Preferences is one of the few operations that differs depending on your operating system. Mac users choose **Dreamweaver, Preferences** from the menu bar; PC users choose **Edit, Preferences** from the menu bar. In most other situations, Dreamweaver commands are almost identical for both Macintosh and Windows users.

To change any other Dreamweaver preferences, click a category on the left and access the options for that category on the right. Select new preferences by clicking an option once; click it again to turn it off (this is called toggling). You can also type in any editable information. After you set your preferences, they become your new default settings.

Here is a brief description of each category in the preferences window.

General: Set default options for documents and editing; for instance, you can set Dreamweaver to reopen recently used documents when Dreamweaver is opened.

Accessibility: Set options to show the Accessibility Attributes when forms, frames, media, and images are inserted into a webpage.

AP Elements: Set default AP element options like background color or determine a background image (see Chapter 14).

Code Coloring: Set the color for Dreamweaver generated code based on document type like ASP or PHP. This is visible in the Code View (see Chapter 11).

Code Format: Set default options for formatting your HTML code (see Chapter 11).

Code Hints: Set default options for Code Hints (see Chapter 11).

Code Rewriting: Determine options for automatic code corrections that Dreamweaver performs when you hand-code a web page (see Chapter 11).

Copy/Paste: Set how Dreamweaver copies and pastes information from another application into the Design view (see Chapter 5).

CSS Styles: Establish default options for creating and editing CSS Rules and determine how the CSS panel responds to a double-click (see Chapter 7).

File Compare: Set a default application for comparing two files.

File Types/Editors: Establish the default editor application for different file types. For instance, you can set Photoshop to automatically be the default editor for editing PNG, GIF, and JPG when in Dreamweaver (see Chapter 8).

Fonts: Set the default font for proportional or fixed fonts and set the font to be used for Code view (see Chapters 5 and 7).

Highlighting: Determine what highlight color is used when different web elements are selected or highlighted in both Design and Code view.

Invisible Elements: Set invisible elements to display in the Design view of Dreamweaver for different tags and elements (see Chapter 9).

New Document: Set the default HTML document type for new web pages (see Chapter 4).

Preview in Browser: Determine the Primary and Secondary browser used for previewing your web pages in Dreamweaver (see Chapter 4).

Site: Establish settings for the Define Site window and FTP default connection options (see Chapter 3).

W3C Validator: Set the default HTML document type to be used for validating your web pages based on W3C rules (see Chapter 17).

Window Sizes: Establish a default window size for new web pages (see Chapter 11).

Exploring the Dreamweaver Workspace

Dreamweaver's workspace is similar to other Adobe products in the Creative Suite series, such as Photoshop and Acrobat. The workspace features panels, toolbars, the Property Inspector, and menu bar (see Figure 2.3).

DREAMWEAVER TIP

The Dreamweaver workspace differs slightly depending on whether you're using a Mac or Windows. In Windows the Application Bar is located on top of the menu bar; on Macintosh the Application bar is located below the menu bar.

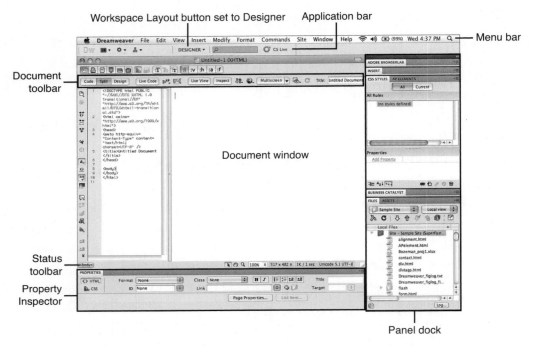

Figure 2.3: The default view of the document window is Designer view.

Overview of Workspace Layouts

Because Dreamweaver is designed to streamline the workflow of web design, it offers different layouts of the workspace to accommodate how people work. The Designer workspace is the default setting, but you can switch to different preset workspaces based on how you like to work.

To switch to a new workspace, click the **Workspace** button in the Application bar and choose the workspace that fits your style of working (see Figure 2.4). Here's an overview of each workspace:

Application Developer: This workspace is arranged to support the workflow of application development.

Application Developer Plus: Similar to the Application Developer workspace but includes more panels and tools to aid in the process of application development.

Classic: Traditional layout of past versions of Dreamweaver.

Coder: This workspace is arranged with the tools and panels essential to hand-coding a web page.

Coder Plus: Similar to the Coder workspace but includes more panels and tools for hardcore coders.

Designer: Default workspace arranged with commonly used panels for website designers.

Designer Compact: Exactly the same as the Designer Workspace but created to fit a lower resolution (such as 1024 x 768) screen.

Dual Screen: This workspace makes use of a dual monitor setup by placing the panels and designer tools on one screen and the Document window on a second screen.

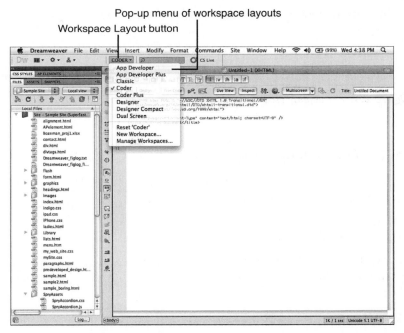

Figure 2.4: The Dreamweaver Coder workspace is set up for people who like to hand-code the HTML for their web pages.

Customizing a Workspace Layout

You can customize and manage any of the workspaces by moving and resizing elements of that layout, including windows, panels, toolbars, and the Property Inspector.

To increase the size of the entire Panel dock, position your cursor on the border between the Panel dock and the Document Window. Your cursor changes to the double arrow tool, which indicates that you're on a border. Click and drag the border to resize the Panel dock. You can resize any of the other Workspace elements by positioning your cursor on its border and dragging to a new size.

To move any Panel, Panel Group, document window, or the Property Inspector to a new location in your workspace, click and drag its Title bar. This undocks the element so you can drag it where you want it. If you want to dock it somewhere else in the Workspace, position it close to the Document window edge and a highlighted gray bar will extend from the edge of the screen with a thin bold line indicating that the element will be docked at that edge of the window.

DREAMWEAVER TIP

If you want to reinstate the default workspace layout, click the **Workspace** button in the Application bar and choose **Reset "Designer"**. (The actual name of the workspace depends on the layout you have active.)

Creating Your Own Workspace

After you've customized your workspace to your needs, you can save it to reuse later. To save your workspace, click the **Workspace** button in the Application bar and choose **New Workspace.** Type a name for your workspace in the New Workspace window and click **OK**.

You can now access your personalized workspace at any time by clicking the **Workspace** button in the Application bar and choosing your personalized workspaces from the list of workspaces.

Overview of Document Window

You perform all web design functions in the Dreamweaver document window. Anything that you type, insert, copy, or paste displays in this window.

The Document window has the following three views:

Design view—Shows how the design will appear in a browser window

Code view—Shows only the HTML code for the web page

Split view—Shows both Design view and Code view (see Figure 2.5)

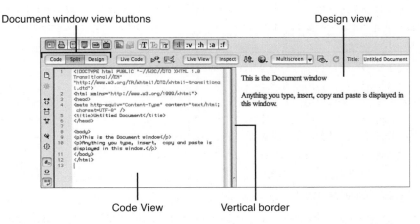

Document window view buttons

Design view

Code View

Vertical border

Figure 2.5: The document window in Split view. You can adjust the size of the Code or Design view by clicking and dragging the vertical border that separates them.

You can change between views by clicking one of the three View buttons on the Document toolbar.

DREAMWEAVER TIP

If you don't like the vertical layout of the split view, you can arrange this horizontally through the menu bar. Choose **View** and deselect the **Split Vertically** menu command.

Document Tabs

When you open or create documents in Dreamweaver, you'll see a document tab at the top of the Document window (see Figure 2.6). The tab lists the name of an individual document. When multiple documents are open, you can switch between documents by clicking the document tab.

Document tabs

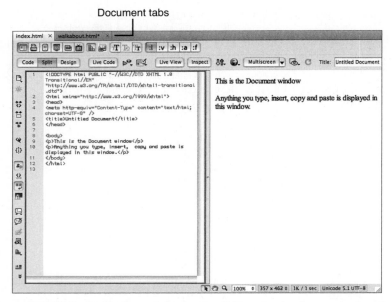

Figure 2.6: You can also close a document by clicking the close button on the tab.

DREAMWEAVER TIP

An asterisk by the document name in the document tab indicates that changes have been made to the document since it was last saved. To avoid losing any changes, save the document. To save all opened documents at one time, choose **File, Save All**.

Overview of Menus and Toolbars

You can find many of the commands and features of Dreamweaver in a toolbar or the menu bar of the workspace (see Figure 2.7).

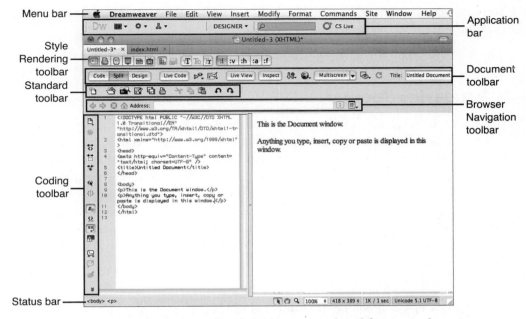

***Figure* 2**.7:** *You can find most Dreamweaver commands and features in the menu bar. On this workspace, all toolbars are visible.*

The Dreamweaver menu bar works the same as in other applications. To use the menu bar, click a menu and then choose a command from the drop-down menu. If you don't want to make a selection from the menu, click in a blank area of your workspace to close the menu, with no choice selected.

Dreamweaver groups toolbars by their function. The six Dreamweaver toolbars are as follows:

- Style Rendering
- Document
- Standard
- Browser Navigation
- Coding
- Status

You can view or hide toolbars by choosing **View, Toolbar** and selecting the toolbar that you want to display.

The following sections walk you through the features of each toolbar type.

Style Rendering Toolbar

Use the Style Rendering toolbar to view your web page based on the type of media in which it will be displayed (see Figure 2.8). For instance, if you want a web page to print nicely, without bad page breaks, you need to create a layout that fits on an 8.5 × 11 inch sheet of paper. The Style Rendering toolbar lets you view your different page layouts for a web page based on various types of media. In our example of a printed page, when you click the **Print Media Type** button, Dreamweaver displays your web page as it would look on a printed page. This lets you fine-tune the style rules that control the printed web page so that it fits nicely on a standard size sheet of paper.

Media types

CSS buttons

Figure 2.8: When you click a Media Type button, your document window displays the web page with the format and page layout created through CSS.

The following media types are represented in the Style Rendering toolbar:

- Screen Media Type
- Print Media Type
- Handheld Media Type
- Projection Media Type
- TTY Media Type (Teletype machine media type)
- TV Media Type

DREAMWEAVER TIP

Hover your mouse over each of the buttons in the Style Rendering toolbar for a ToolTip identifying each individual button.

Document Toolbar

The Document toolbar houses options for controlling your web page. Earlier in this chapter you explored some of the buttons on the Document toolbar: the **Code View**, **Split View,** and **Design View** buttons. You can also use this toolbar to initiate the **Live Code** and **Live View** modes of Dreamweaver (see Chapter 4 for details on using Code view and Live view modes).

You can set the title for a web page in the Document toolbar by typing the name into the Title field. The title of a web page displays in a browser Title bar, serving as the label for the page and making it accessible for search engines for indexing. The title is also read out loud by speech readers, which are devices that help visually impaired users browse the web.

You can use the other features of the Document toolbar to upload and download your web pages to your remote hosting server.

Standard Toolbar

The Standard toolbar is similar to toolbars found on other applications, such as Microsoft Word. It has **New Document, Save, Print,** and **Open** buttons, as well as buttons for **Cut, Copy, Paste, Undo,** and **Redo.** You simply click a button to initiate the feature on the Standard toolbar. By default this toolbar is hidden when you first open Dreamweaver. It is only displayed on a new document or web page. With a new document opened, you must show the toolbar to access it choosing **View, Toolbar, Standard** from the menu bar.

Browser Navigation Toolbar

The Browser Navigation toolbar is active only when you initiate Live view. The Browser Navigation toolbar displays the address of the page you're looking at in the Address field (see Figure 2.9).

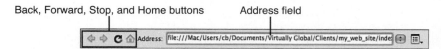

Back, Forward, Stop, and Home buttons   Address field

Figure 2.9: The Browser Navigation toolbar. Live view displays your page as a browser would see it, and the Browser Navigation toolbar lets you work in Dreamweaver as if you were really in a browser.

Coding Toolbar

The Coding toolbar helps you create code. It's a vertical toolbar on the left side of the Document window that's visible only when you're in Code view. The coding toolbar can collapse and expand sections of code. You can use it to highlight code that is wrong and create or delete comments in your code. You can also use the toolbar to indent code and insert snippets of code. (For more on this toolbar, see Chapter 11.)

Status Toolbar

The Status toolbar displays the status of the web page. You can use it to change the magnification of the Document window and to change the screen display type by choosing a new dimension with the Window Size button. The feature I like the most about this bar is the Tag selector. If you click one of the HTML tags listed in this toolbar, you actually select the code in the document for this tag.

Panels, Panels, and More Panels

Panels play a big role in Dreamweaver. With them, you can group similar functionality in one location, called a panel group (see Figure 2.10).

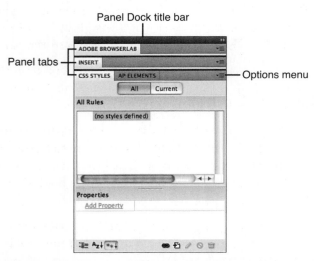

Figure 2.10: The CSS Styles and AP Elements panels are grouped together in a panel group.

All panels and panel groups have common features that support consistent function-ality. All panels have panel tabs. In a panel group, you access a panel by clicking its tab. All panels have an Option menu that contains other relevant commands of that panel.

Panel Basics

You can access any panel through the menu bar by clicking the **Window** menu and then choosing the panel that you want to open. Each **Workspace** layout also has a set display of certain panels that streamline the workflow. For instance, if you're a hardcore HTML programmer, you probably want to use the Coder Workspace layout. This layout displays the Files, Snippets, Assets, CSS Style, and AP Elements panels by default. Even though each Workspace layout has a set panel display, you can customize your workspace by moving, opening, and reorganizing your panels and panel groups. You can group any set of panels together in a panel group.

Managing Panels and Panel Groups

The panel dock consists of panel groups and can be docked to either the top, bottom, left, or right edges of the workspace. You can move the entire panel group by clicking and dragging the title bar. You can drop the panel group away from the panel dock so that it's free floating. You can re-dock the panel group by dragging the title bar of the panel group to the panel dock so that you see a grayed-out bar in the panel dock. Release the mouse button and the panel group re-docks to the panel dock.

You can also reorganize a panel in a panel group. Click and drag the panel tab that you want to move to the left or right of another panel tab. This moves the panel to the new location within the panel group.

You can drag a panel out of the panel group and drop it somewhere else in the workspace; it will be free floating. If you want to group the panel in a different panel group, click the panel tab or title bar of the panel to move and drag the panel into a new panel group. The panel group edge appears highlighted when the panel is in the panel group.

If you want a panel to be its own group, click the tab or title bar of the panel and drag it so that a horizontal bar displays between the panel groups. This drops the panel into the dock as its own panel group.

To collapse or expand a panel, double-click the panel tab. The entire panel group expands if it's collapsed and collapses into just the title bar of the panel group if it's already expanded.

The Panel Options Menu

The Options menu is in the upper right corner of all panels (see Figure 2.11). It contains a menu of frequently used commands or special commands that relate to the active panel.

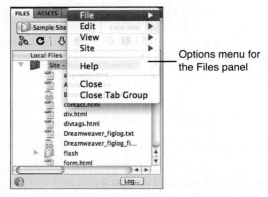

Figure 2.11: *You can quickly access commonly used commands from the Options menu of a panel.*

You can close a panel or panel group with the Options menu in all panels by choosing **Close** from the menu.

Files Panel

The Files panel contains all pages, elements, and assets of your website (see Figure 2.12). It records changes to the location of documents in real time. For instance, if you move a graphic file that you've inserted in a web page to a new folder, the Files panel changes the code in the web page to reflect the new location.

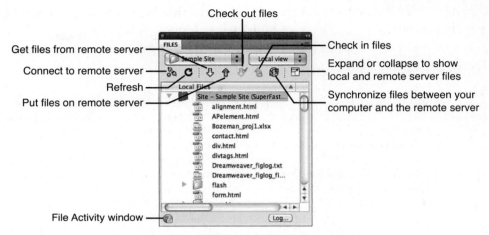

Figure 2.12: You can also view files from any location on your computer in the Files panel.

DREAMWEAVER DON'T

If you use Windows Explorer or the Macintosh Finder to reorganize website files, you break any links that you've set in other documents to the relocated file. Always use Dreamweaver's File panel to reorganize your website files; it retains all links.

You can use the Files panel to access your remote hosting server and post and download files to and from the remote server. You can check in and check out files among multiple designers. You can reorganize your file and folder structure for your website without breaking any links in existing documents. You'll likely use this panel a lot as you develop your website.

You can also adjust the columns in the Files panel. Click on the vertical border between the column headers. Your mouse becomes the double arrow tool. Click and drag to adjust the size of the column. If you want to list a column of data in ascending or descending order, click the column header label just as you would in the Macintosh Finder or Windows Explorer windows. Dreamweaver lists all data content in the column in ascending or descending order.

Insert Panel

You'll use the Insert panel a lot when designing web pages (see Figure 2.13). You can insert all types of web elements and elements with this panel, including graphics, Flash media, tables, and *meta tags.*

DEFINITION

Meta tags are tags in the `<head>` tag of an HTML document. When a web page is viewed in a browser, the `<head>` tag isn't visible to the visitor other than the page title displays in the browser title bar. However, the `<head>` tag is visible to search engines and plays a big role in how search engines index your site. See Appendix D for more information optimizing your website for search engines.

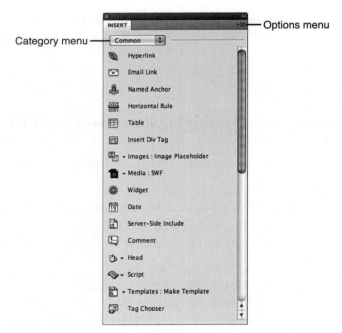

Figure 2.13: The Insert panel contains buttons for inserting elements in your web page.

Insert Panel Categories

The Category menu presents all the categories for the Insert panel (see Figure 2.14). To change to a new category, click the Category menu and choose the new category from the list.

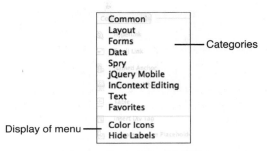

Figure 2.14: The Category menu of the Insert panel. You can change the display of the panel by choosing one of the two display menu options at the bottom of the menu.

You can choose from the following eight categories for the Insert panel:

Common—Holds the most common insert elements

Layout—Holds layout elements, including div tags (see Chapter 13) and AP elements (see Chapter 14)

Forms—Holds form elements, including text fields and submit buttons (see Chapter 19)

Data—Holds data elements such as Sprys and regions (see Chapter 20)

Spry—Holds Spry elements and widgets, such as Spry menu bars and tabbed panels (see Chapter 20)

jQuery Mobile—Holds jQuery Mobile elements for creating queries for mobile devices (see Appendix C)

InContext Editing—Holds template-editing features, including repeating regions and editable regions (see Chapter 16)

Text—Holds text elements for document structure and formatting (see Chapter 5)

Favorites—Enables you to create your own custom Insert menu

Manipulating the Insert Panel

You can drag the Insert panel from the panel dock and position it in another location. You can also change the display of the panel by choosing **Color Icons** or **Hide Labels** from the **Category** pop-up menu (see Figure 2.15).

Figure 2.15: When you choose Hide Labels on the Insert panel, only the button icon for each command is visible.

The Favorite Category

The Favorite category of the Insert panel lets you create a personalized menu of your most commonly used commands. You can add any menu command or button to this menu. To add a button, follow these steps:

1. In the Favorite category of the Insert panel, Ctrl-click or right-click and choose **Customize Favorites** from the list. This opens the Customize Favorites window (see Figure 2.16).

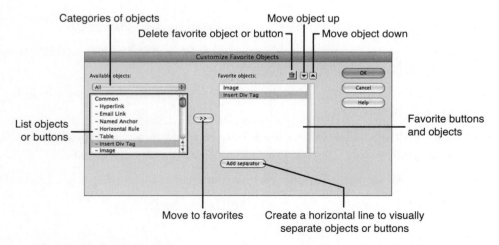

Figure 2.16: You can access all menu commands and buttons in Dreamweaver through the Customize Favorites menu.

2. Choose the category for the object on the left and then select the object in the list below the category menu.

3. To move this object to the Favorite Objects pane on the right, click the **Move** button. The object (or objects) is moved to the Favorite Objects pane and becomes a button for Favorites in the Insert panel. Now these buttons are easily accessible anytime as you work with Dreamweaver.

DREAMWEAVER TIP

You can delete a Favorite button by selecting it from the list on the right and clicking **Delete.** You can also rearrange the order of the buttons by selecting the button and clicking the **Move Object Up** or **Move Object Down** buttons.

Accessing Other Panels

You'll find all Dreamweaver panels under the **Window** menu in the menu bar. Choose the panel you want to use, and it displays in the panel dock. If it's part of a panel group, all other panel tabs set by default to be in this group will also open (see Figure 2.17).

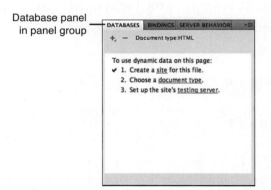

Figure 2.17: The entire panel group opens when the Database panel is selected from the Window menu; this group includes the Bindings and Server Behavior panels.

The Much-Used Property Inspector

The Property Inspector is just that: a feature that inspects the properties of elements in your document. When you select an element such as text or a graphic, the Property Inspector displays the properties for that element, such as bold formatting for text or border settings for an image. You can use the Property Inspector to add or edit properties for these elements. It's a powerful web design tool that you'll use frequently (see Figure 2.18).

Figure 2.18: *The Property Inspector has two modes, CSS and HTML, with each mode supporting different functionality and features.*

The Property Inspector has two modes of functionality: CSS and HTML. Click either CSS or HTML to access the functionality and properties of each mode.

HTML mode offers functionality and properties that establish document structure like paragraphs or headings. You can also apply formatting like bold and italic in HMTL mode. When in this mode, you are actually creating HTML tags in the code (see Chapter 6). You can see these tags by clicking Code view or Split view from the Document toolbar.

DREAMWEAVER TIP

The more HTML code you have for a web page, the larger the file size it will be and the slower it'll load in a browser.

Using CSS mode of the Property Inspector, you can create CSS code for controlling the document structure and element format (see Figure 2.19). Chapter 7 covers this mode.

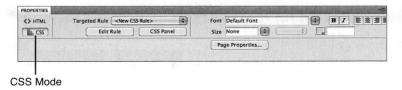

CSS Mode

Figure 2.19: You can create new style rules for formatting your web page through the CSS mode of the Property Inspector.

You can show and hide the Property Inspector by choosing it from the Windows menu.

Application Bar

The Application bar contains features that control the layout view of the Workspace, *extensions*, and *widgets*. It also provides a document search feature and direct access to Adobe's *CS Live* services. This bar is located in a different location of the workspace based on whether you are using a Macintosh or a PC. On a Macintosh, the Application bar is located below the menu bar in the Dreamweaver workspace (see Figure 2.20). On the PC platform, this bar is located above the menu bar.

Application bar

Figure 2.20: You used the Application bar earlier in this chapter when you changed your workspace layout view from Design view to Code view.

You'll use this bar throughout this book.

DEFINITION

An **extension** is a program or application that adds additional functionality to Dreamweaver.

A **widget** is a small program that can be installed and executed from a web page.

CS Live integrates five online services from Adobe. These services further streamline the creative and development process of the entire suite of CS5 products (see Chapter 21).

Tutorial: Setting Up Your Workspace

You need to do a little housekeeping before you start creating the Walkabout Adventure Travel website. This site is for a travel company that offers soft adventure travel. They offer tours to exciting destinations around the world. Your job is to build a website to advertise Walkabout and its tours. As you progress through this book, each tutorial builds upon the previous ones. By the end of the book you will have created a full-featured website for Walkabout Adventure Travel.

To help make the tutorials and instruction as consistent and understandable as possible, this tutorial sets up a common Dreamweaver workspace so that panels and toolbars are in the same location for all users. You will also set up the Insert panel with commonly used buttons so that they're available for use in the rest of the book. Follow these steps:

1. Open Dreamweaver and select **HTML** from the **Create New** section of the **Welcome** window. This opens a blank HTML page.

2. Now you need to set your workspace to the Designer workspace. From the Application bar, click the **Workspace** button and choose **Designer** from the list of workspace layouts.

3. Next, split the view of the document into both Code view and Design view. From the Document toolbar, click the **Split** button.

4. Now set up some favorite buttons in the Insert panel. Click the **Insert** tab in the panel dock. This displays the Insert panel.

5. From the **Category** menu, choose **Favorites**.

6. In the **Favorites** category of the Insert panel, Ctrl-click or right-click to display the pop-up menu and choose **Customize Favorites** from the list.

7. In the Customize Favorites window, click the **Common** category on the left and then select **Image** from the list.

8. Move **Image** to the right Favorite Objects pane by clicking the **Move** button.

9. Repeat steps 7 and 8 to add **Insert Div tag**, **Table**, and **Email Link**.

10. In the Favorite Objects list to the right, select **Image** and then click the **Add Separator** button to create a dashed line below **Image**.

11. Now you can organize your Favorites list of buttons on the right side of the Customize Favorite Objects window. Click **E-mail Link** to select it. Using the **Move Up** button, move this button below **Image** (see Figure 2.21).

Figure 2.21: You can arrange your Favorites buttons in any order you want and even add a divider to separate groups of related buttons.

12. Click **OK** to close the Customize Favorites window.

13. Now switch your view of the Insert panel to icons only by clicking the **Category** button in the Insert panel and choosing **Hide Labels** from the pop-up menu.

Your Dreamweaver workspace and your Favorites category of the Insert panel are now set up (see Figure 2.22).

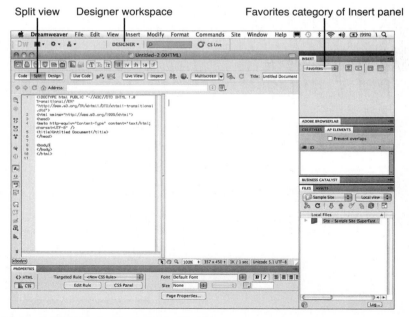

Figure 2.22: Your workspace looks like this.

The Least You Need to Know

- You can use the Welcome Screen to create a new web page.
- You can organize the Dreamweaver workspace by choosing a workspace layout from the Application Bar.
- You can manipulate panels and panel groups by collapsing, moving, sizing, and re-organizing them.
- You can use the Files panel to view all web pages and elements of your site.
- You can create your own customized Favorites category in the Insert panel.
- You can use the Application bar to set layout views and workspaces.
- You can switch between the HTML or CSS mode of the Property Inspector.

Defining Your Site

In This Chapter

- Defining a new site
- Setting your local site folder
- Linking to your remote servers
- Defining advanced site functionality
- Changing and editing a defined site

The first step in creating a new site in Dreamweaver is to define your site. Defining a site sets up the folder, called the *root folder*, for storing all pages, graphics, and elements in your site. Defining a site enables Dreamweaver to manage the site and all pages within the site, as well as create links between pages and other elements.

If you don't define a site, Dreamweaver won't know where to save files that you create. Nor will the program know how to create hyperlinks between files or even where to find graphics that you want to use in your web pages. By defining a site, Dreamweaver can accurately create the pages and set up the links for files and assets in your website pages.

You can also establish the link to the remote server that's hosting your site. Dreamweaver synchronizes the root folder with the host directory of your site. Dreamweaver's goal is to make the web design process work efficiently and seamlessly.

The Web Development Process

A website consists of HTML/HTM files, graphic/media files, folders, and site assets. As a web developer, you first create a new site on your computer and group all files in a root folder. By keeping your files on your computer, you can develop and test your site to get it working as you planned. When you put your stamp of approval on your site, it's ready to be viewed on the web.

When your site is ready, you upload, or post, your site to a *remote hosting server*. Now your site files exist both on your local computer and on the remote server. Your files, folders, and site structure are identical on each location. The hosting server displays your site pages when a visitor to your site requests them through a URL and a domain name.

DEFINITION

The **remote hosting server** allows your site to be visible on the Internet or an intranet running on a Local Area Network or LAN.

By creating a local root folder, Dreamweaver knows where to save files and how to organize, share, and manage files on your computer. When you want to post your files, Dreamweaver makes transferring these files to the remote server a snap.

Defining a Local Site

Before you can define your site, you first need to determine the local site folder that will be the root folder for your site. This folder holds all the files, elements, and assets used in the site. You create this folder on your computer through the New Folder command of your operating system.

With a local folder created for your website, you now can define a new site through the New Site command. You can find the New Site command in the Dreamweaver menu bar by choosing **Site, New Site**. This opens the Site Setup window for your new site (see Figure 3.1).

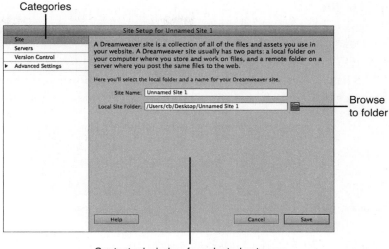

Figure 3.1: The Site Setup window lets you define your new website in Dreamweaver.

Notice that this window is divided into two panes. On the left are category options that are contextually related to the pane on the right. By default, the first category option is the Site category of the Setup window, and it's active by default. The right pane of this window is a contextually sensitive window that displays the Site Name field and the Local Site Folder field associated with the Site category. You can click a different category from the left pane of the Site Setup window and access all features and options associated with this category displayed on the right. The following sections explore the Site Setup dialog box by looking at each category and its features and options.

The Site Category

The Site category is the first category you'll use when defining a site. Through the Site category, located on the left, you can establish the name of your new site and what folder on your computer will store your *site files*. Figure 3.1 shows the Site Setup window with the Site category selected.

DEFINITION

Site files are all the HTML/HTM files, as well as all the graphic and supporting files.

To create a name for your site, type the name of the new site into the **Site Name** field. You may call your site anything you like, with no restrictions (see Figure 3.2).

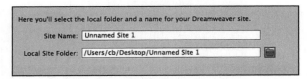

Figure 3.2: To define a site, you must set the site name and the local site folder.

Next, you must establish the folder on your computer to use as the Local Site folder or site root folder. You can either type a path to a folder in the **Local Site Folder** field or click the **Browse to Folder** icon to the right of the field. This opens the Choose Root Folder Window and allows you to navigate to the folder (see Figure 3.3).

Create a new folder ———
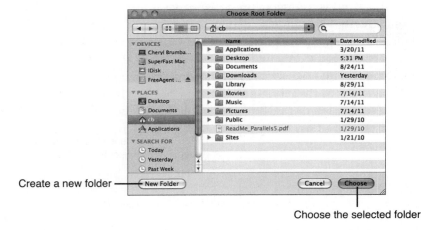
Choose the selected folder

Figure 3.3: You can navigate to any location on your computer through the Choose Root Folder window.

DREAMWEAVER TIP

On a PC, Choose Root Folder Window displays a **Select** button instead of the **Choose** button as shown in Figure 3.3.

If the folder doesn't exist, you can click the **New Folder** button to create a new folder. This opens the New Folder window on a Macintosh (see Figure 3.4) or creates a new folder directly in the Choose Root Folder window on a PC.

Figure 3.4: *The New Folder window. You can name your folder any name that you want but you must follow the naming conventions of your operating system.*

Name the local site folder (root folder) for your site and click **Create** (Mac)/**Select** (PC) to close the New Folder window and return to the Choose Root Folder window to finalize the setup of the local site folder for your new site (see Figure 3.5).

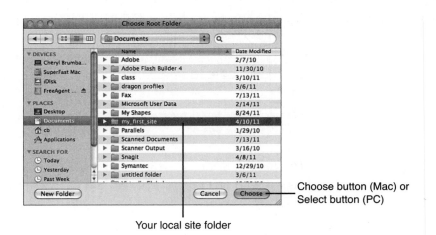

Choose button (Mac) or
Select button (PC)

Your local site folder

Figure 3.5: *Your Local Site Folder is highlighted in the Choose Root Folder.*

You'll see your local site folder highlighted. Click **Choose** (Mac)/**Select** (PC) to establish this folder as your local site folder.

DREAMWEAVER TIP

The most efficient way to define a new site is to create a site name and set a local site folder for your site files and assets. This is all Dreamweaver needs to define a site.

The Servers Category

The Servers Category of the Site Setup window links your local site folder to your remote server. Click the **Servers** category; the contextual screen on the right changes to display server information (see Figure 3.6).

Servers category

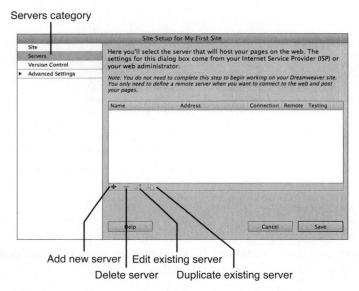

Add new server | Edit existing server
Delete server | Duplicate existing server

Figure 3.6: *The Servers category of the Site Setup window. The remote server hosts your website and makes it visible to others.*

To add a remote server, click the **+** sign, which is the **Add New Server** button. This opens a window that enables you to determine your server and connection type (see Figure 3.7).

DREAMWEAVER TIP

You can set multiple remote web servers by clicking **Add New Server** (+) again and going through the remote server setup process for each new server. You can add as many remote servers as you need to develop and test your site.

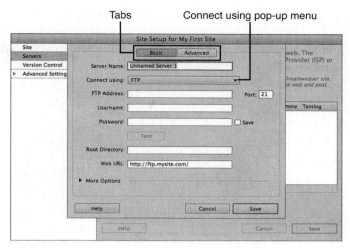

Figure 3.7: The Server and Connection Type window. You can select your Connection type for your remote server in the **Connect Using** *pop-up menu.*

FTP stands for *File Transfer Protocol* and is a standard network protocol for transferring files between local computers and remote hosting servers over the Internet. In Dreamweaver, you can find FTP in the **Connect Using** pop-up menu. With this type of connection, you can upload files to your remote server and download from the remote server to your local computer. See Chapter 17 for details on the FTP server setup process, as well as how to set up other remote server connections.

Version Control

You can set Dreamweaver to connect to a remote server that uses *Subversion (SVN)*. The *Version Control* category of the Site Setup window enables you to create this connection.

DEFINITION

Subversion (SVN) is a version control system. On an SVN, multiple users can collaboratively edit and manage files on a remote web server.

Version Control is a system developed to keep track of different versions of software or files. It typically uses a numbering system to reflect newer versions.

Access dropdown menu

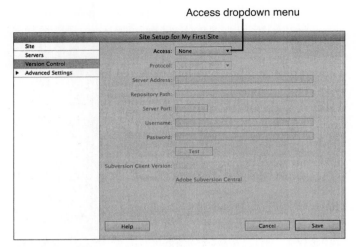

Figure 3.8: By default, the Access option is set to None in the Version Control category of the Site Setup window. On a PC the Cancel and Save buttons are reversed in the order of their display.

To access the Version Control settings, click the **Version Control** category on the left, click the **Access** dropdown menu, and choose **Subversion**. Through the Subversion options and settings, you can set version control settings so that you can share, edit, and manage files with multiple users (see Figure 3.8).

Advanced Settings of the Site Setup Window

The Advanced Settings category is a group of subcategories. If you click the Advanced Settings category, it expands to display all the subcategories that make up the Advanced Settings (see Figure 3.9).

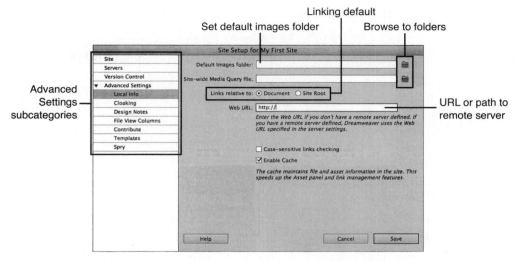

Figure 3.9: Seven subcategories comprise the Advanced Settings Category.

Select one of these subcategories to display its contextual settings on the right.

Local Info

The Local Info subcategory includes the information you need for managing files and links for your site. Table 3.1 provides information about each of the settings and options in the Local Info subcategory of Advanced Settings.

Table 3.1   Local Info Settings

Setting	Overview
Default Images Folder	Enables you to set the default image folder for your site. You can type in the path to your images folder or click the folder to the right of the field and navigate to it.
Links Relative To	Sets up the type of link that Dreamweaver creates to your site assets.
Web URL	Establishes the remote server. If you entered this information in the Site category, it displays here. If you didn't set this information yet, you can do so now. Type the URL to your site's domain name that is hosted on a remote web server.

(continues)

Table 3.1   Local Info Settings   (continued)

Setting	Overview
Case-Sensitive Link Checking	Checks to see if the case of links matches the linked file name. If you are hosting your site on a UNIX server, this option should be selected, as UNIX servers are case sensitive.
Enable Cache	Creates a local cache of all pages and links in your site. This improves the speed at which the pages of your site displays and the speed of link-management tasks.

DREAMWEAVER TIP

The Assets panel works correctly only if the Enable Cache option is active and a cache has been created.

You need to establish the type of link path you'll use in your website. Dreamweaver offers two choices: document-relative paths and site root–relative paths.

By default, Dreamweaver is set to the document-relative path. Document-relative paths are a simple, focused way to link a document because they are based on the linking document. Using Figure 3.10 as an example, if you create a link on your index.html page (the linking document) to your contact.html page (the linked document), the document relative path is **contact.html**.

Figure 3.10: The site named Site2 contains two documents and an images folder that contains one graphic file.

A document relative path is based on the document that is linking (index.html) to another file (contact.html). They exist at the same level in the site, so the document relative path based on index.html as the linking document would be contact.html. If the linked document is in a folder, the path to the document shows the folder in relation to its location to the linking document. For instance, if you created a link on your index.html document to the header.gif in the images folder, you would use **images/header.gif** to indicate the path.

Site root–relative paths are a form of linking that always starts at the root folder of the site and then shows the path to the document. You use this type of path when your site has several remote servers or a main server that hosts multiple sites. If you frequently move HTML files between folders on your site, this type of path is the best choice. A site root–relative path always begins with a forward slash (/), which represents the root folder of the site. Using the Figure 3.10 example, if you created a link on the index.html document to contact.html, you would use this type of path: **/contact.html.** The forward slash tells Dreamweaver to go to the site root folder and then find the contact.html file. To link to the image in the Images folder, the site root–relative path would be **/images/header.gif**.

DREAMWEAVER TIP

A third type of path you can use in Dreamweaver is called an absolute path. Every web page has a unique address or URL. An absolute path is the complete address to a document or linked file. If you linked from your index.html file to the contact.html file, you would use http://www.site2.com/contact.html to create this type of path link.

Cloaking

Cloaking is a setting that enables you to designate certain files or file types that you want Dreamweaver to exclude from certain operations (see Figure 3.11).

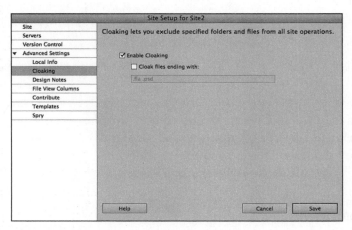

Figure 3.11: *Cloaking hides certain files or file types from Dreamweaver management operations.*

A common use of cloaking is to exclude all Photoshop files, which have the extension of .psd, from Dreamweaver operations. To designate these files, you select the **Enable Cloaking** option and then select **Cloak Files Ending With**. Either type in the name of the files you want to cloak or, to reference many files, such as all Photoshop files, type just the file extension (.psd). Now any time you use the Dreamweaver Put or Get operations, Dreamweaver skips any Photoshop files. Chapter 18 covers the Put and Get operations in detail.

Design Notes

Design notes are useful when you're collaborating with other designers and developers to create a site. You can attach notes to other people collaborating on the site to explain functionality, discuss ideas, or provide instructions (see Figure 3.12).

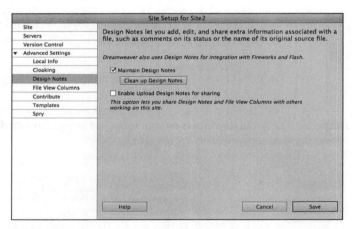

Figure 3.12: The Design Notes window. Design Notes help keep others in the loop on the development of each page of the site.

If you select the **Enable Upload Design Notes for Sharing** option, other designers and developers on your team can read all design notes on your site documents. You can also use Design Notes to integrate with other Adobe CS5.5 products. See Chapter 18 for details about using Design Notes.

File View Columns

The File View Columns setting relates to the Files panel and the display of the columns in this panel. The Files panel displays all the documents, folders, and assets of your site in a columnar format.

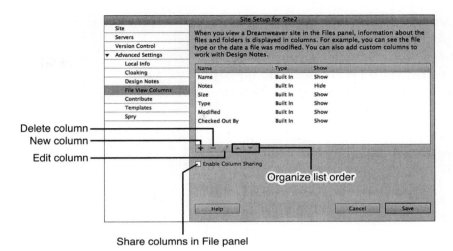

Delete column
New column
Edit column

Organize list order

Share columns in File panel

Figure 3.13: *The File View Columns window. You can show and hide columns in the Files panel by double-clicking the show or hide option for a column.*

DREAMWEAVER TIP

If you select Enable Column Sharing, you can share the format of your Files panel with other designers and developers on your team, just as you can with design notes.

By using the tools in the lower-left corner of the right contextually sensitive screen of **File View Columns**, you can create, delete, organize, and edit columns in the Files panel (see Figure 3.13). To add a new column, click the **+** button, which opens a new window for designating another column.

Contribute

The **Contribute** category of the Site Setup window enables you to prepare a site for use with Adobe Contribute. *Adobe Contribute* is a web-publishing and site-management tool that allows others to access, edit, and author website content. To enable a website to work with Contribute, select the **Enable Contribute Compatibility** option (see Figure 3.14).

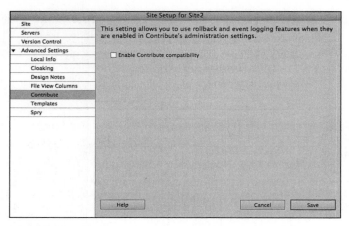

Figure 3.14: *The Enable Contribute Compatibility option sets up your site for use with Contribute functionality and features.*

When you enable Contribute, the Design Notes and Check In/Check Out options are also automatically enabled. If your connection to the remote service doesn't support Contribute, a message appears indicating that the current connection isn't compatible with Contribute (see Figure 3.15).

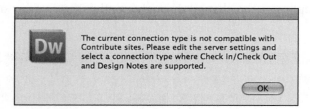

Figure 3.15: *This message indicates that you need to choose Server settings, such as FTP, that are compatible with Contribute.*

If your remote server is compatible with Contribute, a message appears indicating that Design Notes and the Check In/Check Out options will be enabled (see Figure 3.16).

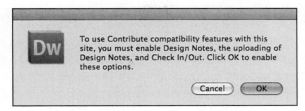

Figure 3.16: If you have a connection type that supports Contribute but didn't turn on the Design Notes or Check In/Check Out options, Dreamweaver automatically turns on these features through this message.

Click **OK** to enable Contribute and the other collaborating Dreamweaver features. Your site is now set to work with Adobe Contribute.

Templates

Templates are a powerful time-saving feature of Dreamweaver that Chapter 16 covers in detail. This option is enabled by default (see Figure 3.17). You can create a template from an existing web page or from scratch. You can apply a template to existing pages in your site or you can create new web pages from it. Using templates helps keeps your design consistent throughout the site. If you change the template, Dreamweaver automatically replicates the change throughout all pages on your site that are based on the template.

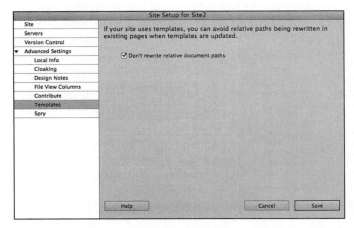

Figure 3.17: The Templates subcategory of the Advanced Settings. Templates are a useful tool when developing websites and pages in Dreamweaver.

Spry

The Spry widget is another nice feature of Dreamweaver. A Spry widget is a web page element that lets users interact with the page content. Spry widgets come in different forms. Five Spry widgets are included with Dreamweaver; to access them, go to **Insert, Spry.** Chapter 20 covers Spry widgets in detail.

When you use a Spry widget, Dreamweaver automatically creates a folder in your site root folder named SpryAssets folder. This folder holds all the supporting code, graphics, and CSS required to create the widget in your web page.

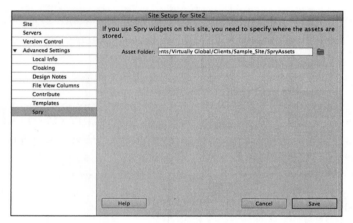

Figure 3.18: *Spry widgets consist of Spry assets, which need to be stored in an Asset folder within your defined site.*

You can change the location of the SpryAssets folder by either typing the path to a SpryAssets folder in another location or clicking the folder on the right of the Asset Folder field and navigating to the location of another SpryAssets folder (see Figure 3.18).

Finalizing Site Setup

When you've set your categories and subcategories and established and defined your site information, click the **Save** button in the lower-right corner of the Site Setup window. This finalizes your site setup by saving your defined site. After you save the defined site, it appears in the Files panel (see Figure 3.19).

Figure 3.19: *The Files panel holds all the pages and site assets for your website.*

With a site defined, you can begin to create and develop your site's web pages.

DREAMWEAVER TIP

You can modify the settings for any site you've defined by choosing **Site,
Manage Sites** from the menu bar.

Modifying a Defined Site

Now that your site is set up and defined, you're not limited to those settings. You can
edit and modify site definition settings using the Manage Site command. You can
access the Site Setup window in the following ways:

- In the menu bar, choose **Site, Manage Sites**.

- In the Files panel, select the **Site** menu and then choose **Manage Sites** (see
  Figure 3.20).

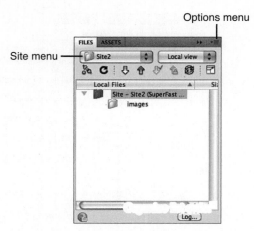

Figure 3.20: *You can access the Site Setup window through the Files panel and the Site menu.*

• In the Files panel, select the **Options menu** and then select **Manage Sites** (see Figure 3.20).

• In the Application bar, select the **New Site** command and then choose **Manage Sites** (see Figure 3.21).

Figure 3.21: *The Site button in the Application bar. The Manage Sites and New Site commands are available to you in many different locations in Dreamweaver.*

Regardless of which technique you use to choose **Manage Sites**, doing so opens the Manage Sites window (see Figure 3.22).

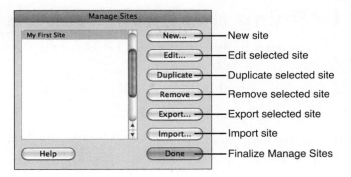

Figure 3.22: As you develop more sites, the Manage Sites window lists all sites you've defined.

You use the Manage Sites window to define a new site, edit existing sites, duplicate or remove a site, and import and export sites. Here's an overview of what you can do using the Manage Sites window:

- To create a new site, click **New**. This opens the Site Setup window.

- To edit an already defined site, select the site on the left of the Manage Sites window and then click **Edit**. This opens the Site Setup window with all the information that you originally set up when defining your new site.

- To duplicate an existing site, select the site on the left and then click **Duplicate**.

- To remove a defined site, select the site on the left and then click **Remove**.

- To export a site, select the site on the left and then click **Export**. In the Exporting window that displays, choose your export settings.

- To import a site, click **Import** and navigate to the site that you want to import into Dreamweaver.

- When you've established all your settings for your defined sites, click **Done** to exit the Manage Sites window and apply the settings.

Tutorial: Defining the Travel Website

Before you begin to create the first page of your Travel website, you need to define the site in Dreamweaver. Follow these steps:

1. Open Dreamweaver so that the Welcome Screen displays.

2. From the menu bar, choose **Site, New Site**.

3. This opens the Site Setup window (see Figure 3.23). Type **Walkabout Travel** for the site name.

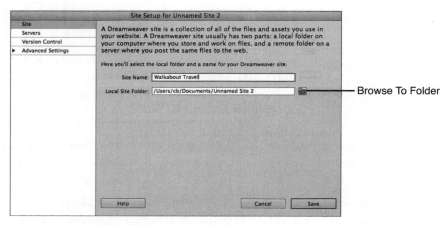

Browse To Folder

Figure 3.23: The Site Setup window for Walkabout Travel. You can name your site anything you want, with no restrictions on naming conventions.

4. Next, you need to determine the root folder for your site. Click the **Browse To folder** to the right of the Local Site Folder field and navigate to your desktop.

5. Click the **New Folder** button to create a new folder on your desktop. Type **Walkabout Site** in the Name of New Folder field. Click the **Create** (Mac)/ **Select** (PC) button to create the folder (see Figure 3.24).

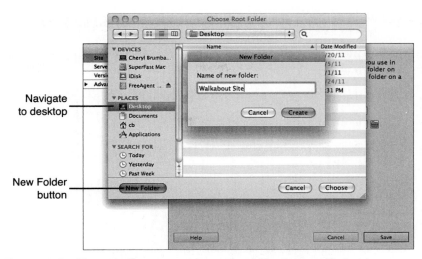

Navigate
to desktop

New Folder
button

Figure 3.24: *You typically want to create a root folder in a specific location on your computer, but for ease of instruction, here you create the Walkabout folder on the desktop.*

6. In the Choose Root Folder window, click the **Choose/Select** button to set the folder as your root folder for your site (see Figure 3.25).

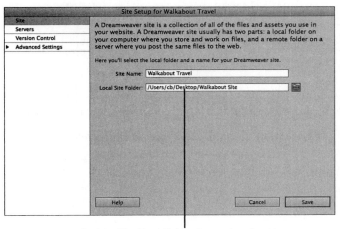

Path to Site Root Folder located on Desktop

Figure 3.25: *Your Site Setup window should look similar to this figure.*

7. Next, you define an **Images** folder for the site. Expand the Advanced Settings category by clicking the **Advanced Settings** category to expand it. Make sure the **Local Info** subcategory is selected (see Figure 3.26).

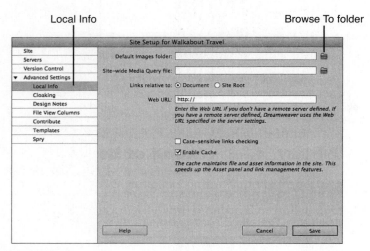

Figure 3.26: You can create a new folder for your images by clicking the **Browse To folder** *to the right of the Default Images folder field.*

8. To create a new folder for your site images, click **Browse To folder** and create a new folder.

9. Type **images** in the New Folder Window and click the **Create/Select** button to create this new folder in your root folder for the Walkabout site.

10. In the Choose Image Folder window. With the **images** folder highlighted, click the **Choose/Select** button to set **images** as your default images folder.

11. Leave the **Links Relative To** option set to **Document.**

12. Make sure the **Enable Cache** option is selected (see Figure 3.27).

Document option

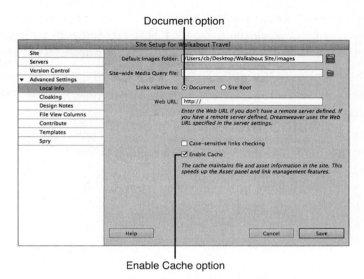

Enable Cache option

***Figure 3.27**: If you have a remote server to host your website, type the URL of the remote server in the Web URL field to establish a connection.*

13. To finalize site setup, click **Save** in the Site Setup window to save all your settings for defining the Walkabout site.

14. This returns you to the Manage Sites window. Click **Done** to close this window.

15. The Files panel displays your new site (see Figure 3.28).

***Figure 3.28**: The Files panel displays the site files and file structure for Walkabout Adventure Travel.*

The Least You Need to Know

- The first step in developing a website in Dreamweaver is to define your site.
- You define a site by creating a new site in the Site Setup window.
- The most direct way to access the New Site command is through the Dreamweaver menu bar Site, New Site command.
- The most efficient way to define a site is to establish your site name and identify the root folder in the Local Info category of the Site Setup window.

Building Your First Web Page

The chapters in this part provide step-by-step instructions for creating your first web page. You find out how to add basic content and create document structure to that page.

This part also introduces you to many features and elements you can use to add pizzazz to your page, including CSS style sheets for formatting your page and adding images, links, and tables.

Creating Your First Web Page

In This Chapter

- Creating your first web page
- Applying HTML format headings
- Setting page properties
- Saving a web page

Now that you've defined your website (see Chapter 3), it's time to create a web page for it. You can use Dreamweaver's Define Site process to save your pages, create links, and store any images that you create.

This chapter walks you through the process of starting your first web page.

Creating a New Web Page

You can create a new web page (which, if you're using HTML to make the page, is also called an HTML document) in Dreamweaver in any of the following ways:

- Select **HTML** from the **Create New** section of the Welcome Screen.
- Choose **File, New** from the menu bar.
- Click the **New** button from the Standard toolbar.

Each of these techniques creates a new web page.

Creating a New Document with Default Settings

As you learned in Chapter 2, when you create a new web page through the Welcome Screen, you are creating a document based on the document preferences that you've set for Dreamweaver.

From the Welcome Screen, under the **Create New** section, select **HTML** (see Figure 4.1).

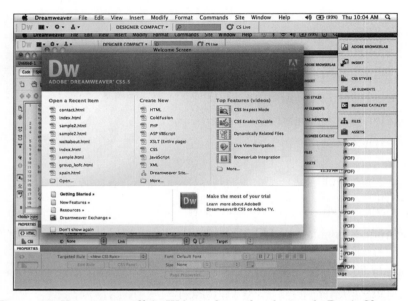

*Figure 4.1: You can turn off the Welcome Screen by selecting the **Don't Show Again** option in the lower-left corner.*

This is the most direct way to create a new web page document, but you're stuck using the default setting.

You can also create a new document using a different version of HTML. As discussed in Chapter 1, numerous versions of HTML exist. Dreamweaver gives you the option to choose different versions of HTML for your new web pages; if you go this route, you need to determine the version of HTML that supports the functionality you want for your web page.

Creating a New Document with User-Defined Settings

If you want to use options other than the Dreamweaver default settings, use one of the following two techniques to create your new web page:

- From the Standard toolbar (see Chapter 2), click the **New** button (see Figure 4.2).

- From the menu bar, choose **File, New.** The keyboard equivalent is **Cmd/ Ctrl+N**.

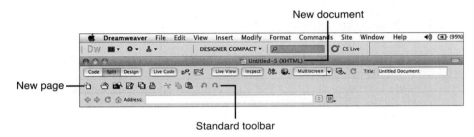

Figure 4.2: From the Standard toolbar you can Open, Save, Print, Cut, Copy, and Paste, as well as undo and redo.

Both techniques open a new HTML document (see Figure 4.3).

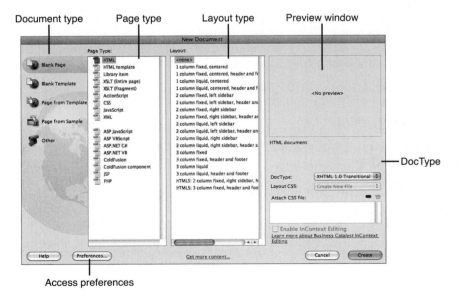

Figure 4.3: The New Document window offers category choices on the far left that, when selected, display contextually relevant options to the right.

DREAMWEAVER TIP

When you create a new web page, any toolbars that you set to display are located at the top of the New Document window. To display other toolbars, choose **View, Toolbars,** located in the menu bar.

You can create many different types of new web documents, including HTML documents, template documents, or CSS documents, in New Document window. The New Document window is divided into five sections: Document Type, Page Type, Layout Type, Preview Window, and DocType (see Figure 4.3). Each section, except for the far-left Document Categories, is context sensitive to what you select in the section directly to the left.

DREAMWEAVER TIP

Dreamweaver provides many different types of layouts for creating a new document. Under the Layout Type section of the New Document window is a listing of sample layouts based on many popular design layouts. Select a layout, and the Preview window displays a preview of the page.

Start by selecting the Document Type category, at the far left. You can choose from one of the following options:

- **Blank Page**—Creates blank page
- **Blank Template**—Creates a blank template
- **Page from Template**—Creates a page from an existing template
- **Page from Sample**—Creates a page from a sample page
- **Other**—Creates non-HTML page types

Simply click the document type that you want to use to create a new web document. Each document type displays different options in the context-sensitive sections to the right. The **Blank Page** option is selected by default.

After you establish your document type, you can choose a page type. Dreamweaver displays context-appropriate settings based on your selection. For example, if you are creating a new HTML page, when you select **HTML** from the Page Type section, you can choose a default layout for the document from the Layout column of the New Document window.

Preset Document Layouts

Adobe provides some of the more popular HTML page layouts for your new web page. Each of these layouts is based on CSS, which Chapter 15 covers. You have a choice of fixed or liquid layouts (see Figure 4.4).

Fixed layouts are structured to give you a fixed page width in which to display your content. The width doesn't change in dimension based on the size of the user's browser window. Fixed layouts give you more control over your page structure and design.

Liquid layouts expand or contract based on the size of the user's browser window. All the page content must be designed to flow and display based on the size of the browser window. As a designer, when you use this type of layout, you need to design your page to look good no matter how wide or tall the browser window is set. In other words, your design must be able to flow to fill the browser window.

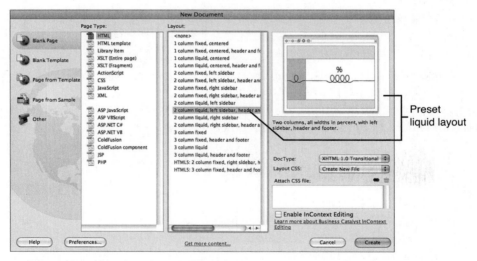

Figure 4.4: After you choose HTML from the Page Type column, you can choose your layout type.

When creating a blank HTML page, you can choose from 19 different layout options in the New Document window. Each of these layouts offers a different display of the various areas of a web page, including the header/banner, sidebars, and footer.

Setting DocType

With your layout determined, you can set your web page's DocType. This option sets the type of HTML you'll be using for all new documents on your site (see Figure 4.5).

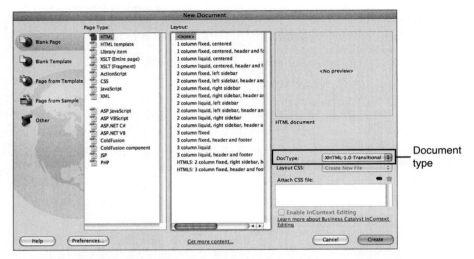

Figure 4.5: *Choose your document type in the New Document window. The default setting is XHTML 1.0 Transitional.*

You can choose from the following document types:

- None
- HTML 4.01 Transitional
- HTML 4.01 Strict
- HTML 5
- XHTML 1.0 Transitional
- XHTML 1.0 Strict
- XHTML 1.1
- XHTML Mobile 1.0

The default Dreamweaver setting is XHTML 1.0 Transitional, but you may choose any other type of HTML you need by selecting it from the list. The difference between Strict and Transitional involves the type of HTML tags and properties supported. A Transitional document supports some older HTML tags and properties that the Strict versions have phased out. So if your document has older tags and prop-erties from earlier versions of HTML, they might still work in your document if you use Transitional types of HTML. (To learn more about HTML types, go to www. wikipedia.com and type in "HTML.")

DREAMWEAVER DON'T

Avoid selecting **None** for the **DocType** of HTML. This setting can cause a browser to display your document in what is called Quirks mode, and your design might not display as you intended.

After you've determined your settings for your new page, click the **Create** button to create the page.

Your new page now awaits your creative touch! Notice all the HTML code that Dreamweaver automatically generated in Code view (see Figure 4.6). This HTML code adheres to the type of HTML you chose for the DocType.

Code generated by Dreamweaver   Design view of new page

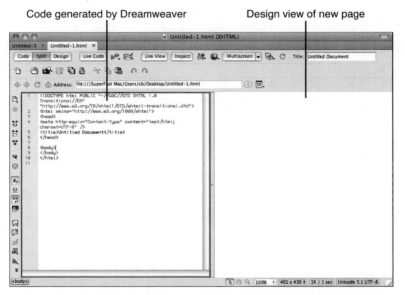

Figure 4.6: *A split view of your new page, showing both the HTML code in Code View (on the left) and the Design view (on the right).*

Setting Page Properties

The new document is basically a blank slate for which you determine all the properties. When you create a website, you need to set the default page properties for page elements such as the font-family, page background color and image, link colors, and page margins.

To access the document's page properties, choose **Modify, Page Properties** from the menu bar. This displays the Page Properties window (see Figure 4.7).

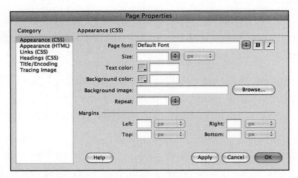

Figure 4.7: The page properties apply to only the active document.

Typical of other windows you've been introduced to, on the left of the Page Properties window is a category of options that, when selected, display the associated settings on the right. Click the individual settings option and select your choice to set up your page properties.

The Page Properties window has two choices for default page properties: CSS or HTML. If you choose **Appearance (CSS),** the page properties that you determine are coded as CSS in the web page. If you choose **Appearance (HTML),** all settings that you determine are coded as HTML (see Chapter 1 for general information about HTML and CSS).

DREAMWEAVER TIP

It's good practice to set your Appearance settings in CSS and not HTML. CSS is much more flexible because it can be exported to an external style sheet for linking with other HTML documents (see Chapters 7, 12, and 15).

Appearance (CSS)

The Appearance CSS creates CSS code in the HTML <head> tag at the start of the HTML code of the web page (see Figure 4.8).

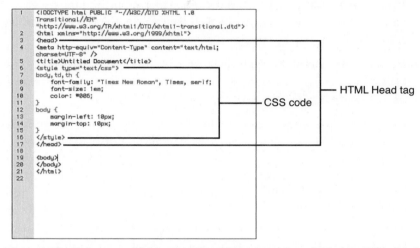

Figure 4.8: Code view of CSS code. This CSS code applies a background color and a left and top margin of 10px to the body tag of the HTML document.

DREAMWEAVER TIP

When you set page properties through Appearance (CSS) to a page that is already linked to an external style sheet, Dreamweaver will not overwrite any tags that have been set for the same properties in the external style sheet (see Chapter 12 for more information about external style sheets).

When working in Appearance (CSS) mode, you can choose the following settings on the Page Properties window:

- **Page Font**—This is the default font used for all text on your page. Select your *font-family* for your page and apply Bold or Italic.

DEFINITION

A **font-family** is a group of fonts that have similar displays. Based on the visitor's computer and the fonts that they have installed, the font-family dictates which font to use. For instance, in the font-family "Times New Roman, Times, Serif" if the visitor has Times New Roman on their computer, this font is used for the display of the web page text. If they don't, then the next font in the list is used. If they do not have this second font installed, the machine default font of serif is used for the text on the web page.

- **Size**—Set the font size and determine the size unit.

- **Text Color**—Click the color palette button and select a color for the text on the page, or type in the *hexadecimal* number for the color.

- **Background Color**—Click the Color Palette button and select a background color for the background of the web page. Your background can be a solid color or an image.

- **Background Image**—Type the path or browse to a background image. The background image displays in the background of a page. All text and images on the page display on top of the background image.

- **Repeat**—Choose the type of tiling for the background image for your page. A background image can be stationary and only display at the top of the page or it can be set to repeat. If you have a long web page and you want to have the background image visible for the entire page, you need to repeat the image so that it tiles down the page. You can repeat a background image for both x and y coordinates so that it tiles both vertically and horizontally. Or you can set it to repeat for just the x coordinate so that it tiles horizontally across your page. If you set the repeat to just the y coordinate, it tiles the image vertically down the page.

- **Margins**—Set left, top, right, and bottom margins.

> **DEFINITION**
>
> **Hexadecimal** is a six-digit number that's associated with a color for display on a screen. It is a standard way to represent color for both your computer's color system and colors on the Internet.

Appearance (HTML)

When you set Appearance (HTML) settings, you are actually setting HTML tags that are embedded in the code of the active document. These settings apply to the page and increase the file size of your document.

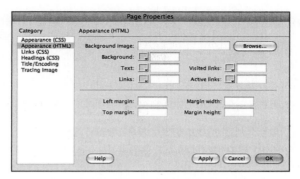

Figure 4.9: *The Appearance (HTML) option enables you to set colors for your links states.*

Here's an overview of each setting in the Appearance (HTML) category of the Page Properties window (see Figure 4.9):

- **Background Image**—Type the path or browse to a background image.

- **Background Color**—Click the Color Palette button and select a background color.

- **Text**—Set the default color of the text by clicking the Color Palette button and selecting a color.

- **Links**—Set the default color of linked text by clicking the Color Palette button and selecting a color (see the next section for details on links).

- **Visited Links**—Set the default color of visited links by clicking the Color Palette button and selecting a color.

- **Active Links**—Set the default color of active links by clicking the Color Palette button and selecting a color.

- **Margins**—Set left, top, right, and bottom margins.

Links (HTML)

The web is popular due to its ability to link to different documents, web pages, and websites via hyperlinks. Most web pages are built using HTML, and part of HTML's power is the hypertext link. When you click a link on a web page, it takes you to another location within that website, to a new website altogether, or to a document such as a PDF file. Links are the power behind the sharing of information that the web does so well.

Links in an HTML document have the following three states:

- **Static**—A link that exists on a page and hasn't been clicked
- **Visited**—A link that has already been clicked, and the linked content visited
- **Active**—A link that the visitor is clicking

You can set different colors to represent each of the link states to help visitors navigate your page. For instance, if they click a link and then return to the web page with the link, that link displays in a different color, indicating that they have already visited this link.

Browsers have a standard setting for displaying a link. By default, a browser displays linked text with an underline. Browsers also apply a default color scheme to links based on their state: static, active, or visited. Blue applies to the static state, red to the active state, and purple to the visited state. You can use the link properties settings to establish different fonts and colors for all the states of a link.

Links (CSS)

The Links (CSS) setting determines the properties for all CSS-coded links. These properties are coded as CSS in the <head> tag of the HTML document.

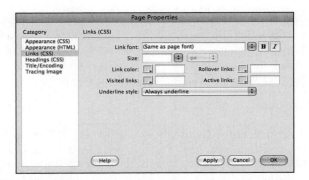

Figure 4.10: In this document, the default font setting for static link text is set the same as the page font.

The Links (CSS) setting has these properties (see Figure 4.10):

- **Link Font**—Set the default font-family for all links on the web page. By default, the Same As Page Font setting is set, but you can change this to any font-family and also apply Bold or Italics.

- **Size**—Set the font size for links.

- **Link Color**—Set the default color of linked text by clicking the Color Palette and selecting a color. You can also type the Hexadecimal color equivalent number in the Link Color field.

- **Visited Links**—Set the default color of visited links by clicking the **Color Palette** button and selecting a color or typing the Hexadecimal color equivalent number in the Visited Links Color field.

- **Rollover Links**—Set the default color of *rollover links* by clicking the **Color Palette** button and selecting a color or typing the Hexadecimal color equivalent number in the Rollover Links Color field.

- **Active Links**—Set the default color of active links by clicking the **Color Palette** button and selecting a color or typing the Hexadecimal color equivalent number in the Active Links Color field.

- **Underline Style**—Set the format for displaying link text with or without an underline. This applies to the various states of a link.

> **DEFINITION**
>
> A **rollover link** displays differently when the end user hovers the mouse over a link; this link state is also referenced as a *hover link*. **Underline style** determines how link states are indicated in the document—with an underline or not.

Headings (CSS)

The Headings (CSS) setting determines the appearance of your headings on your web page. Headings range from Heading 1 to Heading 6 (see Figure 4.11). The supporting HTML uses the tags `<h1>`, `<h2>`, `<h3>`, and so on to designate a heading or headline. You can set a different font and color for each of these headings to really make your headings stand out. You can set the font-family for all headings to be the same as the page font or a different font. You can also determine the font size and color of each individual heading. (See Chapter 6 for more about HTML heading tags and formats.)

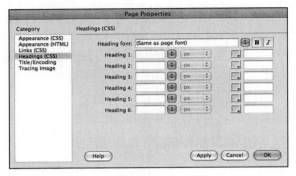

Figure 4.11: In the Headings (CSS) category of the Page Properties window, you can set the font for all heading tags. You can also apply bold or italic formatting to the heading font.

Title/Encoding

The Title/Encoding category enables you to set the document title, as well as the HTML document type and associated encoding settings (see Figure 4.12). The document *encoding* type is specific to the HTML language used to create your web page and relates to the *Unicode Normalization Form* to use with the encoding type.

DEFINITION

Encoding in an HTML document is the process of converting text into a numeric or symbol representation. A browser interprets these numeric codes and decodes it back to text in its display of the web page. The default setting Unicode (UTF-8) for the document encoding represents all text characters and is the common choice.

Unicode Normalization Form dictates the form for the encoding method.

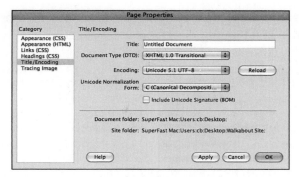

Figure 4.12: When you set a title in the Title/Encoding category of the Page Properties window, it displays at the top of the browser window in the title bar.

Tracing Image

The Tracing Image category allows you to insert an image of your web page to use as a guide for your page design (see Figure 4.13). The image is for your reference only, as the page designer; browsers don't display this image.

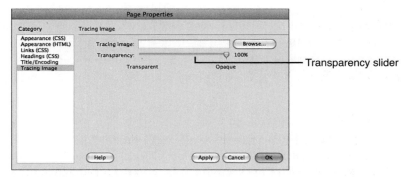

Figure 4.13: You can set the transparency of the guide image by adjusting the Transparency slider in the Tracing Image category of the Page Properties window.

Finalizing Your Page Properties

After you've determined all the page properties for your web page, you need to finalize these settings. To do this, click the **OK** button. The Page Properties window closes and all settings are applied to the active document, as CSS code in the HTML Head tag and/or as HTML tags directly in the HTML code.

> **DREAMWEAVER TIP**
>
> You can click the **Apply** button in the Page Properties window at any time to apply properties that you've set as you work through the settings. Your Page Properties dialog box doesn't close, but the active document reflects the new settings. Applying the properties as you work through the settings helps you fine-tune your settings without having to close and then reopen the Page Properties dialog box to adjust the page settings.

Saving Your Page

After you've created and designed your page, you must save it. You'll find the Save command in the menu bar under **File, Save**. You can also use the **Save** button from the **Standard toolbar** to save your document (see Figure 4.14).

Figure 4.14: The Standard toolbar displays in the active document window.

The asterisk by the document name in the title bar of the web page indicates that the web page needs to be saved. When you save a web page, this asterisk disappears, indicating that the most recent version of the document has been saved.

File Naming Conventions

Because a web page is based on HTML code, you must follow some naming conventions for it. First, if the page is a home page of your site, you must name it one of three names for a browser to recognize it as a home page:

- home.html

- default.html (Windows server home page naming convention)

- index.html

Your file names shouldn't have any spaces or special characters, such as asterisks, commas, periods, or parentheses. Many special characters and symbols represent something else in HTML code, and if your document is named with these symbols, the browser won't interpret your file name correctly and won't be able to display the page. The only special symbol you can use in a file name is the dash. For example, you could use *my-first-page.html* for an HTML document; all browsers understand this convention.

DREAMWEAVER DON'T

Avoid using uppercase in your document names. UNIX doesn't recognize uppercase letters, and if your website is hosted on a UNIX server, it might not interpret the document name correctly.

Using File Extensions

An HTML document can have a file extension of *.html* or *.htm*. In the past, the file extension of *.html* was associated with the Macintosh platform and the .htm extension was associated with the Windows platform due to extension conventions of Windows. If you're using Windows XP or higher, you can use either file extension as Windows limits for file extensions to three characters.

Using Save As Command

To rename an already saved document, choose **File, Save As** in the menu bar. The Save As window opens, prompting you to specify the new file name in the Save As: field; you also have the option to save the file in a new location (see Figure 4.15).

Expands the window to display
navigation or browse features

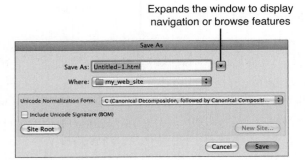

Figure 4.15: Click the button to the right of the Save As field to expand the window and display the navigation or browse feature of both Macintosh and Windows operating systems.

After you've established your file name and save location, click **Save** to close the window and save the file under a new name.

Previewing Your Page

As you develop and design your page, you should preview it occasionally to see how it will look in a browser. All browsers interpret code in their own way, and although this interpretation is almost identical for all browsers, they interpret and then display your HTML and CSS somewhat differently.

You can use any of the following Document toolbar buttons to preview your page (see Figure 4.16):

- Live View
- Live Code
- Preview/Debug in a Browser

DREAMWEAVER TIP

When designing web pages, it's a good practice to preview your pages frequently on a variety of browsers. You can use Live Preview to approximate different browsers, but nothing replaces seeing the page in an actual browser window.

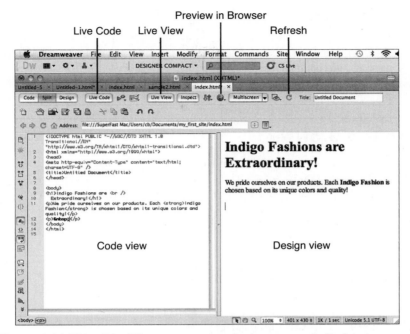

Figure 4.16: Using Live View, you can view the document as it displays in a browser.

The following sections take a closer look at each of these preview options.

Using Live View and Code View

With Live view, you can preview your web page based on your default browser right in Dreamweaver. You can switch between Live view and Design view at any time by clicking the **Live View** button. The Live View button highlights in blue when it's active. You can toggle back to Design view by clicking the **Live View** button again.

You can make edits to a document displayed in Live view, but you must make the edits in the HTML code displayed in Code view. When you turn on Live view, the Property Inspector grays out, indicating that you can't use these settings. You can't edit the Design view display while in Live view.

Also, if Live view is active and you make any changes to the HTML code, you need to refresh the Live view display by either clicking in the Design view display or clicking the **Refresh** button in the Document toolbar.

DREAMWEAVER TIP

Make sure you exit Live view before proceeding with the rest of this chapter. The Design view is disabled when Live view is active. So if you are working on a page and can't access the web page in Design view, check to see if Live view is enabled. Turn it off to get full editing capabilities in Dreamweaver.

Previewing in a Browser

The best technique for seeing how your document will display in a browser is through the **Preview/Debug in a Browser** button, located in the Document toolbar. When you click this button, it expands to a menu of browsers from which to choose (see Figure 4.17).

Figure 4.17: You can add and remove browsers from this menu through Dreamweaver Preferences.

Choose the browser from the pop-out menu; Dreamweaver displays the page in your browser of choice. If the browser isn't opened yet, Dreamweaver launches the browser and displays the page. You must have the browser installed on your computer but you can customize the browser list to reflect all installed browsers through the Dreamweaver Preferences.

Setting Up Primary and Secondary Browsers

You can set up primary and secondary browsers for the Preview/Debug in a Browser command. The primary browser is the one that you're targeting with your design—in other words, it's your first choice for previewing your web pages. The secondary browser is the browser you'll use to preview your web pages after you preview them in the primary browser.

You can set your primary and secondary browsers through the **Edit Browser List** menu choice in the **Preview/Debug in a Browser** button (see Figure 4.17).

> **DREAMWEAVER TIP**
>
> I like to use keyboard commands for accessing many of the Dreamweaver commands. One I use a lot is the keyboard equivalent for previewing your web page in both the primary and secondary browsers. The keyboard equivalent for Preview in the Primary Browser is Opt+F12 (Mac)/F12 (PC). You can only use a secondary browser if you're using a Macintosh. To preview a web page in the secondary browser on a Macintosh, use Cmd+F12.

Click **Edit Browser List** to open Dreamweaver preferences, displaying the Preview in Browser category (see Figure 4.18).

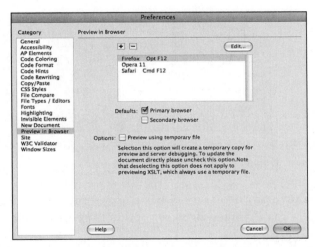

Figure 4.18: *You set your primary and secondary default browsers in the Dreamweaver preferences.*

Here are some ways you can edit the browser list:

- **To add a new browser**—Click the **+** button. This opens the Add Browser window (see Figure 4.19). Name the browser in the Name field. In the Application field, type the path or use the **Browse** button to navigate to the browser application you want to add to the list.

Figure 4.19: *The Add Browser window. Select a default setting to make the new browser a primary or secondary browser.*

- **To delete a browser from the list**—Click the browser from the list to select it, and then click the − button.

- **To access the browser list in one window**—Click the **Edit** button. This opens the Edit Browser window (see Figure 4.20).

Figure 4.20: *You can change the location of the browser application file through the Edit Browser window.*

- **To set a primary browser**—Click a browser from the list to select it, and then select the **Primary Browser** option from the Defaults section.

- **To set a Secondary Browser**—Click a browser from the list to select it, and then select the **Secondary Browser** option from the Defaults section. (This is a Macintosh-only setting. If you're using Dreamweaver on a PC, you only have the Primary browser for previewing).

- **To create a temporary copy of your document in a browser**—Click the box next to **Preview Using Temporary File.**

DREAMWEAVER TIP

BrowserLab is a free Adobe application that lets you see a browser preview of your web page while you're working in Dreamweaver. You don't need to post your page to your remote server to see the browser preview of your page. To open BrowserLab, log in to it at http://browserlab.adobe.com. This service generates a static image of how your web page appears in the browser. You can't click any of the page links or interact with the page (see Chapter 17 for more information about BrowserLab).

Tutorial: Creating a Web Page for the Travel Site

In the tutorial in Chapter 3, you defined your travel site so that Dreamweaver knows where to save pages, how to set up link paths, and where to find images. If you did not complete that tutorial, you'll need to define a site for Walkabout Adventure Travel before you can complete this tutorial.

This tutorial guides you through the process of creating your first web page for Walkabout Adventure Travel website. Follow these steps to create this page:

1. Open Dreamweaver and access your defined travel site by opening the Files panel and choosing **Walkabout** from the Site pop-out menu (see Figure 4.21).

Site pop-out menu

Figure 4.21: *You can also switch to any other defined site through the Site pop-out menu.*

2. On the Welcome Screen, in the Create New section, click **HTML** (see Figure 4.22).

Creates a new HTML page

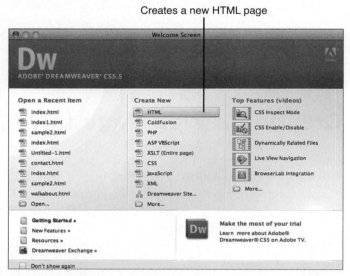

Figure 4.22: *The HTML page you create through the Welcome Screen reflects the version of HTML that you set in your Dreamweaver Preferences.*

3. In the Untitled new page that opens, click in the Title field at the top of the web page and type **Walkabout Adventure Travel Welcomes You!** (see Figure 4.23).

Page Title field

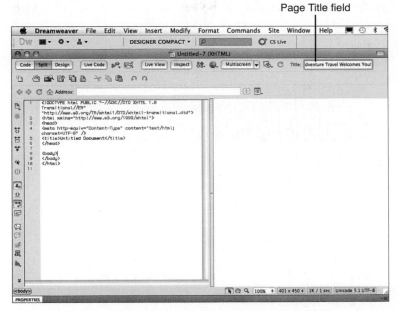

Figure 4.23: *The Page Title field sets the title for the web page. This title is displayed in the title bar of the browser window when the page is viewed through a browser.*

4. Open Page Properties by choosing **Modify, Page Properties** from the menu bar.

5. In the Page Properties window, click the **Appearance CSS** Category and select **Times New Roman, Times, Serif** from the drop-down menu to the right of the Page Font field.

6. To set the font size, click the **Size** field and type **1**. Then click the size menu and select **em** from the list.

7. Set the font color by clicking the **Text Color** palette button next to Text Color and select Hexadecimal number **#360,** which is a green color. (Alternatively, you can click in the Text Color field and type **#336600** or the shorthand version **#360.**)

8. Set the background color to the Hexadecimal number of #cc9 by clicking the **Background Color** palette button and choosing the pale-green color from the palette (or you can click the **Background color:** field and type **#cccc99** or **#cc9** (see Figure 4.24).

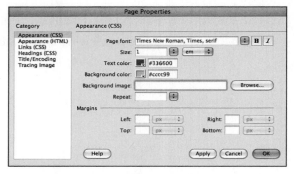

Figure 4.24: Your Page Properties settings should match this figure.

9. Click **OK** to close the window. The Dreamweaver Design view changes to reflect the new background color.

10. Click the **Save** button from the Standard toolbar to save your file.

11. In the Save As window, name the file **walkabout.html** in the Save As field.

12. Click the **Save** button to save the new web page.

Access your Files panel, and you'll see the new web page listed in your defined Walkabout Travel site (see Figure 4.25).

Figure 4.25: Your new site is listed in the Files panel.

The Least You Need to Know

- The most direct way to create a new web page is to select HTML on the Welcome Screen.
- Dreamweaver automatically generates the supporting HTML code behind the WYSIWYG display of Design view.
- Set your Page Properties to format and set default settings for your web page.
- Test the display of your web page by previewing it through Live view or in a browser.

Adding Text to Your Page

In This Chapter

- Adding, modifying, and deleting text
- Correcting mistakes
- Importing, exporting, copying, and pasting data
- Adding special characters
- Adding date and time features
- Checking your spelling

Now that you know how to create a new web page, it's time to add some content to that page. In this chapter, you'll find out how to add text, special characters, and the date and time to your web page. You can add many of these features by typing directly into the page or by using the Dreamweaver menus and toolbars.

Note: As you learned in Chapter 2, Design view of Dreamweaver displays your web page similar to how it will appear in a browser window. Code view shows only the HTML code for the page. Split view shows both Design view and Code view. Please switch to Split view in your Dreamweaver window as you work through this chapter.

Adding Text

Adobe developed Dreamweaver to make web design a simple process. This starts with the simplicity of adding text to your page. When you are working in the design mode, you type your text where you want it to display, just as you would in most word processing applications. When you reach the end of a line, keep typing; Dreamweaver wraps your text to the next line, based on the size of your Design view screen.

Notice that, in the Code view window, Dreamweaver displays the supporting HTML for the text that you just typed in the Design view window (see Figure 5.1). You can also add new code or modify code in the Code view window, but you need to know HTML to do this.

HTML code for paragraph of text

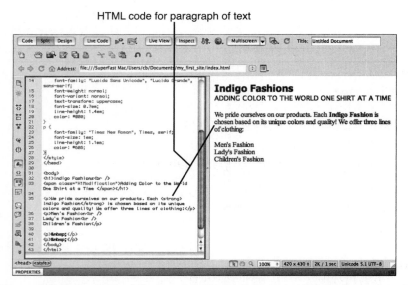

Figure 5.1: *Code view and Design view. In the Code view window, the paragraph tag,* `<p></p>`, *surrounds the text, designating it as a block of text.*

When you're ready to end a paragraph, press the **Return** (Mac)/**Enter** (PC) key on your keyboard. This creates a block of text. Dreamweaver automatically creates a paragraph break with a set amount of line space between the lines of text in the paragraph (officially called the *line height*), as well as default space between paragraphs or blocks of text (see Figure 5.2). Line height can be compared to leading in print.

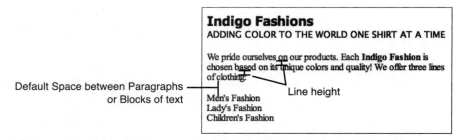

Default Space between Paragraphs or Blocks of text

Line height

Figure 5.2: *When you press the* **Return** *(Mac)/**Enter** (PC) key, Dreamweaver creates a block of text with a set default line height between the lines of text in the paragraph, and sets default space between the following paragraph or block of text.*

DEFINITION

The **line height** between lines of text in a paragraph is a generic default setting that each browser interprets with its own amount of space. While most browsers have a similar line height, they do have slight differences. You can set an exact value for the line height by creating a style rule in CSS.

Sometimes you might want an actual line break rather than a paragraph break. A line break is used to avoid the default space between blocks of text. For instance, you might use a line break between a header and a slogan on a web page. A line break is just a break in the lines of a block of text or paragraph. The line of text displays beneath the line break, with no additional spacing (see Figure 5.3).

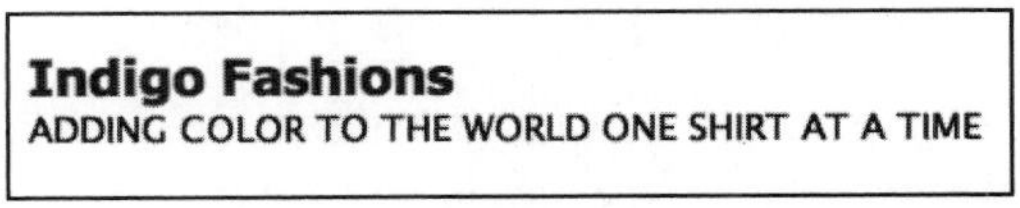

Indigo Fashions
ADDING COLOR TO THE WORLD ONE SHIRT AT A TIME

Figure 5.3: *Notice the line break between the slogan and the heading on this web page.*

To create a line break, hold down the **Shift** key while pressing the **Return** (Mac)/ **Enter** (PC) key.

Changing and Modifying Text

To modify text, you first need to set your cursor by clicking next to the text you want to change. You can delete individual characters by pressing the **Delete** key or add new text by typing. If you want to delete or change an entire word or lines of text, highlight the text by using your mouse to click and drag over the text you want to select. To select an entire word, double-click it. To select the entire paragraph, triple-click it. When you've selected the text, start typing to replace it with new text.

Another way to select multiple words or lines of text is to use the **Shift-click** method. Set your cursor in front of the text to be selected and, while pressing the **Shift** key, click at the end of the text you want to select. Dreamweaver highlights everything between the two clicks.

Using the Undo and Redo Commands

The **Undo** and **Redo** commands are handy tools for modifying your web page. Use the Undo command to undo your last action. Use the Redo command to redo an action that you just undid. You can access these commands in the following places:

- On the menu bar, choose **Edit, Undo** or **Edit, Redo**.

- On the Standard toolbar, click the **Undo** button or the **Redo** button (see Figure 5.4).

Figure 5.4: The Undo and Redo buttons on the Standard toolbar are toggle buttons. The former undoes your latest action, and the latter redoes an Undo action.

- On your keyboard type **Cmd/Ctrl+Z** for Undo and **Cmd/Ctrl+Y** for Redo.

If you just typed a line of text that you want to rephrase, click the **Undo** button from the Standard toolbar. Dreamweaver deletes the line of text. If you change your mind and decide that the deleted line of text was really what you wanted to say, click the **Redo** button to reinstate your original line of text.

DREAMWEAVER TIP

You can use the Undo command to go back several actions by initiating it repeatedly. By default, Dreamweaver is set to undo the last 50 actions. You can change this undo level in your Dreamweaver Preferences in the **General** category, **Maximum Number of History Steps** option.

Using the History Panel

You just learned that you can use the Undo command repeatedly to undo several previous actions. You can also use the History panel to "go back in time" to step through each action of your page development. The History panel is accessible by choosing **Window, History** (see Figure 5.5).

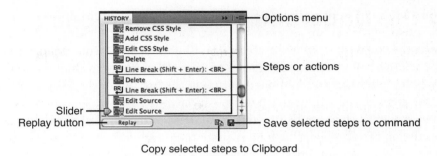

Figure 5.5: *The History panel keeps track of all your steps as you develop your web page.*

The History panel records all your actions or steps from the time you created or opened a web page. If you click and drag the scroll tool on the panel, it backtracks through your steps of development. Dreamweaver undoes each step and displays the results as you go back in time. You can also click on the scrollbar next to a step to move directly to that step.

To move to a step, click the step to highlight it. To replay all the steps from that step on, click the **Replay** button. For instance, if you need to insert a company logo at several different locations on your page, position your cursor at the first location and insert the logo. Then you can use the History panel to repeat this step at several other locations on the page. Just set your cursor where you want the next image of the logo to be placed and in the History panel, select the step for inserting the logo and click the **Replay** button to replay this step. Dreamweaver automatically inserts the logo at the new location. You can select multiple, sequential steps (series of actions) by shift-clicking between the starting step and the ending step. When you click **Replay**, the selected steps all replay in order.

DREAMWEAVER TIP

You can also highlight a series of steps in the History panel by simply dragging through these steps.

Adding Steps to the Clipboard

The Dreamweaver Clipboard keeps track of your cut or copied data. This could be text, images, or even actions from the History panel in Dreamweaver. When you initiate a paste command, Dreamweaver pastes the most recent data on the Clipboard.

To add a group of steps to the Clipboard, you first must identify the series of steps on the History panel that you want to copy. You do this by clicking and dragging through the steps you want to select and highlighting them. You can also use the Shift-click method to select your group of steps. With the steps highlighted, click the **Copy Selected Steps to Clipboard** button at the bottom of the History panel. This saves the steps to the Clipboard. Next, position your cursor or select the web element that you want the steps applied to and paste them into your web page. Because the steps exist on the Clipboard, you must paste them right after you copy them, but you can paste them as many times as you need at different locations in the active web page or in another web page.

Saving Steps As a Command

You can use the History panel to save a series of steps as a command. This feature enables you to re-create content or format properties with a simple keyboard command. Highlight the steps you want to save and click the **Save Selected Steps As a Command** button at the bottom of the History panel (see Figure 5.6).

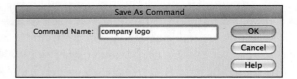

Figure 5.6: When you create a command name for your series of steps, you can use this command on any other page in the site.

When you're ready to apply the saved series of steps, position your cursor where you want to apply the steps, or select the element you want to apply the steps to, choose the **Command** menu from the menu bar, and select your command name at the bottom of the menu (see Figure 5.7).

Figure 5.7: When you save a series of steps as a single command, you can access this new menu command through the Commands menu.

Clearing History Panel Steps

When you're working in a very complex web page, you might need to free up some memory or disk space. The History panel relies on memory and disk space from your computer to keep track of all the steps. You can clear your History panel of all actions to free up memory and disk space. To clear the History panel and all steps, click the **Option** menu in the upper-right corner of the History panel and select **Clear History** from the list. A message appears indicating that all undo steps will be removed and memory and disk space will be cleared. This action can't be undone, so if you're sure you're ready to clear the History panel click the **Yes** button. Clearing the History panel does not affect the development of your web page; it just deletes your previous steps.

DREAMWEAVER TIP

You can also right-click a selected series of steps in the History panel and choose **Clear History** from the pop-up menu.

Copying and Pasting Text

Another technique for getting text into your web page is to copy it from another document and paste it into your page. You can copy text from a Dreamweaver document, a website, or a word processing application like Microsoft Word. If you can select the text and copy it, you can paste it into Dreamweaver.

Follow these steps to copy text from any other document and paste it into your Dreamweaver web page:

1. Open the document with the information to be copied.

2. Select the information you want to add to your web page and then copy it. You'll find the **Copy** command in the **Edit** menu of most applications.

3. Open Dreamweaver and the web page to which you want to paste the information.

4. Position your cursor where you want the new information to go and choose **Edit, Paste** to paste the information into your document.

DREAMWEAVER TIP

You can also drag and drop content from Word or Excel into your web page. Select the data in Word or Excel and then, with your web page visible, drag it into the web page. You must be able to see both application windows to use this technique.

Using Paste Special

Dreamweaver offers a variety of paste options based on whether you want to paste just plain text or formatted text. To access these commands, choose **Edit, Paste Special** (see Figure 5.8).

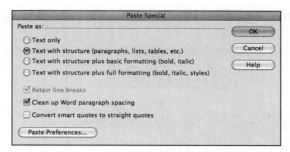

Figure 5.8: *Four different Paste options exist under the Paste Special command; each option pastes different types of information.*

Under the Paste As section, you'll find the following paste options:

- **Text Only**—Pastes only the text, with no formatting.

- **Text with Structure (Paragraphs, Lists, Tables, etc.)**—Pastes text with paragraph returns and other document structure required for lists and tables.

- **Text with Structure Plus Basic Formatting (Bold, Italic)**—Pastes text along with limited formatting and document structure.

- **Text with Structure Plus Full Formatting (Bold, Italic, Styles)**—Pastes text with full formatting and document structure.

After selecting one of the preceding Paste As options, you can apply these additional settings (see Figure 5.8):

- **Retain Line Breaks:** Keeps line breaks throughout the copied text.

- **Clean Up Word Paragraph Spacing:** Clean up Word paragraph spacing deletes the extra paragraph spacing that other applications might use for text. This option is available if you have either the **Text With Structure** or **Text With Structure Plus Basic Formatting** option selected.

- **Convert Smart Quotes to Straight Quotes:** Convert smart quotes to straight quotes by selecting this option.

With your Paste Special options selected, click **OK** to paste the copied text into your web page.

Pasting Excel Spreadsheet Information

You can paste Excel spreadsheet information and data into your web page using Dreamweaver (see Figure 5.9). You use the same process as when copying and pasting text. To retain the format and document structure of your spreadsheet data, use the **Paste Special** command and choose the **Text with Structure Plus Full Formatting (Bold, Italic, Styles)** option.

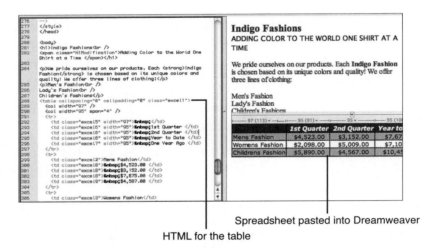

HTML for the table

Spreadsheet pasted into Dreamweaver

Figure 5.9: *This spreadsheet was created in Microsoft Excel and pasted into this web page.*

Notice the supporting HTML shown in the Code view of Figure 5.9. To create the document structure to display a table in HTML code, you need to use the following tags:

- Table tag: `<table></table>`
- Table row: `<tr></tr>`
- Table data: `<td></td>`

The CSS code for this table is automatically imported into the HTML <head> section of your document (see Figure 5.10).

Figure 5.10: The Paste Special command automatically translates formatting in the original document into CSS code in the Dreamweaver document.

Importing Word and Excel Documents (Windows Only)

If you have a PC, you can import an entire Word or Excel document into a web page. (Dreamweaver for Macintosh doesn't.) You can find the import command in the **File, Import** menu. To import a Word or Excel document, follow these steps:

1. Open the web page document into which you want to import the data.

2. In Design view, position your cursor in the web page where you want to place the data.

3. Choose **File, Import, Word Document or Excel** document. Dreamweaver imports the file.

Cleaning Up Word HTML

You can generate an HTML document using Microsoft Word's Save As feature, but you can get weird characters and strange code *syntax* in your HTML. Fortunately, Dreamweaver offers a clean-up feature just for Word documents. In the menu bar, choose **Command, Clean Up Word HTML** (see Figure 5.11).

DEFINITION

Syntax is the arrangement and order required in the construction of a programming language's code.

Figure 5.11: The Clean Up Word HTML command removes unnecessary HTML code that Word generates when converting a document to a web page.

This opens the Clean Up Word HTML window, which has two tabs: Basic and Detailed (see Figure 5.12).

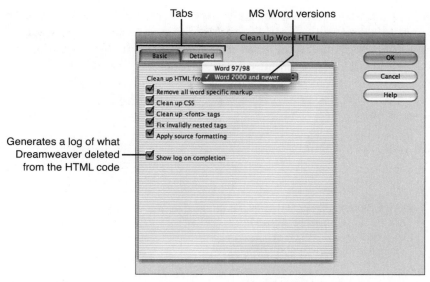

Figure 5.12: You can choose between two versions of Word through the Clean Up HTML From option.

The Basic tab offers several options for removing certain types of code. The Detail tab (see Figure 5.13) offers even more detailed options.

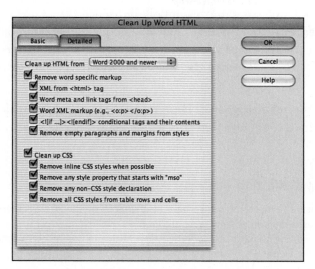

Figure 5.13: The Detail tab of the Clean Up Word HTML window. You can choose a version of Word and then select specific Microsoft code that you want Dreamweaver to remove.

After you've selected your settings, click **OK**. Dreamweaver cleans the code of unwanted Microsoft-only HMTL code. If you've selected the **Show Log On Completion** option, you'll see an overview window listing what Dreamweaver removed from the code (see Figure 5.14).

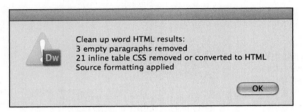

Clean up word HTML results:
3 empty paragraphs removed
21 inline table CSS removed or converted to HTML
Source formatting applied

OK

Figure 5.14: Dreamweaver cleans the document of unnecessary or Word-only HTML code. This cleanup deletes this code from your web page, reducing the lines of code required to represent the web page.

Click **OK** to close this overview window. The code should now be standard with World Wide Web Consortium (W3C) conventions and requirements (see Chapter 1).

Creating Special Characters

You can insert special characters and symbols such as copyright and trademark symbols into your web page. Both symbols and special characters are accessible by choosing **Insert, HTML, Special Characters** in the menu bar (see Figure 5.15). First, position your cursor in the location you want the item to be inserted; then select the special character from the menu list. The special character is inserted into the web page.

Highlight any special character in Design view and then look at the associated HTML code that's highlighted in your Code view. Each character has its own unique HTML code.

DREAMWEAVER TIP

If you want to insert multiple consecutive spaces in your HTML document, you must set your Dreamweaver preferences to allow multiple spaces. In Dreamweaver preferences, click the **Allow Multiple Consecutive Spaces** option under the General category.

Figure 5.15: *You can insert any of these special characters into your web page.*

Adding the Date and Time

Another nice feature to add to a web page is the date you created the page. Position your cursor in the location where you want to place the date on your web page before you initiate the Date command. In the menu bar, choose **Insert, Date,** or click the **Date** button on the Insert panel (see Figure 5.16) to open the Insert Date window (see Figure 5.17).

Insert date ——— Date

Figure 5.16: The Insert panel offers quick access to many useful features, including the Insert Date feature.

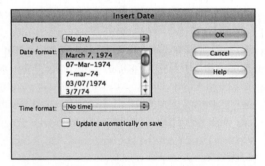

Figure 5.17: Use the Insert Date window to set your Date and/or Time to update every time the file is saved.

You can choose from among a variety of time and date formats.

Spell-Checking Your Web Page

You should run a spelling check on your web page before you publish it. To start the spelling check, choose **Commands, Check Spelling.** Dreamweaver begins checking the document for spelling errors. If Dreamweaver finds a word that isn't in its dictionary, the Check Spelling window lists the word and gives you five options (see Figure 5.18).

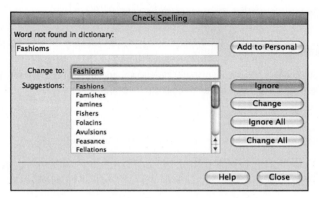

Figure 5.18: *If you need help, click the Help button in the Check Spelling window.*

If the flagged word is spelled wrong, Dreamweaver offers a suggested spelling in the Change To field. If the suggested word is not correct, you can click a different word from the Suggestions list. The Change To field will reflect the word you choose, and you can then click any of the buttons to the right. Here's an overview of each button and its function:

- **Ignore:** Ignores any suggestions and keeps the flagged word as is.

- **Change:** Changes the flagged word to the word listed in the Change To field.

- **Ignore All:** Ignores all instances of the flagged word throughout the entire document.

- **Change All:** Changes all instances of the flagged word throughout the entire document to the word listed in the Change To field.

- **Add to Personal:** Adds the word to Dreamweaver's spell-check dictionary.

Tutorial: Adding Text to Your Travel Web Page

Walkabout Adventure Travel has a site defined and one web page created at this point in the book. Let's add some text and other web elements like horizontal rules, a date, and special characters to the page. From this point forward in this book and the following tutorials, you can find the files that accompany and support each chapter's tutorial at www.idiotsguides.com/dreamweaver.

> **DREAMWEAVER TIP**
>
> Each chapter has its own tutorial with supporting files. This allows all readers a common starting point for each chapter tutorial. You can download all tutorials at www.idiotsguides.com/dreamweaver.

Follow these steps to add text to your travel site web page:

1. Define the **Chapter05** folder in the **Tutorial** folder as a new site. To do this, choose **Site, New Site** from the menu bar to open the Site Setup window.

2. In the **Site Name** field, name the site **Chapter05 Travel.** In the **Local Site** folder field, navigate to the **Chapter05** folder in the **Tutorial** folder on your desktop. Then under Advanced setting click the **Local Info** subcategory and set the images folder as the default image folder.

3. Click the **Advanced Settings** category and select the **Local Info** subcategory. In the **Default Images** field, navigate to the **images** folder in the Chapter05 folder.

4. In the Files panel, double-click the **walkabout.html** page to open it in Dreamweaver. Click anywhere in the page to set your cursor and type the following text:

   Walkabout Adventure Travel is your Group Tour Specialist for Seniors!

5. From your keyboard, press the **Return/Enter** key to create a new line, and then type the following text (see Figure 5.19):

   ```
   We customize all our tours with our clients in mind. This means
   we take care of all the details so that you can enjoy your
   travel experience to its fullest.
   ```

6. Press the **Return/Enter** key to create another new line, and add the following text:

```
Custom Designed with You in Mind!
```

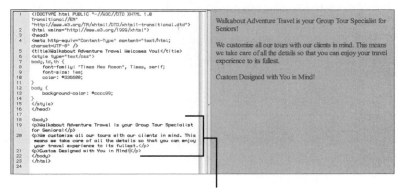

Code for the new text you just added.

Figure 5.19: *This figure shows Split Screen view with your new text. Notice all the code that Dreamweaver generated in the Code view.*

7. Press **Return/Enter** to create a new line. Next, choose **Insert, HTML, Horizontal Rule.** This inserts a horizontal rule below the text of the web page.

8. Select the horizontal rule by clicking it.

9. In the Property Inspector, click in the **Width** field and type **95.** Then click on the **Unit** pop-up menu and select % to set the horizontal rule to 95% of a browser window. Leave the Height field blank to use the default setting of 1px (see Figure 5.20).

Width   Unit pop-up menu

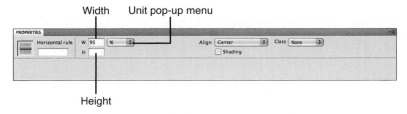

Height

Figure 5.20: *The Width and Height fields both adhere to the unit type that you select in the Property Inspector from the Unit pop-up menu.*

DREAMWEAVER TIP

When you use a percentage as the unit for a web page element, you're setting the element relative to the browser window in which it is viewed. When you set the width to 100%, it fills the browser window horizontally all the way across the window. When you set it to 50%, it fills only half of the window's width.

10. With the horizontal rule still selected, in the Property Inspector, click the **Align** pop-up menu and select **Center** so that the horizontal rule is centered in the middle of the web page.

11. Also in the Property Inspector, deselect the **Shade** option to turn off this feature. You have just customized your horizontal rule.

12. Click to set your cursor below the horizontal rule. Now you will create a footer area for the web page and add copyright information and a date.

13. To insert a copyright symbol in the line below the horizontal rule, choose **Insert, HTML, Special Characters, Copyright** from the menu bar.

14. Add the following text after the copyright symbol: **Copyrighted 2011 by Walkabout Adventure Travel**.

15. Press **Shift-Return/Enter** on your keyboard to create a new line directly below the copyright line.

16. To add the date for when the document is saved, open the **Insert panel** (see Figure 5.21) and, under the **Common** category, click **Date.** This opens the Insert Date window.

Figure 5.21: *Your Insert panel may look different if you have Hide Labels or Color Icons turned on.*

17. In the Insert Date window, select the **March 7, 1974** format and then select the **Update Automatically on Save** option (see Figure 5.22).

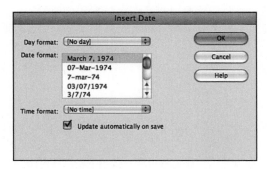

Figure 5.22: *The date will automatically be updated each time you save your web page.*

18. Click **OK** to close the Insert Date window. Today's date displays directly below the copyright information.

19. Save the web page by clicking the **Save** button on the Standard toolbar or by choosing **File, Save** from the menu bar.

Congratulations! You've added more information to the first page of the Walkabout Travel site.

The Least You Need to Know

- You can add text to your web page by typing it in, or by copying and pasting material from other sources. If you're using Windows, you can import entire Word or Excel documents.
- Use paragraph breaks and line breaks to create blocks of text or document structure for a web page.
- Use the History panel to backtrack through your actions or steps of development for a web page.
- You can add special characters and the date/time to a web page.
- You can spell-check your web page.

Creating Paragraph and Document Structure

In This Chapter

- Formatting bold and italic text
- Structuring paragraphs and headings
- Creating bullet, numbered, and definition list
- Creating complex lists with many levels
- Modifying lists and list items

A web page consisting of just plain text isn't very interesting—and it might even be so dull that it actually drives visitors away from your site. Adding a little document structure to the web pages of your site—things like paragraphs and headings, as well as text formatting like bold and italic—gives it some visual pop that encourages visitors to stick around and explore.

In this chapter, you learn how to create document structure for paragraphs and apply bold and italic to blocks of text using Dreamweaver's Property Inspector. With the Property Inspector, you can apply text format either in HTML code or through style sheets using CSS.

Adding Some Pizzazz to Your Web Page

Using the Indigo Fashions page from previous chapters as an example, compare a plain-text version (see Figure 6.1) and a version with some formatting (see Figure 6.2).

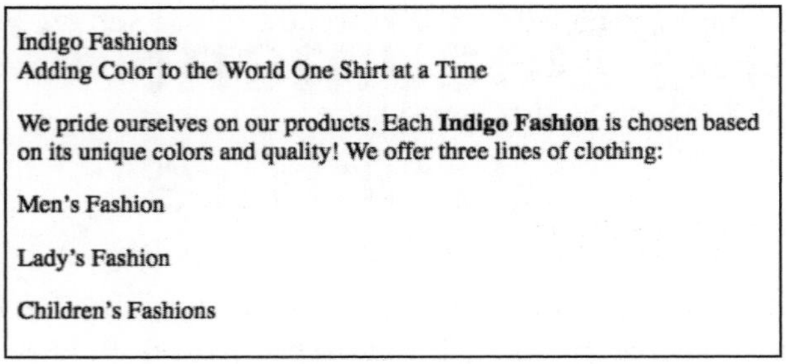

> Indigo Fashions
> Adding Color to the World One Shirt at a Time
>
> We pride ourselves on our products. Each **Indigo Fashion** is chosen based
> on its unique colors and quality! We offer three lines of clothing:
>
> Men's Fashion
>
> Lady's Fashion
>
> Children's Fashions

Figure 6.1: This page has no formatting and appears stagnant and dull.

Now compare the plain-text page with a version of the site that has document structure applied to the paragraphs, as well as text formatting applied to text.

> # Indigo Fashions
> ADDING COLOR TO THE WORLD ONE SHIRT AT A TIME
>
> We pride ourselves on our products. Each **Indigo Fashion** is chosen based
> on its unique colors and quality! We offer three lines of clothing:
>
> - Men's Fashion
> - Lady's Fashion
> - Children's Fashions

*Figure 6.2: After applying a few tags and formatting, the site draws in the viewers
and invites exploration.*

HTML Revisited

You learned about the differences between HTML and CSS in Chapter 4. Now it's time to take a closer look at HTML to see how you can use it to create document structure.

As you know, the Property Inspector has two modes, the HTML mode and the CSS mode. You can toggle between the two modes by clicking the associated button. When you click a button from the Property Inspector, Dreamweaver creates the HTML tags required to support the feature. Design view displays your page with the applied format and the Code view displays the supporting HTML code.

In HTML mode, tags are coded in HTML code. If you set the Property Inspector to CSS, your formatting is coded in CSS and is placed in the documents `<head>` tag at the start of the HTML code of the web page.

Creating Paragraphs

By default, Dreamweaver formats text in a paragraph or text block referred to as a *block level element.* Just like in word processing, when you press **Return/Enter,** you create a new paragraph. Dreamweaver automatically adds the HTML paragraph tags to the block of text, distinguishing it as a paragraph.

> **DEFINITION**
>
> In a web page, browsers display web elements as either block or inline, with both being part of the document flow. **Block level elements** display as rectangular blocks that don't break across lines. Block level elements can have margins and width and height settings applied to them. An example of a block level element is a paragraph. **Inline elements** are part of the flow of information of the document and can't have margins or width and height properties applied to them; they can also break between lines. An example of an inline element is a list item, which is covered later in this chapter.

The following example is a block of text in HTML code:

> `<p>`We pride ourselves on our products. Each Indigo Fashion is chosen based on its unique colors and quality. We offer three lines of clothing:`</p>`

The paragraph tags, `<p>` and `</p>`, tell browsers to display this as a block of text.

When you type text in a web page, Dreamweaver creates the supporting HTML code, which you can see in the Code view. As soon as you press the Return/Enter key on your keyboard, Dreamweaver inserts `<p> </p>`, which is the `<p>` tag surrounding the code for a blank line of text. When you start typing the paragraph information, the **" "** code is replaced with what you're typing.

DREAMWEAVER TIP

Browsers automatically add space between block level elements, such as the <p> tag and heading tags such as <h1> (see the next section for detail on heading tags). Browsers also have a default setting for line height or the space between lines of text in a paragraph. Before the adoption of CSS, this caused headaches for web designers because they couldn't control their content layout and were restricted to this set amount of space between paragraphs and lines of text. But now, with CSS, you can control both line height and space between paragraphs (see Chapter 7).

Just as an entire web page resizes in width and height to fit the browser window, an HTML block of text within a website resizes based on the browser window. Since browser windows vary in size, you must create a design that looks good in any type of display. One of the challenges of web design is to create a layout that looks good in any browser window.

Applying Alignment to Paragraphs

Aligning paragraphs in Dreamweaver is similar to aligning paragraphs in Microsoft Word or any other word processing program. You can align a paragraph left, right, center, or fully justified (see Figure 6.3). You can apply paragraph alignment through CSS or through HTML code. You learn how to align paragraphs using HTML code here; see Chapter 7 for details on using CSS to control your paragraph alignment.

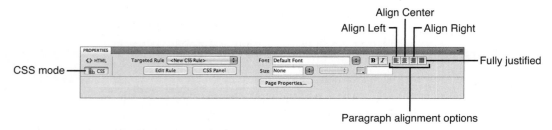

Figure 6.3: You can use the Property Inspector or the menu bar (Format, Align) to access these paragraph-alignment commands.

Here is an overview of each form of justification.

- **Align Left:** A block of text that's vertically aligned along the left margin.
- **Align Center:** A block of text in which each line is centered between the left and right margins.
- **Align Right:** A block of text that's vertically aligned along the right margin.
- **Fully Justified:** A block of text with vertically aligned left and right margins.

By default, the `<p>` tag creates a paragraph that is aligned left. The HTML code for the other paragraph alignment is as follows:

- `<p>`—HTML code for left justified
- `<p align="right">`—HTML code for right justified
- `<p align="center">`—HTML code for center justified
- `<p align="justify">`—HTML code for fully justified alignment

To apply paragraph alignment, follow these steps:

1. Click in the paragraph to which you want to apply paragraph alignment.
2. From the menu bar, choose **Format, Align**, and then select the desired alignment (Left, Right, Center, Justified).

The new paragraph alignment appears in Design view. Look in Code view, and you'll see the HTML code that creates the paragraph alignment.

Indenting Paragraphs

You can create block quotes using the `<blockquote>` tag to indent both sides of a paragraph (see Figure 6.4). This works well in HTML to draw attention to the paragraph.

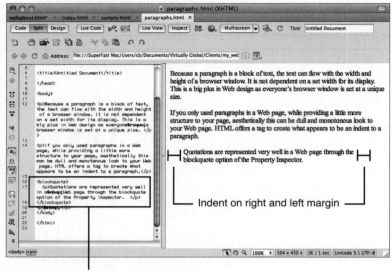

Block quote tag surrounding the paragraph tag

Figure 6.4: *The* `<blockquote>` *tag creates an indent on both the right and left margins of this paragraph.*

To create a block quote, use the Property Inspector in HTML mode and follow these steps:

1. Click anywhere in the paragraph that you want to indent.

2. In the Property Inspector, in **HTML** mode, click the **Blockquote** button (see Figure 6.5).

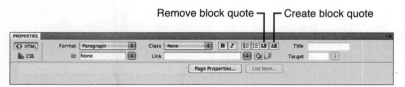

Figure 6.5: *You can undo a block quote by clicking the Remove Blockquote option.*

DREAMWEAVER TIP

A block quote isn't the same as a paragraph indent. A block quote indents both sides of the paragraph. A paragraph indent only indents the left side of the first line of text. To create a paragraph indent you need to use CSS (see Chapter 15 for details).

Controlling Document Structure

A page consisting of paragraph after paragraph is monotonous. To alleviate the monotony, you can use HTML document structure tags to apply precreated format to your blocks of text. This gives you more control over your page design and look.

Dreamweaver has eight document structure tags, including the paragraph tag you already learned about. You can access all the tags in the Property Inspector under **HTML** mode from the **Format** pop-up menu (see Figure 6.6).

Figure 6.6: Each tag formats a block of text.

DREAMWEAVER TIP

When you type text in a web page, Dreamweaver codes it with the **None** format setting for document structure. As soon as you press the **Return/Enter** key on your keyboard, Dreamweaver inserts the paragraph tag, `<p> </p>`, surrounding the block of text.

Browsers interpret each of the eight types of document structure tags and display them with their default settings for font, font format, font size, and line height (see Figure 6.6).

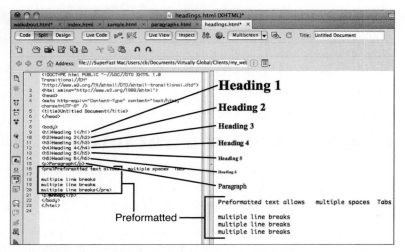

Figure 6.7: *Browsers display each of these heading tags based on the browser's default settings and interpretation of the tags.*

To apply a document structure tag, follow these steps:

1. Click to set your cursor in the block of text. This could be an entire paragraph or just a headline.

2. From the Property Inspector, click **HTML** mode.

3. Click the **Format** pop-up menu and select the document structure tag.

Dreamweaver applies the format to the paragraph. The Design view of Dreamweaver reflects this new formatting.

DREAMWEAVER TIP

You don't need to select the entire paragraph to which you want to apply the formatting. Set your cursor somewhere in the block of text, and Dreamweaver applies the format to the whole paragraph.

Headings

To add a little more pizzazz to a page of print, you can create headlines or topics. *Heading tags* in HTML create headlines that help divide the text content on your page, giving it structure. Six types exist, as follows:

- **Heading 1:** HTML `<h1>` tag (the largest and most prominent heading)
- **Heading 2:** HTML `<h2>` tag
- **Heading 3:** HTML `<h3>` tag
- **Heading 4**: HTML `<h4>` tag
- **Heading 5:** HTML `<h5>` tag
- **Heading 6:** HTML `<h6>` tag (the smallest and least prominent heading)

DEFINITION

Heading tags in HTML represent headlines and help structure content based on the importance of a topic. The most prominent heading is the Heading 1 tag, the Heading 2 is slightly smaller, and each of the others gets smaller based on numerical order to Heading 6, which is the smallest.

A rule of thumb for print and web design is to put your most important headline early in the web page and apply the Heading 1 tag to it. This tag signals the most important topic. As you continue to segment your information on the page, you apply a Heading 2 to a subtopic of the Heading 1 or as a less important topic of the overall page content.

DREAMWEAVER TIP

You can also use the menu bar to apply heading format by choosing **Format, Paragraph Format, Heading (1–6)**.

To apply a heading tag to a headline in your web page, follow these steps:

1. Click the headline to which you want to apply the Heading tag. This focuses Dreamweaver on this block of text.

2. Click the **HTML** mode of the Property Inspector.

3. Click the **Format** pop-up menu and choose the heading you want to apply to the headline.

4. If you need to change a headline, click in the headline to be changed and then select the new format from the **Format** pop-up menu in the Property Inspector.

Dreamweaver displays the headline based on its default settings for the line height and space between paragraphs. Each heading tag is represented in a browser based on the browser default settings for font, font size, and line height, so your Dreamweaver display may differ from the browser display. You can control the format of a heading through CSS (see Chapter 7).

DREAMWEAVER DON'T

If you use the **None** paragraph format, you're leaving your paragraph structure up to the browser's interpretation. This can create weird formatting that displays your paragraphs poorly.

Using Lists

Lists offer another way to create document structure (see Figure 6.8). Use lists in web design to segment your information into numbered or bulleted items.

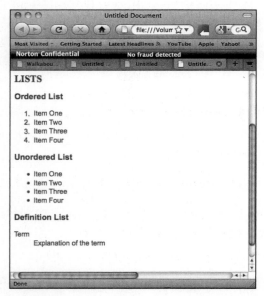

Figure 6.8: Each of these lists lets you structure your page content to help clarify it and present it with a different structure.

HTML supports the following types of lists:

- **Ordered lists**—A numbered list; the HTML tag is `<ul>`.

- **Unordered lists**—A bulleted list; the HTML tag is `<ol>`.

- **Definition lists**—A list consisting of a keyword and a definition; the HTML tag is `<dl>`.

Each list type has formatting applied for the font, font size, font style, and line spacing (see Figure 6.9).

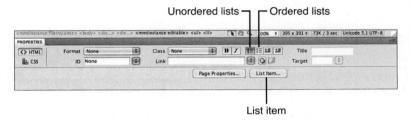

Figure 6.9: *The Property Inspector showing the different types of lists you can create. Notice the HTML tags for each list type in Code view on the left side of the screen.*

The Definition list isn't accessible through the Property Inspector. Choose **Format, List, Definition List** from the menu bar to create this type of list.

Unordered and Ordered Lists

Unordered lists segment information into bullet points. Ordered lists use numbers or letters to designate each item. Both an unordered list and an ordered list are block level elements. The process for creating unordered and ordered lists is similar. Follow these steps to create an unordered or ordered list:

1. Create a new line where you want your bulleted list to start.

2. In the Property Inspector, click either **Unordered List** or **Ordered List,** depending on which type of list you want. This defines the list type.

3. Type your first list item for the list.

4. Press **Return/Enter** to create a new list item and type your next item. Continue this process until you have all list items.

5. Press **Return/Enter** twice to end your list.

The HTML tags that represent the list begin by defining the type of list, either `<ul>` for Unordered List or `<ol>` for Ordered List, and then each list item is created through the `<li>` tag (see Figure 6.10).

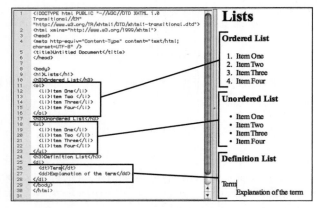

Figure 6.10: *HTML tags and Design view of the three list types.*

DREAMWEAVER TIP

You can also find the Unorder List and Order List commands in the menu bar by choosing **Format, List.**

Definition Lists

Definition lists in HTML format a paragraph into a keyword term followed by a definition. This type of list is ideal for technical terminology and glossaries. The HTML code is similar in structure to ordered and unordered lists, but the process for creating these lists differs slightly.

To create a definition list, follow these steps:

1. Set your cursor in a blank line where you want your definition list to begin.

2. In the menu bar, choose **Format, List, Definition List**.

3. Type your keyword term and then press **Return/Enter** to create a new line that is slightly indented to the right.

4. Type your definition for the keyword and again press **Return/Enter** from your keyboard. This creates your first list item for your definition list.

5. Repeat steps 3 and 4 to create all list items for your definition list.

DREAMWEAVER TIP

By default, list items display directly below each other, with no line spacing. You can't use HTML to add more line spacing; however, you can assign a margin and line height for list items using CSS.

Using Letters Instead of Numbers

By default, Dreamweaver uses numbers for ordered list items. To replace numbers in a list with letters, follow these steps:

1. In an ordered or unordered list, click in one of the list items to set your cursor. If you don't select a list item first, the List Item button in the Property Inspector is grayed out (unavailable).

2. Click **List Items** in the Property Inspector. This opens the **List Properties** window (see Figure 6.11).

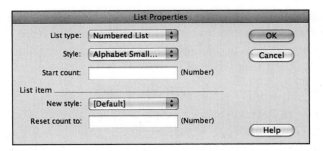

Figure 6.11: The List Properties window consists of two sections: List Type settings at the top and List Item settings at the bottom. Changing the list type in the upper section of the List Properties window affects the entire list.

3. Click the **List Style** menu and choose the style you want for your list (see Figure 6.12). The entire list items display with the new style.

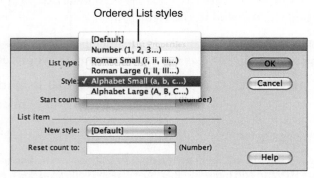

Ordered List styles

Figure 6.12: You can change any list to another type through the List Styles pop-up menu.

4. If you want to start your list with a specific number or letter, type a number into the **Start Count** field.

DREAMWEAVER TIP

When you change the list type or list item style to a new list type, Dreamweaver automatically changes the HTML list tag to the new tag.

Nesting List Items

You can also create nested list items, which are lists inside another list. For example, if you have a grocery list with three items—milk, eggs and fruit—and you want to expand upon the fruit item by including specific types of fruit, you can use a nested list for the kinds of fruit, as follows:

- Milk
- Eggs
- Fruit
  - Bananas
  - Apples
  - Oranges

You can use the List Properties window to create nested lists, and you can set different properties for each nested list item (see Figure 6.13).

Suppose you have a bulleted list and you want to nest three numbered items underneath one of the bulleted items. You can do this through the List Item section of the List Properties window by following these steps:

1. Click at the end of the list item under which you want to create a nested numbered list.

2. Press **Return/Enter**.

3. To indent the nested list, click **Indent** from the Property Inspector.

4. Type your nested list items; press **Return/Enter** at the end of each nested list item.

5. With your cursor anywhere in the nested list items, click **List Style** on the Property Inspector.

6. In the List Properties window, select the **List Type** and **List Style** options you want for your nested list.

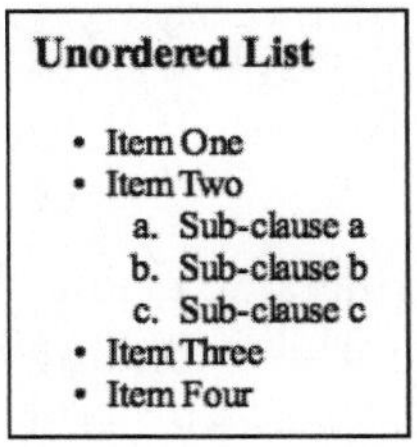

Unordered List

- Item One
- Item Two
    a. Sub-clause a
    b. Sub-clause b
    c. Sub-clause c
- Item Three
- Item Four

Figure 6.13: *You need to indent your nested list items to create new margins for your nested list.*

DREAMWEAVER TIP

If you want to change just one list item style in an ordered or unordered list, click to insert your cursor in the list item that you want to change and then, from the lower section of the List Properties window, select the new style from the **List Style** pop-up menu.

Deleting Lists

You can delete a list or list item in two different ways. You can highlight the HTML code for the list in Code view and delete it by pressing the **Delete** key. Or, in Design view, you can select the list and/or list item(s) and press the **Delete** key. Either technique deletes the list item(s) or entire list based on your selection.

To convert a list into a paragraph, highlight the list in the Design view of Dreamweaver, and in the Property Inspector click the associated List button. The list is converted into a series of paragraphs or block level elements.

Text Format

Adding bold or italic formatting to text using Dreamweaver is similar to performing these actions in most word processing programs. First, highlight the text you want to apply format to and then, in the Property Inspector, click the HTML mode and apply the new text format by clicking either the **Bold** or **Italic** buttons. You get these results:

- **Bold**: Creates <strong></strong> tag in the HTML surrounding the selected text.

- **Italic**: Creates <em></em> tag in the HTML code surrounding the selected text.

Applying both bold and italic formatting creates both tags in the HTML code with one tag nested inside the other and surrounding the selected text.

Tutorial: Creating Document Structure for the Travel Page

Let's add some document structure and format to the travel web page you've been working on. You can download all supporting tutorials at www.idiotsguides.com/dreamweaver. Follow these steps:

1. Define the **Chapter06** folder in the **Tutorial** folder as a new site. To do this, choose **Site, New Site** from the menu bar to open the Site Setup window.

2. In the **Site Name** field, name the site **Chapter06 Travel**. In the Local Site Folder field, navigate to the **Chapter06** folder in the **Tutorial** folder on your desktop. Under Advanced Settings, click the **Local Info** subcategory and set the images folder as the default image folder.

3. Click **Advanced Settings** and select the **Local Info** subcategory. In the **Default Images** field, navigate to the **images** folder in the Chapter06 folder.

4. In the Files panel, double-click the **walkabout.html** page to open it.

5. Click to set your cursor in the first paragraph on the page.

6. In the Property Inspector, click HTML mode.

7. Apply a Heading 1 to this paragraph by selecting the **Format** pop-up menu and choosing **Heading 1** from the list.

8. Click to set your cursor in the third paragraph—"Custom Designed with You in Mind!".

9. Apply a Heading 2 to the third paragraph by selecting the **Format** pop-up menu and choosing **Heading 2** from the list.

10. Apply bold format to the text **"we take care of all the details"** in the second paragraph by highlighting this text and then clicking the **Bold** button in the Property Inspector.

11. Save your web page by clicking the **Save** button in the Standard toolbar. Your web page should look like Figure 6.14.

Figure 6.14: Your Walkabout Travel web page should look like this figure

The Least You Need to Know

- You can add structure to your document by applying heading tags and creating lists and list items.
- HTML tags are used to create document structure; these tags are embedded in the HTML code.
- You can format text by embedding HTML tags in the code or through CSS.
- HTML mode of the Property Inspector has two text format buttons: Bold and Italic.
- When you apply bold or italic through the Property Inspector's HTML mode, HTML tags are embedded in the code.

Formatting with Cascading Style Sheets

In This Chapter

- Using the CSS Styles panel to create CSS Tag and Class style rules
- Using the Property Inspector to create CSS Tag and Class style rules
- Working with Type and Block properties
- Using the CSS Rules Definition window to edit a CSS style rule
- Using the properties section of the CSS Styles panel to edit a CSS style rule

A Cascading Style Sheet is basically a document that contains style rules. In the context of web development, a *style rule* is a set of format and layout options that you can apply to your website text, images, and other elements to control format, positioning, and layout (see Chapter 1 for more information about CSS).

Introduction to Cascading Style Sheets

Many software applications have used style rules for years. These are typically called *Styles,* and they contain style rules for formatting options. For example, Microsoft Word and Adobe InDesign use style rules to control formatting of text in print documents. The difference between Dreamweaver Cascading Style Sheets and other application Styles is that in Dreamweaver, the style rules apply to web elements. They enable web designers to apply formatting such as font, font size, colors, borders, cell padding, and backgrounds with much more precision and control than using HTML tags. And as with HTML, new CSS tags and code appear with each release of CSS, giving you more power over your designs and web pages as the technology advances.

CSS is its own language, with syntax similar to HTML (see Figure 7.1).

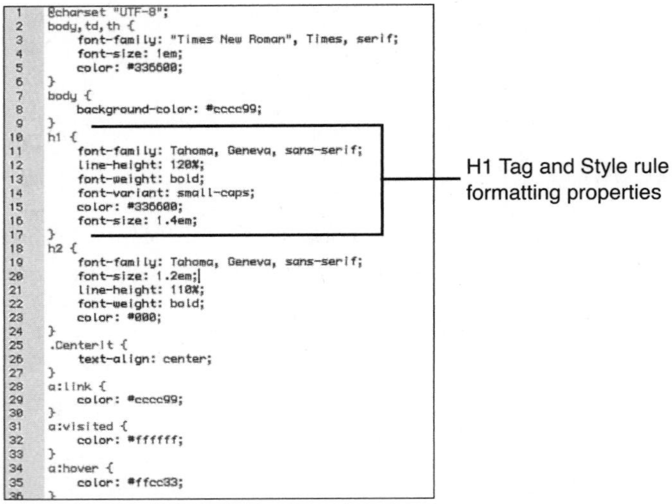

```
1   @charset "UTF-8";
2   body,td,th {
3       font-family: "Times New Roman", Times, serif;
4       font-size: 1em;
5       color: #336600;
6   }
7   body {
8       background-color: #cccc99;
9   }
10  h1 {
11      font-family: Tahoma, Geneva, sans-serif;
12      line-height: 120%;
13      font-weight: bold;
14      font-variant: small-caps;
15      color: #336600;
16      font-size: 1.4em;
17  }
18  h2 {
19      font-family: Tahoma, Geneva, sans-serif;
20      font-size: 1.2em;
21      line-height: 110%;
22      font-weight: bold;
23      color: #000;
24  }
25  .CenterIt {
26      text-align: center;
27  }
28  a:link {
29      color: #cccc99;
30  }
31  a:visited {
32      color: #ffffff;
33  }
34  a:hover {
35      color: #ffcc33;
36  }
```

H1 Tag and Style rule formatting properties

Figure 7.1: *An example of CSS code syntax. The formatting properties for an* <h1> *(Heading1) tag are wrapped in the CSS code for HTML tags and other page elements.*

There are three types of Cascading Style Sheets (CSS):

- **External style sheet:** always its own document with a .css extension

- **Internal style sheet:** part of the HTML document that has the styles embedded within the <head> tag in the <style> tag

- **Inline style sheet:** a style rule embedded within the line of a document, such as **Indigo Fashions**.

You can use the CSS Panel to create internal and external style sheets.

Advantages of CSS over HTML Formatting

Before the introduction of CSS, designers used HTML to create formats for fonts, borders, and other page elements. Web designers could be only as creative as the HTML tags and their capabilities allowed. Designers formatted fonts through the ever popular `<font>` tag and all its attributes (see Figure 7.2).

```
<p><font size="2" face="Arial, Helvetica, sans-serif">
Paragraph 1</font></p>
```

Figure 7.2: Look at all the code that's needed to format a particular font through the HTML `<font>` tag.

Unfortunately, the HTML `<font>` tag has properties that are open to a browser's interpretation. For example, there isn't an attribute for the `<font>` tag to control line height; instead, the browser's settings determine line height. As you can see, HTML tags provide limited control over basic elements of your design.

DREAMWEAVER TIP

The W3C has been phasing out many HTML tags since the introduction of CSS. Many browsers no longer support these phased out HTML tags. As a consequence, in Dreamweaver CS5.5, the `<font>` tag isn't readily available. To find this tag in the menu bar, choose **Format, Font**.

CSS gives you much more control over your page designs. Aside from taking advantage of the wonderful properties it brings to the format of your fonts, you can establish page margins; precisely format borders, lists, links, and images; set padding and alignment; and, using the Div tag, create divisions for page layout and then apply formatting to these divisions.

As an added bonus, CSS can help you minimize the size of your HTML document files. If you're using an external CSS style sheet, your web page has less code, which makes it smaller and thus quicker to download.

Setting CSS Preferences

Let's take a look at the CSS Preferences for Dreamweaver (see Figure 7.3). Open the Dreamweaver Preferences by **Dreamweaver, Preferences** (Mac)/**Edit, Preferences** (PC) from the menu bar. Click the **CSS Styles** category on the right. You can customize these default CSS Styles settings based on how you like to work.

Shorthand settings for CSS Styles

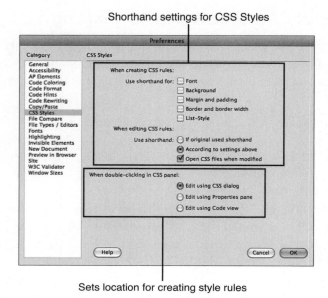

Sets location for creating style rules

Figure 7.3: By default, Dreamweaver uses the CSS Preferences dialog box for creating style rules and properties.

You can choose from among the following major sections for options relating to how Dreamweaver creates and writes CSS code:

- **When creating CSS rules:** Choose settings for Dreamweaver to automatically convert the code to shorthand version. You can set options for converting code used for Font, Background, Margin and padding, Border and border width, or List-Style.

- **When editing CSS rules:** Set options for controlling how rules are edited. This setting is again for using the shorthand setting for your edits to CSS style rules.

- **When double-clicking in the CSS panel:** Set options for which CSS tool to use for editing style rules. This could be the CSS dialog window, the Properties pane, or just the Code view. The default setting is the CSS dialog box, which you initiate through the CSS panel (see the following section).

DREAMWEAVER TIP

If you turn on shorthand settings for the CSS code, you might run into problems with older browsers that don't understand the shorthand.

Creating CSS Style Rules

By default, Dreamweaver creates style rules through the CSS Styles panel (see Figure 7.4).

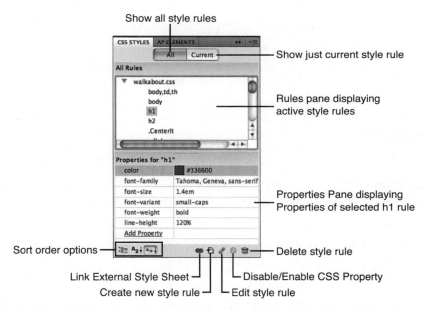

Figure 7.4: When you select the style rule in the Rules pane, the bottom Properties pane displays all properties of the rule.

Using the CSS Styles panel is the most popular and complete way you can create style rules, but you can also use the Property Inspector in CSS mode to create rules on the fly (see Figure 7.5).

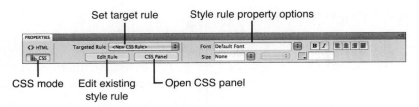

Figure 7.5: You can use the Property Inspector to create style rules as you are designing your page.

Style rules are grouped by selector types (see Figure 7.6).

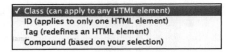

Figure 7.6: Selector types for classifying style rules.

You need to determine which of the following four selector types you're using when you create a style rule.

- **Class**—Rule that you can apply to any HTML element, such as making one word in a paragraph bold and red.

- **ID**—Rule that applies to only one HTML element, such as applying margins and cell padding to a layout area for an advertisement.

- **Tag**—Rule that redefines an HTML element, such as a <h1> tag.

- **Compound**—Rule that is based on multiple page elements or tags. This type of style rule only applies to <h1> tags in the content <div> tag; it will not apply to any other <h1> tag (this is an advanced concept for CSS and is explained more in Chapters 12 and 15).

Each selector type has its own associated properties and affiliated HTML tags. Each of these selector types has a specific use when creating format, design, and layout for a web page. In this chapter, you learn about the Tag selector style rule and the Class selector style rule. You'll learn about the ID and Compound selector style rules in Chapters 12 and 15.

Creating Tag Style Rules

Use the Tag style rule in CSS to create specific formatting for your individual HTML tags, like the <p> tag or the <h1> tag. You designate the rule type first, and then you associate the properties you want to apply to the designated HTML tag. You can create properties for fonts and font attributes, margins, borders, cell padding, and text alignment.

Using the Property Inspector

To create a new Tag type style rule through the Property Inspector, follow these steps:

1. In the **CSS mode** of the Property Inspector, select **New CSS Rule** from the **Targeted Rule** pop-up menu.

2. Click in the **Font** field and choose a font-family from the list (see Chapter 4 for more information about font-families).

3. This opens the New CSS Rule window (see Figure 7.7). Under **Choose a Contextual Selector Type for Your CSS Rule**, click the pop-up menu for **Selector Type.** Choose the **Tag (Redefines an HTML Element)** option.

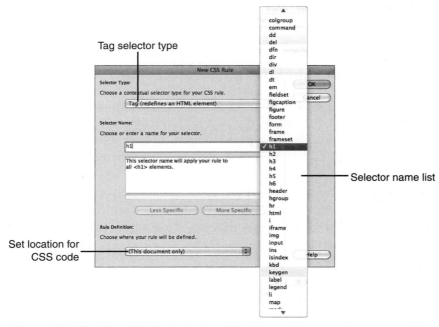

Figure 7.7: *The New CSS Rule window. The Selector Name area lists many of the commonly used HTML tags.*

4. In the **Selector Name** area of the window, click the arrow button to the right of **Choose or Enter a Name for Your Selector**. A pop-up menu displays all the associated HTML tags. Choose an HTML tag from the list. You can also just type a tag in the field.

5. In the **Rule Definition** area of the window, click the pop-up menu and select the location for the CSS code. You can choose to create a new external style sheet by selecting **(New Style Sheet File),** or select **(This Document Only)** to create the CSS code in the <head> tag and then wrap it in the <style> tag of the active document.

DREAMWEAVER TIP

If you've already created an external style sheet for your site, it's listed in the pop-up menu of **Rule Definition**. You can select any of your defined style sheets for your root site through this menu list.

6. Click **OK** to create the rule.

7. If you chose to create a new style sheet in the **Rule Definition** area of the New CSS Rule window, the **Save Style Sheet File As** window opens, allowing you to choose where to save your new style sheet document.

8. With the rule created, add the properties for the new style rule by choosing other options from the Property Inspector. Dreamweaver automatically updates these properties and adds them to your style rule.

If you're in Design mode or Split mode of Dreamweaver, the updates appear on your web page based on the associated style rule with the new properties and attributes you selected. Open the CSS Styles panel to see your new style rule for the HTML tag you're controlling. For instance, if you click the new h1 rule, the properties associated with it appear in the Properties pane of the CSS panel (see Figure 7.8).

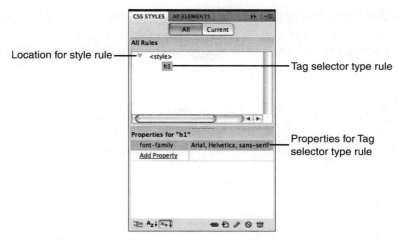

Location for style rule

Tag selector type rule

Properties for Tag selector type rule

Figure 7.8: *You must click the triangle (Mac) or + symbol (PC) to expand the style location to see the style rules associated with that style sheet location.*

Using the CSS Panel

The primary benefit of using the Property Inspector to create style rules is moving through the process so quickly. However, the Property Inspector doesn't present all the properties available for your style rule. As a consequence, most web designers use the CSS Styles panel to create their style rules. You've already seen how you can use the CSS Styles panel to review an existing rule and its properties. Now let's look at how to use the CSS Styles panel to create a new Tag style rule.

To create a Tag style rule, follow these steps:

1. Open the CSS Styles panel by choosing **Window, CSS Styles**.

2. At the bottom of the panel, click the **New CSS Rule** button. This opens the New CSS Rule window.

3. To set the Tag style rule for the new rule, type or choose a selector name from the pop-up menu under the **Selector Name** area.

4. Now you need to set the location for the style rules from the **Rule Definition** area of the window. You can use an internal style sheet by choosing **This Document Only**, or you can create a new style sheet by choosing **New Style Sheet**.

DREAMWEAVER TIP

You can type a tag into the Selector Name field instead of choosing the name from the pop-up menu list under the Selector Name area of the New CSS Rule window.

5. Click **OK** to set your choices for the new rule. This opens the CSS Rule Definition window (see Figure 7.9). If you chose to create your style in an external style sheet, the Save Style Sheet File As window appears, prompting you to set the location of the new style sheet. Click **Save**.

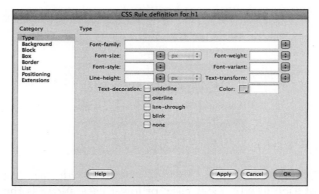

Figure 7.9: The CSS Rule Definition window. The properties on the right change to reflect the properties associated with the category that you choose on the left.

6. In the CSS Rule Definition window, select your properties by first clicking the category on the left and then setting your properties on the right.

7. When you're finished setting your properties, click **OK** to create the style rule. The new Tag selector type style rule appears in the CSS Styles panel.

This process creates a new style rule and associates it with a CSS style sheet.

The CSS Rule Definition window offers eight categories for setting the properties for your style rules. Two of these categories—**Type** and **Block**—are commonly used with the Tag style rule. The following sections explore those two categories in detail; refer to Chapter 12 and 15 for an overview of the remaining categories.

Using the Type Category and Setting Associated Properties

The Type category of the CSS Rules Definition window offers formatting options that you can set as properties and then apply to the text and font on your web page. Figure 7.9 shows all the formatting options available. These options are properties of the font tag in CSS.

Here's a quick overview of each option for the Type category:

- **Font-family:** Defines a font-family.
- **Font-size:** Defines a font size.
- **Font-style:** Defines a font style; Normal is the default setting.
- **Line-height:** Defines the space between each line of text in a block of text.
- **Font-weight:** Sets the font weight. Normal is the default, but you can select various amounts of bold format.
- **Font-variant:** Sets small caps or normal (default setting) for your font.
- **Text-transform:** Transforms your text to all title case (capitalizes the first letter of each word), upper case, or lower case. None is the default setting.
- **Text Color:** Click the **Color** button to access the color palette or type a hexadecimal number in the color field.
- **Text-decoration:** Set decoration settings for the display of text. None is the default setting.

Understanding Fonts and Web Design

As covered in Chapter 4, font-families are groups of fonts used to format your document. For the first time in many years, Adobe added new font-families to Dreamweaver because computers these days ship with more fonts pre-installed on the computer. You can create your own font-family by choosing **Edit Font List** from the Font-family option in the Type category. This displays the Edit Font List window, where you can create your own font-family.

Font size varies based on the viewer's browser settings for the display of that font. Most browsers are set to display fonts at a default setting of 16 pixels (px). However, anyone can change the browser settings to display fonts in a larger or smaller size.

This makes your job as a web designer really tough, but the Font-size options give you a bit more control.

You can set a font from predetermined sizes through the **Font-size** pop-up menu on the right of the Font-size field (see Figure 7.10).

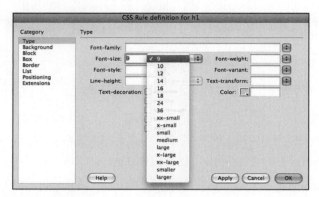

Figure 7.10: *You can choose preset font settings in the Font-size pop-up menu.*

Options include pixel sizes ranging from 9 to 36—9px is so small that it's almost unreadable, whereas 36px is very large and really stands out on your page. When your font size is based on a pixel, your text displays similarly across all browsers and operating systems.

Various unit sizes appear below the pixel sizes on the menu. Unit sizes relate to the old font size attributes associated with the HTML `<font>` tag. The medium setting is about 14 pixels in size. The smaller and larger settings are based on the page default setting that you establish for your font size. Whatever you set your page font size to, these two settings will make it bigger or smaller.

You can also type a number into the font-size field and then choose a unit of measurement from the Unit pop-up menu (see Figure 7.11).

Unit pop-up menu

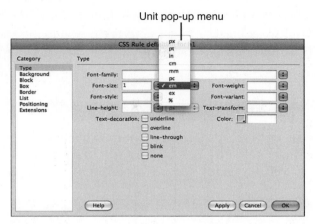

Figure 7.11: You can choose preset font units in the Font-unit pop-up menu.

The Unit pop-up menu lists measurement units for font size. Pixel (px) and point (pt) are fixed units, meaning that your site visitor can't increase the size of the web page text. You might say, "Great!" but this doesn't allow someone with visual disabilities to adjust browser settings to increase font size. If you're designing a website for the general public or for the government, this is a big "no-no" and goes against the Americans with Disabilities Act (ADA) of 1990, Section 508, which guarantees accessibility to all public website content. To be on the safe side, use relative measurements that allow for font adjustments in a browser.

Font units that are commonly used in web design are the relative fonts, like **em** or **%** (percentage). Here is a description of these relative font units:

- **Em:** An em unit is a size based on the default font size of the browser. For instance, if a browser has a default font size of 16px, 1 em is 16 pixels, 2 ems is 32 pixels, 3 ems is 48, and so on.

- **% (Percentages):** Percentages are a percentage of the default font size. For instance, if a browser has a default font of 16 pixels, a percentage of 100% equates to 16 pixels. A 90% default size is 14.4 pixels.

DREAMWEAVER DON'T

Macs render fonts smaller than PC machines, so avoid using a small font-size on a PC. For instance, if you use a PC and set your font size to 10px, it might be readable on a PC but unreadable on a Mac.

The font units of centimeters (cm), millimeters (mm), and inches (in) don't relate well to a computer displays and pixels. These units are rarely used for web design. Also, the ex font unit isn't recommended anymore for web design and is being phased out of CSS.

Setting Block Properties

Use the Block category of the CSS Rule Definition window to apply formatting to the area surrounding an element or a block of text (see Figure 7.12). This includes the text alignment, as well as vertical space of a block of text or a web element.

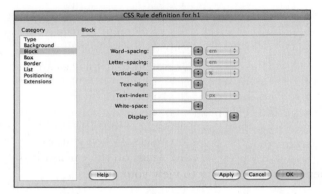

Figure 7.12: Use the Block category to manage word and letter spacing, to create custom typography in a web page.

DREAMWEAVER TIP

To see many of the Block category features, you must use Live view or preview the page in a browser. Dreamweaver's Design view is limited in its ability to display many of these Block attributes.

Here's a description of each property in the Block category:

- **Word-spacing**—Sets the space between words in a block of text. You can use both positive and negative measurements.

- **Letter-spacing**—Sets the space between letters of a word. Highlight the word or set of letters and create the CSS rule. You can use both positive and negative numbers.

- **Vertical-align**—Sets the vertical alignment of a web element or block of text. This is how the element displays in a line based on baseline, sub, super, top, text-top, middle, bottom, and text-bottom.

- **Text-align**—Sets the alignment of a block of a web element or a block of text. You can set a text-align of left, center, right, justified.

- **Text-indent**—Sets a paragraph indent for your first line of text in a text block. Dreamweaver displays this in Design view only when it is applied to an HTML tag for a block element.

- **White-space**—Sets how white space displays around an element or block of text.

- **Display**—Determines whether an element is displayed and how it's displayed. Display controls the type of box from the box model concept (see Chapter 1). You can change a block level element to display as an inline element. Choose **None** to hide an element.

Many of these options in the Block category set properties and attributes that not all browsers support, particularly older browsers. When you use these settings, be sure to test your page in many browsers and focus on the earliest browsers that you think your web audience might be using to view your site.

Creating Class Style CSS Rules

The Class selector rule is the second type of selector we focus on in this chapter (see Figure 7.13).

You can apply the Class selector style rule to an individual HTML element or a block of text. For example, if you want to make certain words in a block of text bold and red, you can create a Class style rule with these properties and then apply it to individual words in a block of text.

Although you can name your Class selector rule anything you like, as long as it's a single word, the name should indicate the function of the rule. In Figure 7.13, this class rule bolds and centers the web element or text block to which it is applied. Click **OK** to open the CSS Rule Definition window and then set your properties.

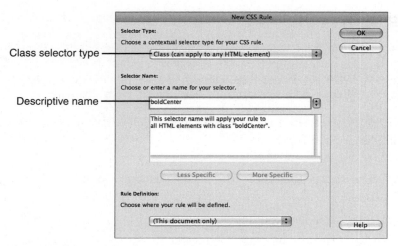

***Figure* 7.13:** *You can name your Class selector rule anything you want, as long as it's one word.*

Applying a Class Style Rule

After you've created a Class style rule, you apply it to your web page content by first selecting the web element in the Document window. Then, in the Property Inspector in CSS mode, click the **Class Field** pop-up menu and choose the rule from the menu (see Figure 7.14).

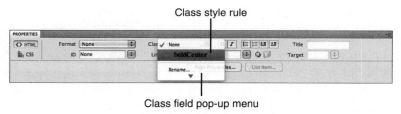

***Figure* 7.14:** *The Property Inspector with a Class style rule. You can apply a Class style rule to different HTML elements on your web page. There's no limit to the number of times you can apply a Class rule.*

Removing a Class Style Rule

To remove an applied Class style rule, simply select the web element that has the rule applied to it and then, in the Property Inspector in CSS mode, click the **Class** field pop-up menu and select **None** from the list. This removes the CSS class rule from the HTML element.

You can also simply delete the HTML code for the Class rule. Don't forget to delete the closing tag for the rule as well.

Editing CSS Style Rules

The beauty of CSS style rules is that you can edit them by changing, deleting, and adding properties for existing rules. You can edit a style rule in the CSS Styles panel, or you can change the actual code of the rule. You can also use the Property Inspector to quickly edit existing rules.

Using the CSS Styles Panel

After you've created your style rules, you can see them in the CSS Styles panel (see Figure 7.15).

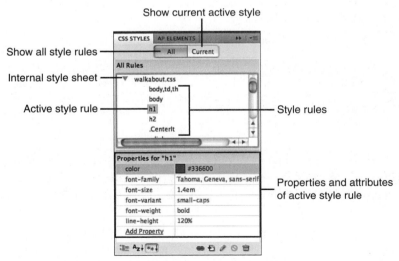

Figure 7.15: You can adjust, change, and create new properties for any defined style rule in the CSS Styles panel.

This panel has two modes: the Show All Style Rules mode and the Current Style Rules mode. You can access these two modes by clicking the associated button on the top of the panel. In the Show All Style Rules mode, when you click a style rule from the top section of the panel, you see all the properties and attributes you have defined for the rule in the lower section of the panel. Click on the property or rule to change it or delete it. Click on the property name on the left in the lower section of the panel to select it, and then click the attribute setting on the right to access other attributes associated with this property (see Figure 7.16).

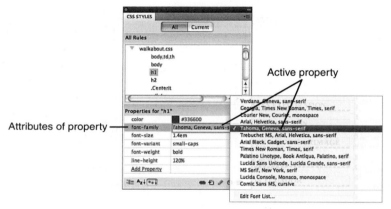

Figure 7.16: If you know the property setting, you can also just type its name in the appropriate field to set it as a new attribute.

DREAMWEAVER TIP

Not all properties can display in all browsers. Older browsers might not understand newer CSS properties for style rules. If a browser doesn't understand a property, it just skips it and doesn't display it.

To add a new property to the rule, click the **Add Property** link at the bottom of the list of defined properties. This opens a menu that displays the commonly used CSS rule properties available to you in Dreamweaver (see Figure 7.17).

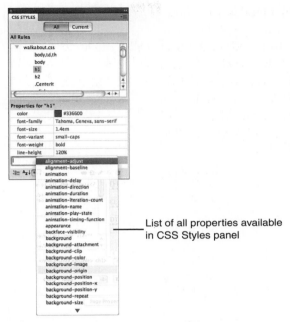

List of all properties available
in CSS Styles panel

Figure **7.17:** *This list doesn't contain all CSS properties defined by the W3C, but it does contain most of the more commonly used CSS properties.*

Using the CSS Rule Definition Window

You can also edit style rules and their properties through the CSS Rule Definition window. Once you've created your rules, you can double-click that style rule in the CSS Styles panel, or select the rule and then click the **Edit Rule** button at the bottom of the CSS Styles panel (see Figure 7.4). This opens the CSS Rule Definition window. Click the category for the property you want to change and then select the new attribute.

You can also use the Property Inspector to change a rule. Simply click the text block or element that has a rule applied, and then make any changes in the Property Inspector.

Editing the CSS Code

Once you become familiar with CSS and its code, you can go directly into the CSS document and hand-code your style rules and properties. You can view an attached external style sheet by clicking the style sheet name from the Document toolbar at the top of the document window and then viewing the code in Dreamweaver's Code view (see Figure 7.18). If you're using an internal style sheet, click the **Source** button at the top of the Document window and, in Code view of Dreamweaver, find the code in the <head> tag of the active HTML document and edit it.

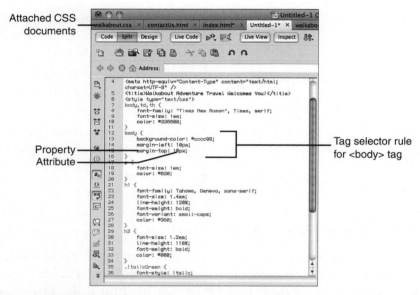

Figure 7.18: Select the property or the attribute, and type the new setting for your rule.

DREAMWEAVER TIP

You can add new rules and their properties by typing the rule in the CSS code. Dreamweaver helps you with the creation of this code through Code Hints (see Chapter 11). You must use the proper names and syntax of CSS code for a browser to understand it.

Tutorial: Using CSS to Format the Travel Site

The best way to truly understand CSS is to use it. So let's move on to the tutorial so you get a chance to create your own style rules and style sheets and then apply these rules to your travel website. I recommend rereading this chapter after you work through this tutorial, as it will make better sense after some hands-on practice.

From this point forward, you need to define the Walkabout Travel site based on the associated chapter folder inside the Tutorial folder that's available for download at www.idiotsguides.com/dreamweaver. Each chapter has its own tutorial folder with all the necessary files to support the instructions.

1. Define the **Chapter07** folder in the **Tutorial** folder as a new site. To do this, choose **Site, New Site** from the menu bar to open the Site Setup window.

2. In the **Site Name** field, name the site **Chapter07 Travel**. In the Local Site Folder field, type the path or navigate to the **Chapter07** folder in the **Tutorial** folder on your desktop.

3. Click the **Advanced Settings** category and select the **Local Info** subcategory. In the Default Images field, type or navigate to the **Images** folder in the Chapter07 folder.

4. Click **Save** to save the new defined site.

5. Open the **walkabout.html** page by double-clicking it from the Files panel.

6. Open the CSS Styles panel. Note that, due to the development of this file up to this point in the book, Dreamweaver has automatically created two internal style rules. Click the **All** mode at the top of the panel and then click the **body,td,th** rule to select it. (The compound style rule body,td,th is listed because the walkabout.html file has it embedded within the `<head>` tag as an internal style sheet. This is also true for the `<body>` tag style rule.)

7. In the properties section of the CSS Styles panel, click the **font-size** property and double-check that **1em** is the unit; if a different unit is selected, change it to **1em** by clicking it and typing **1** in the size field and choose **em** from the Unit pop-up menu.

DREAMWEAVER TIP

When you set a default font size in the Page Properties (see Chapter 4), you establish this as the base unit size for the web page. All other relative font units, like em, ex, or %, that you apply to a text block HTML tag are based on this default font unit size.

8. Now let's create a style rule for the <p> tag that changes the text color to brown. Click the **New CSS Rule** button at the bottom of the CSS Styles panel (see Figure 7.19).

New CSS rule

*Figure 7.19: CSS Styles panel buttons. You can delete any style rule by selecting the rule and clicking the **Delete CSS Rule** button.*

9. This opens the New CSS Rule window. In the **Selector Type** pop-up menu, choose **Tag (Redefines an HTML Element)**.

10. In the **Selector Name** field, click the pop-up menu button by clicking the arrows to the right of the field and choose the **p (paragraph)** tag.

11. Make sure the **Rule Definition** is set to (**This Document Only**). Click **OK** to open the CSS Rule Definition window.

12. In the **Font-size** field, type **1** and select **em** from the **Font-unit** pop-up menu.

13. In the **Type** category, click the **Color Palette** button and choose a brown color. Click **OK** to create these properties for the <p> tag. Your Document window reflects the new CSS Tag style rule.

DREAMWEAVER TIP

If you want to change or add a property to a defined rule, double-click the rule from the CSS Styles panel to open the CSS Rule definition window and edit or set your properties.

14. Now let's create a new style rule for the H1 tag. Click the **New CSS Rule** button at the bottom of the CSS Styles panel. Set the **Selector Type** to **Tag (Redefines an HTML Element)**. Type **H1** in the **Selector Name** field. Make sure the **Rule Definition** is set to (**This Document Only**), and then click OK.

15. In the CSS Rule Definition window, change the settings for the H1 rule to match Figure 7.20.

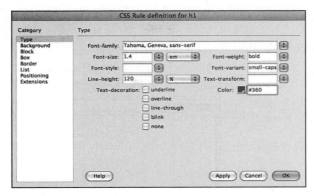

Figure 7.20: *Your CSS Rule Definition settings for the Type category should match this figure. If you're using a PC, you'll see shorthand for the Hexadecimal number for the color—#360.*

DREAMWEAVER TIP

The small caps property doesn't display in Design view of Dreamweaver; you need to click the **Live View** button to see this property display. You can't edit in Design view with **Live View** turned on, so turn it off by clicking it again. You can also preview your page in a browser to see the Live View property.

16. Now let's create a style rule for the <h2> tag. Create a new Tag selector style rule for the <h2> tag. Set your Type category settings as follows:

    Font-size: 1.2 em

    Font-weight: bold

    Color: #000000

    Line-height: 110%

17. Click **OK** to close the CSS rule definition window and set this style rule for the <h2> tag.

18. Next, let's create a Class selector style rule. Create a new CSS rule, but this time, set the Selector type to **Class (Can Apply to Any HTML Element)**.

19. Type **italicGreen** in the **Selector Name** field. Click **OK** to define the rule and open the CSS Rule Definition window.

20. Set the **Type** category to have a **Font-style** of italic and a **Color** of #336600. Click **OK** to set the properties for this Class style rule.

21. Now let's apply this class rule to make the words "with You" stand out in the third paragraph. In the Document window, highlight **with You** to select it. In the Property Inspector, click the **Class** pop-up menu and choose the **italicGreen** style rule from the menu. The words "with You" turn green and display in italic format.

22. Save your web page by choosing **File, Save** from the menu bar.

The Least You Need to Know

-   You can use the CSS Styles panel or the Property Inspector to create CSS Tag and Class style rules.
-   You can edit a CSS style rule using the CSS Rules Definition window or the properties section of the CSS Styles panel.
-   Use the CSS Rules Definition window to set Type and Block properties for style rules.
-   Use the CSS Rules Definition window to edit a CSS style rule.
-   You can use the Properties pane of the CSS Styles panel to edit a CSS style rule.

Adding Images to Your Page

In This Chapter

- Optimizing your images to compress and convert them to a web graphic format
- Inserting images into your web page
- Modifying and editing web graphics
- Making quick edits to graphics using the Property Inspector's editing tools
- Inserting rollover images
- Applying CSS style rules to control the appearance and layout of web graphics

Up to this point, we've focused exclusively on adding and formatting text on your web page. In this chapter, we turn our attention to images. Images include charts, photos, illustrations, clip art, advertising, and backgrounds. Essentially, anything you can save as a JPG, GIF, or PNG file counts as an image in the world of web design. Even a single image on your web page can communicate a message or establish a mood.

Optimization and Web Graphic File Types

Before you insert an image into your web page, you should optimize it. Optimizing an image involves sizing it to the physical dimensions you want it to display in your web page, setting the resolution for display on a monitor, and choosing the appropriate file format.

Monitors have different screen resolution based on their platform. A Macintosh has a PPI (pixels per inch) resolution of 72, and a PC is typically set at a PPI resolution of 96, though they can be changed with some advanced knowledge of the operating system. A good all-purpose resolution is 84 PPI; it's halfway between the two platforms and displays well on both of them.

Another feature of optimizing is choosing the appropriate web file format for your image based on its level of complexity in color and detail. The following graphic file formats are frequently used in web design:

- **JPG**—A *bitmap* compression format commonly used in web design. This format works great for photos and other complex images with lots of detail and colors. This compression is called *lossy.*

- **GIF**—A bitmap *lossless* compression format that works great for images with blocks of solid colors, such as buttons. GIF is limited to 256 colors.

- **PNG**—A compression format used by Adobe Fireworks that combines the best qualities of both JPG and GIF formats. Its compression is similar to that of JPG, but PNG also supports the lossless compression format of a GIF for optimizing an image and the transparent attribute of a GIF. Internet Explorer 6.0 and earlier versions of this browser don't support the PNG format.

DEFINITION

A **bitmap** is an image created through a pixel-by-pixel representation of the image.

Lossless is a compression format that doesn't lose any of the original image's detail.

Lossy is a compression format in which colors and detail are combined during compression, resulting in a loss of the original file's detail and color quality.

After you've optimized your image, you can insert it into your web page.

DREAMWEAVER DON'T

You can use high-resolution images in a web page, but the monitors and displays show the image only in 72 or 96 PPI. Using higher-res images just adds unnecessary file size to your page and causes your page to download slower than necessary.

Inserting Images

Dreamweaver provides the following options for inserting images into a web page:

- From the menu bar, choose **Insert, Image**.

- From the Insert panel, choose the **Common** category from the drop-down menu and click the **Image** button (see Figure 8.1).

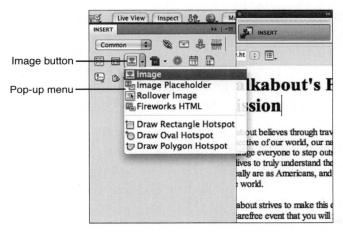

Figure 8.1: If you click the arrow to the right of the image button, you can select additional options for inserting other web elements.

- Drag an image from the Files panel into the active web document in the Document window.

- Drag an image from the Assets panel into the active web document in the Document window.

Any of these techniques inserts the image into your web page using HTML code. Your image appears in Design view of Dreamweaver; Code view displays the HTML code for inserting an image into a web page (see Figure 8.2).

HTML <img /> tag and src attribute

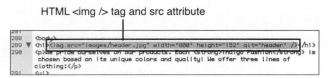

Figure 8.2: HTML code for inserting an image into a web page. The `<img />` tag uses the attribute of src to determine the path to the image file. You can also add other properties that control the image's size, border, margins, and padding.

The `<img />` tag is what's called an empty tag; you use it to determine the path to the source image. You can set other properties for the `<img />` tag to format and control the image. For instance, you can create a border around the image. You can also set alignment properties to control where the image is located on the page and how text flows or wraps around the image. You create these image formats through Cascading Style Sheets (CSS) and `<img>` properties (covered later in this chapter).

Accessibility and Images

If you insert an image into your web page through the menu bar command **Insert, Image**, or through the Insert panel **Common** category and **Image** button, Dreamweaver automatically opens the Image Tag Accessibility Attributes window (see Figure 8.3).

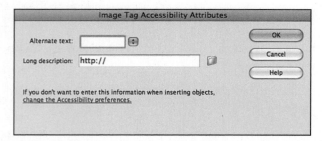

Figure 8.3: The Image Tag Accessibility Attributes window. The Alternate text lets you create a description for your image.

This window enables you to add *alternate text* describing your images. This alternate text is accessible to screen readers that people with low vision use to read web pages. The screen reader reads the alternate text aloud to the user, which gives the visitor more information about the content on the web page.

DEFINITION

Alternate text is the text that displays when you turn off image display in a browser or when you hover your mouse over an image in a web page. Screen readers for visually impaired users read the alternate text aloud.

Alternate text is a searchable attribute that search engines use to index the content of a web page and then rank the page. To add alternate text, type a short description in the Alternate Text field. You can provide even more information about the image by adding a link to a .txt file that resides on your site. This .txt file would contain more information about the image. You can use this attribute to help establish Search Engine Optimization (SEO) by setting the alternate text to a keyword phrase you are targeting (see Appendix D). (The Long description feature is only partially supported by Mozilla FireFox.)

You can turn off the Accessibility feature through Dreamweaver Preferences. In the Preferences window, choose the Accessibility category on the left. Select the options for when to display the Image Tag Accessibility Attributes window, based on the web element that's inserted into your page.

Inserting a Placeholder

Dreamweaver lets you add a placeholder in your page where you plan to insert a graphic later. You can insert a placeholder for this image through one of the following techniques:

- From the menu bar, choose **Insert, Image Objects, Image Placeholder**.

- From the Insert panel, choose the **Common** category, click the **Image** button, and, from the pop-out menu, choose **Image Placeholder**.

Both of these actions open the Image Placeholder window (see Figure 8.4).

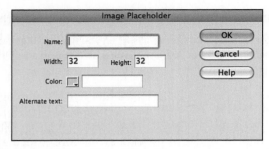

Figure 8.4: *The Image Placeholder window lets you set the name of the image, the placeholder size, the background color, and the alternate text.*

 DREAMWEAVER DON'T

Don't confuse the Name of an image and the alternate text for the image; they aren't the same. The Name of an image is an object name associated with the image. This Name can be used and called in JavaScript or other web languages. The alternate text provides more information about an image.

You can set the attributes of the image placeholder to represent the size of the real image, as well as give the placeholder an object name and a background color. You also can set alternate text for an image placeholder.

When you click **OK**, the placeholder displays in Design view and representing code appears in Code view (see Figure 8.5).

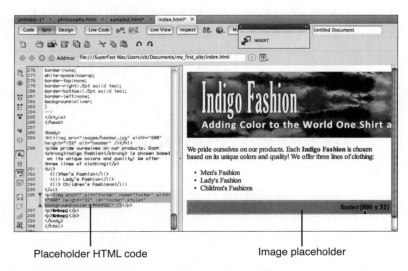

Placeholder HTML code   Image placeholder

Figure 8.5: *An image placeholder in Dreamweaver's Design view and Code view.*

When you insert an image placeholder, Dreamweaver creates the HTML code using the `<img />` tag but doesn't define a graphic file as the source because it's an empty tag. You can set other properties and attributes when you establish the link to the graphic file.

To add the real graphic to the image placeholder, click the image placeholder to make it the active object on your page; then, in the Property Inspector, set the path to the graphic image you want to use in place of the placeholder (see Figure 8.6).

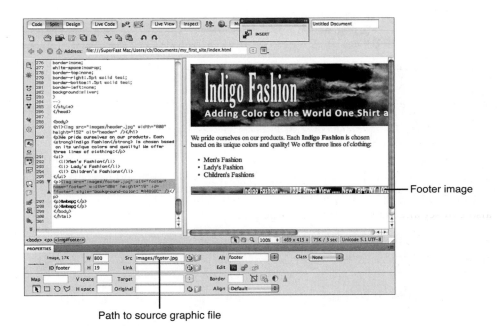

Figure 8.6: The HTML code now has an image source file defined.

A real image replaces the placeholder image.

Inserting Images from Other Adobe Software

With each release of the Creative Suite of software, Adobe provides better integration of features and functionality among the various software applications. This means that you can easily add images from Photoshop, Illustrator, Flash, and Fireworks in their native file type. The following sections explain the different processes for inserting graphics from other Creative Suite and Adobe applications.

Photoshop and Illustrator

Photoshop and Illustrator files use similar processes for generating web graphics. You can use any of the following three techniques for inserting images created in these two applications:

- Convert to a web graphic
- Copy and paste
- Use Smart Objects

The first technique is to convert your Photoshop or Illustrator image into an optimized web graphic file format of GIF, JPG, or PNG. Photoshop has various web generating features available for converting your images. For instance, you can use the slice tool to create slices of a design or image in Photoshop, and then optimize these images through the **Save for Web & Devices** command (see Figure 8.7).

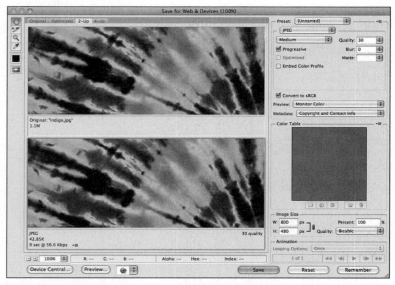

Figure 8.7: The Save for Web & Devices window in Photoshop. You can use the various settings for optimizing your image in the web graphic format that best suits your image.

In Illustrator, use the **Export** command and then optimize and export the web graphic. With the image in web graphic format, you can then use the **Insert** command to add it to your Dreamweaver web page.

> **DREAMWEAVER TIP**
>
> I recommend creating a graphics folder in your root website directory and saving all your original images in the folder. This groups your native graphic files in your root directory, making it easy to find and edit them throughout the design process.

You can also use the copy and paste technique to insert images into your web page. With this technique, you can select the entire image in Photoshop or Illustrator, or get more focused and choose just certain layers or objects. To copy and paste an image from Photoshop or Illustrator, follow these steps:

1. Copy your entire image or just certain objects or layers using the **Copy** command in each application.

2. Open or access your web page in Dreamweaver and click your cursor in the location on the web page where you want the image. Choose **Edit, Paste** from the menu bar to open the Image Preview window (see Figure 8.8).

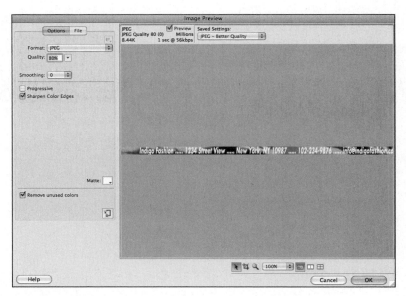

Figure 8.8: The optimization settings for converting the image change based on the web graphic format you choose.

3. In the Image Preview window, select the format for your web graphic first and then choose the settings that best optimize your image for web viewing. Click **OK**.

4. In the Save Web Image window that opens, save the optimized web image in the images folder of your site root folder.

5. In the Alt Text window, type a description of the image in the **Image Description (Alt Text)** field (see Figure 8.9). Click **OK** to close the window. The image displays in your web page.

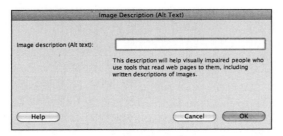

Figure 8.9: Provide a short description of your image for the alternate text.

Updating Pasted Images

Pasted Photoshop or Illustrator images maintain a link to the original Photoshop .psd file. When you edit the original graphics image, you can ensure that the changes are reflected on your web image in your web page. To set up this feature, use the Property Inspector and Roundtrip Edit button (see Figure 8.10).

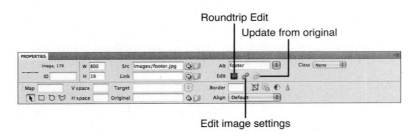

Figure 8.10: The Roundtrip Edit button reflects the native application image based on what you used to create the original image.

Follow these steps to edit the original graphic that's linked to the pasted web image:

1. Select the image in your web page that you created through a copy and paste.

2. In the Property Inspector, click the **Roundtrip Edit** button. This opens the application in which the image was created, as well as the original image.

3. Make your changes to the image in the graphic application and then click **Save** to save the file. Changes and edits automatically update into the pasted web image. Dreamweaver reapplies the original optimization settings that you set when you pasted the image into your web document. It also resaves your web image in the image folder.

You can use roundtrip editing on images created in other Adobe graphic applications, including Flash and Fireworks.

Inserting Smart Objects

You can also insert an entire .psd file into your Dreamweaver web page as a Smart Object. A Smart Object is an object that remembers its link to the original file. Any changes you make to the Photoshop file are updated to the Smart Object in Dreamweaver. This is a nifty way of synchronizing the development of the original graphic with the Dreamweaver image.

To create a Smart Object, follow these steps:

1. Use the **Insert, Image** command and navigate to the .psd file to insert a native Photoshop file with a .psd extension into your web page.

DREAMWEAVER TIP

You can also insert a Photoshop file through the drag and drop technique of the Files panel. You must be able to see the .psd file in the Files panel, so you need to first save it in your root site folder.

2. This opens the Image Preview window so that you can optimize the image as a web graphic. Select the web graphic format that best represents your image, choose the appropriate optimization settings, and click **OK**.

3. In the Save Web Image window, type a name for the Smart Object in the Save As field, and then navigate to the **images** folder of your site and click **Save** to save the web graphic in this folder.

4. In the Alternate Text window, type the Alt text for this image in the Alternate text field. Click **OK**. The image displays in your web page.

> **DREAMWEAVER TIP**
>
> If you need to edit your optimization web image settings, select the image in the web page and then click the **Edit Image Settings** button in the Property Inspector. This displays the Image Preview window.

Notice that this Smart Object image has a different look to it and a regular web graphic. The green symbol with cycling arrows in the upper-left corner indicates that the original graphic and the Smart Object are in sync (see Figure 8.11).

Smart Object symbol ———

Figure 8.11: *The green color of the arrow symbol indicates that the original graphic and the Smart Object are in sync.*

Updating Smart Objects

A Smart Object maintains a link to the original graphic file. If you make changes to the original graphic file, the cycling arrow symbol changes to red, as a visual indicator that the Smart Object image needs to be updated. To update the Smart Object image, select it and then click the **Update from Original** button in the Property Inspector (refer to Figure 8.10).

Fireworks

Adobe Fireworks is kind of a hybrid application for both graphic design and web design. It combines many of the features of a graphics software application with basic web design functions.

A Fireworks file is a PNG file by default. You can insert a PNG file as a web image, but because some browsers don't recognize this file type, it's better to export the graphic image from Fireworks as a JPG or GIF image. You can insert these files directly into your page.

To learn more about Fireworks, read *The Complete Idiot's Guide to Adobe Fireworks*.

You can use roundtrip editing with Fireworks files. You can use Fireworks to create your web design and layout, as well as menu and drop-down menu items. You can then export your work as an HTML page. When you open the HTML page in Dreamweaver, the link for all objects created in Fireworks is maintained, and you can move between the two applications for the entire site development.

Working with Images

After you insert an image into your web page, you can perform some basic edits. You can change the physical dimensions of the image by cropping it, you can adjust its brightness, and you can delete the image. As mentioned earlier in this chapter, you can use roundtrip editing with Smart Objects to edit any web graphics image in its native application, no matter what application created the original file.

Using the Property Inspector to Edit Images

Anytime you select an image in a web page, the Property Inspector reflects information about the image (see Figure 8.12).

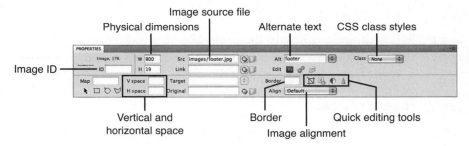

Figure 8.12: The Property Inspector has many options for formatting and modifying your web image.

The Property Inspector provides options for modifying and formatting your image. Here's an overview of many Property Inspector options (the remaining Property Inspector image settings are covered later in this book):

- **ID**—Assigns a name to your image. Each name must be unique, meaning that no other images on your page can have the same name; names also must be a single word without special characters, except for the underscore (_).

- **W/H**—Reflect the height and width of the image. When you insert an image, Dreamweaver automatically calculates its physical dimension. You can change the dimension of the image by adjusting these fields, but you're changing the view of the image only through distortion.

- **Src**—Indicates the source file path. You can change the source file by typing a new path or browsing to a new source file.

- **Alt**—Provides Alternate text describing the image, for accessibility purposes.

- **Class**—Applies Class CSS style rules to your image. You can set alignment, margins, cell padding, and borders to any image.

- **V space/H space**—Set the vertical and horizontal space along the edges of an image. These options also create additional HTML code for this spacing.

- **Border**—Determines the thickness of your border by typing a number. This is a pixel-based unit.

- **Editing tools**—Enable you to quickly crop, resample, adjust brightness/contrast, and sharpen the inserted web graphic. These tools permanently alter the web graphic.

- **Align**—Sets how your image aligns with other page objects in the same line.

The following sections explore the Align, Height, and Width features in further detail.

Modifying Image Size

When you change the height or width of an image through the Property Inspector, the browser interprets these measurements and distorts your image. If you use this feature to reduce or increase the image's physical size, the image displays at that size, but you are simply distorting the image instead of actually resizing the physical dimensions. As a consequence, the image appears fuzzy and out of focus.

When the height and width sizes don't match the web image, the Property Inspector displays these dimensions in bold with a circular arrow symbol (see Figure 8.13). Click the arrow symbol to restore the web graphic to its original size.

Figure 8.13: The units in the height and width field display in bold and with a circular arrow symbol to indicate that they've been altered.

Setting Image Alignment

You can use the Align field of the Property Inspector to position your web graphic so that it's aligned to the left or right of a text block. This creates the effect of the text wrapping around the image. To align your image with text, follow these steps:

1. In Design view, click to set your cursor at the beginning of a block of text.

2. From the menu bar choose **Insert, Image**.

3. Click the graphic in the Design view to make it active.

4. In the Property Inspector, click the **Align** pop-up menu and choose either **Right** or **Left**. Your web graphic aligns itself either to the left or to the right of the block of text (see Figure 8.14).

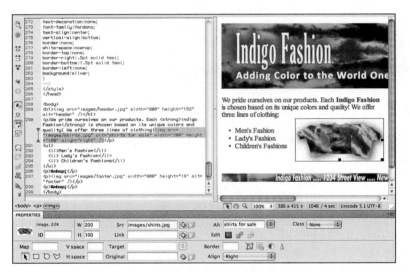

Figure 8.14: This image is right-aligned, so it displays to the right of the bulleted list.

Using the Editing Tools

The Property Inspector's Quick Editing tools enable you to edit your graphic directly in Dreamweaver (see Figure 8.15). You don't need to have another graphic editing application installed on your computer to make these edits.

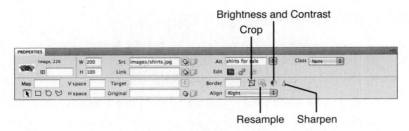

Figure 8.15: The Quick Editing tools in the Property Inspector let you edit any image that's in your web page.

DREAMWEAVER TIP

Any edits that you make to your web graphic using the Property Inspector editing tools are permanent. You can't undo your edits.

The Crop Tool

You can crop—or trim—an image in your web page to focus only on the area of the image that you want to show. Use the **Crop** tool to crop an inserted web graphic. In Design view, select the image you need to modify. Click the **Crop** tool in the Property Inspector. A message displays indicating that you're going to permanently modify your image and can't undo this action (see Figure 8.16). If you want to proceed, click **OK**; your image displays with adjustable crop markings (see Figure 8.17).

*Figure 8.16: You can permanently turn off the display of this warning window by selecting the **Don't Show Me This Message Again** option.*

Figure 8.17: *Adjust the area for your graphic display by clicking and dragging the handles for the crop area.*

Set the new image area by clicking and dragging the handles of the crop markings. When you have the crop area set as you want it, double-click anywhere in the cropped image. Your image adjusts to the new size.

The Resampling Tool

If you resize an image with the Crop tool or through the W/H field in the Property Inspector, you need to resample it so that its image file fits the new physical dimensions of the image in your web page. Resampling adds or eliminates pixels from the resized image. The Resampling tool resamples the image, which reduces its file size and improves the speed of the page download. To do this, in the Design view select the resized image by clicking it and then click the **Resample** tool. A message appears warning that you are about to make permanent changes to your image; to proceed, click **OK**.

DREAMWEAVER TIP

When you resample a resized image in your web page, the circular arrow that displays by the W/H field of a resized image (see Figure 8.13) goes away, indicating that the source graphic is the same size as the web page image.

The Brightness/Contrast Tool

You can make adjustments to both the brightness and the contrast of a web graphic. Simply select the image and then click the Brightness/Contrast tool in the Property Inspector. This opens the Brightness/Contrast window (see Figure 8.18).

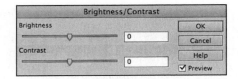

Figure 8.18: You can see your adjustments to the brightness and contrast of your web graphic on the image in real time if you have the Preview option selected.

Click and drag the sliders for brightness and contrast to adjust their settings, or just type the number for the adjustment to the brightness and contrast of the image. Put a check in the box beside **Preview** to see all modifications in real time on the image. Double-click anywhere in the image to save the settings.

The Sharpen Tool

The Sharpen tool adjusts the focus of your image by increasing the contrast of the image edges. It works the same as the other Quick Edit tools. Select your image and click this tool in the Property Inspector. This opens the Sharpen window (see Figure 8.19).

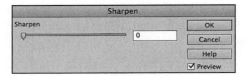

Figure 8.19: The Sharpen window. Drag the slider to increase or decrease the Sharpen setting. You can also type a number between 1 and 10 in the Sharpen field.

Adjust the slider or type a number between 1 and 10. Click **OK** to apply the new sharpening amount directly to the image.

More on Roundtrip Editing

Earlier in this chapter, you learned how to use the Roundtrip Edit button in the Property Inspector to edit Smart Objects and images inserted into a web page in Dreamweaver. You can use this feature for any web graphic in your page, regardless of the graphics software application that created the image.

In your Dreamweaver Preferences, you can establish the application you want to use as your default graphic editing application for roundtrip editing. Open Dreamweaver Preferences (see Chapter 2) and choose the **File Types/Editors** category (see Figure 8.20).

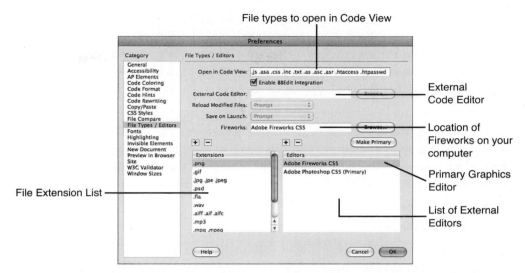

Figure 8.20: You can establish an external graphics editor as a default application to use for Roundtrip Editing in Dreamweaver Preferences window.

The external graphics editor is the application you want Dreamweaver to use to edit any of your page graphics when you use Roundtrip Editing. To set an external graphics editor, follow these steps:

1. Open Dreamweaver Preferences by choosing **Dreamweaver, Preferences** (Mac) or **Edit, Preferences** (PC) from the menu bar. Click the **File Types/ Editors** category on the left (see Figure 8.20).

2. In the Editors list in the bottom right of the Preferences window, you'll see a list of the graphics applications installed on your computer. If you need to add another graphics application that you have installed, click the plus sign. This opens the Select External Editor window.

3. In the Select External Editor window, navigate to your application, select it, and then click **OK**. This adds the application to the Editors list.

4. If you want to delete a graphics application that you no longer use from this list, first select it, and then click the **minus** button.

You can have multiple external graphic editor applications in the Editors list (see Figure 8.20). You can establish one of these as your Primary Editor, which typically is the application you like to use for graphic design. When you establish a Primary

Editor, this application is the one Dreamweaver uses for all Roundtrip editing. To establish a Primary Editor, click the application name from the Editor list that you want to set as the Primary Editor, and then click the **Make Primary** button. This application becomes the Primary Editor and you'll see (Primary) to the right of the listed application name. This application will open whenever you initiate roundtrip editing.

The Extensions list is a listing of file types that are opened for each external graphic editor application. For instance, you can establish that Photoshop is your Primary Editor for opening JPG, GIF, and PSD graphics and that Fireworks is your Primary Editor for opening PNG file types. To add or delete file types from each external graphic editor application, follow these steps:

1. Go to Dreamweaver Preferences, choose **File Types/Editors** and in the Editor list, click an external graphics editor application to select it.

2. In the Extensions list, click a file extension to select it. The list of extensions is associated with the selected external graphics editor.

3. Click the **minus/plus** button above the Extension lists to delete/add that extension.

After you establish an external graphics editor, you can use it to edit any web graphic image you've inserted into your web page. As with Smart Objects, you must first select the image in your web page. In Design view or Split view, click the web graphic to make it active and then, in the Property Inspector, click the **Roundtrip Edit** button. This launches your external graphics editor and opens the web graphic in that application. Make your edits with the graphics application, save it, and then close the window. When you return to Dreamweaver, it automatically updates your web graphic to reflect your recent changes. Dreamweaver also reapplies any optimization settings you established for the original web graphic.

Deleting an Image

To delete an image from your web page, select it on the page and press the **Delete** key on your keyboard. In Code view, you can also highlight the **<image src>** HTML tag and all its properties and attributes, and then press **Delete**.

Inserting Rollover Images

A rollover image is a special type of image that integrates JavaScript code with two related images. One image is used for the active state of the rollover image—this image displays on the page—and the other image is for the rollover state. This rollover image is visible only when someone hovers the mouse over the active image. You can use this for two-state buttons, advertisements, or any other graphic feature in which you want to communicate more information in the rollover state.

To begin the process of inserting a rollover image, either choose **Insert, Image Objects, Rollover Image** from the menu bar or, on the Insert panel, choose **Rollover Image** from the **Insert Image** pop-up menu.

Either command opens the Insert Rollover Image window (see Figure 8.21).

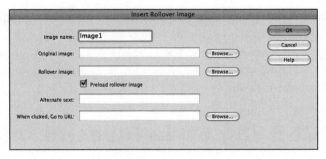

Figure 8.21: The Insert Rollover Image lets you set a graphic for the Original image (active state) and the Rollover image (Rollover state). You can also establish Alternate text and a hyperlink to another document for your rollover image.

Use the fields in this window to configure your rollover image. Here's an overview of the fields:

- **Image Name**—The same as the Image ID name. This name must be one word and unique on the page. Don't use any special symbols except the underscore (_).

- **Original Image**—Type the file path or click the **Browse** button and navigate to the image you want for the active state.

- **Rollover Image**—Type the file path or click the **Browse** button and navigate to the image you want for the rollover state.

- **Preload Rollover Image**—Checked by default. Instructs the browser to preload the rollover image before it is displayed.

- **Alternate Text**—Adds accessibility text describing the image for visually impaired users.

- **When Clicked, Go to URL**—Links the image to another web document or HTML page. This is typical hyperlink functionality. When a user clicks the rollover image, the linked HTML page displays.

DREAMWEAVER TIP

Both the rollover image and the original image need to be the same physical dimensions in height and width. If the two images are different sizes, Dreamweaver distorts the rollover image to match the size of the original image.

When your images and options are set, click **OK** to create the rollover image. Dreamweaver generates the code for this rollover functionality. To see the rollover effect, click the **Live View** button in the Document toolbar and hover your mouse over the rollover image. The original image for the active state of the rollover image changes to reflect the rollover image.

Applying CSS Tag Style Rules to Images

You can apply CSS to enhance the display of your image within the web page design. You do this by creating a Tag selector style rule for the `<img />` tag so that all your images are formatted with the same properties and attributes (see Chapter 7 for details on the Tag style rule). As with other Tag selector rules, you can use the CSS Styles panel to create your style rule.

The following steps outline the process for creating a Tag selector type style rule for the `<img />` tag.

1. In the CSS Styles panel, click the **New CSS Rule** button at the bottom of the panel. This opens the New CSS Rule window.

2. In Selector Type, choose **Tag (redefines an HTML element)** from the pop-out menu.

3. Under Selector Name, type **img** in the field to target the `<img />` HTML tag.

4. In the Rule Definition section, choose where your rule will be defined. For an internal style sheet choose **(This document only)** from the pop-out menu; for an external style sheet choose **(New Style Sheet File)**.

5. Click **OK** to close the window. This opens the CSS Rule Definition window.

6. Dreamweaver uses the categories of Background, Box, and Border to apply format to an image in the web page. To select a category, click it in the Category list.

Here's an overview of each of these categories:

- **Background**—Sets the background color for the image object, or sets the image as a background

- **Box**—Sets padding and margins for your image display

- **Border**—Creates a border around your images

DREAMWEAVER TIP

When you create a Tag style rule for the `<img />` tag, your style rules apply to all inserted images. If you store your rules in an internal style sheet, the style rules apply only to that page. If you use an external style sheet (see Chapter 12), all pages attached to the external style sheet reflect the style rule format on all images throughout your site.

If you want to apply a style to just one web graphic, you can create a Class style rule and apply that rule to the image through the Property Inspector and the Class button.

The following sections explore each of these formatting and layout options in more detail.

Box

The Box category of the CSS Rule Definition window lets you set box model options for an image (see Figure 8.22). As noted in Chapter 1, this is the visual model used for the rectangular boxes that hold or contain web page elements; it entails the cell padding, or space, around the image, as well as the margin, or space between your image and other web page elements like text blocks (see Chapter 5), tables (see Chapter 10), or AP elements (see Chapter 13).

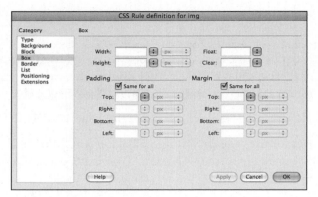

Figure 8.22: The Box category of the CSS Rule Definition window. You can set Padding and Margins to be the same amount by selecting the Same for all option.

The Box category lets you set the options that relate to the display of an image (or other web elements) in your web page. Here's an overview of each option.

- **Width/Height:** Sets the physical dimensions of the image through width and height properties. If you set dimensions that are different than the graphic image, you are distorting the image.

- **Float:** Determines how other web page elements display around an image. For instance, if you have a block of text and you want to have an image display to the right of the block of text, in the **Float** field select **Right**. The image floats to the right of the text block and the text flows around the image.

- **Clear:** Determine the sides of an image that don't allow AP elements to be located (see Chapter 13 for a discussion of AP elements). For instance, if an AP element displays on the clear side of an image, this image moves below the AP element.

- **Padding:** Establish the space that surrounds an image. If you select the **Same for All** option, you can access only the **Top** field for Padding. When you type a number in one of those fields, all the fields below it reflect the same number. If you want to set different numbers for each of the Cell Padding options, deselect the **Same for All** option and type individual settings for each option.

- **Margin:** Establish the space that surrounds an image. If you select the **Same for All** option, you can access only the **Top** field for Margin. When you type a number in one of those fields, all the fields below it reflect the same number. If you want to set different numbers for each of the Margin options, deselect the **Same for All** option and then type individual settings for each option.

Borders

The Border category has options for creating a border style for all four sides of the web element, as well as setting the width and color of the border (see Figure 8.23).

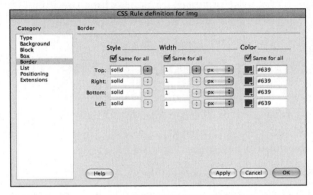

Figure 8.23: The Border category of the CSS Rule Definition window. You can create a variety of borders by setting options for each of the three properties: Style, Width, and Color.

You can set three properties—Style, Width, and Color—for each side (top, right, bottom, and left) of a border. Click the arrow to the left of each option and select the border property from the pop-out menu. If you select the **Same for all** option, all edges of the image are set to the same setting.

Figure 8.24 provides a visual explanation of how both the Box and Borders categories can be used to display an image to the right of a block of text.

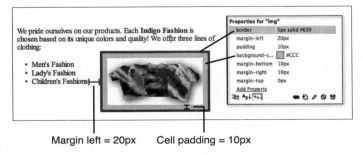

Figure 8.24: This image has a right alignment setting, causing it to float to the right of the bulleted list block of text.

Notice that the image border is 10 pixels away from the edges of the image. This is accomplished through a padding setting of 10 pixels. The border is set to display at 5 pixels in width and a solid style with the color of #639 (shorthand syntax for hexadecimal #663399). The margin settings establish the space that's displayed outside the border in relation to the block of text. This positions the image to the right of the text block with a margin of 20 pixels between both elements.

Tutorial: Adding Images to the Travel Site

Any good travel website features pictures of beautiful scenery and happy, relaxed people enjoying their vacations. So it's time to add some web graphics to our Walkabout Travel website. So far, you've created one page for the site walkabout.html. Let's add the Walkabout logo and other images to this page.

Follow these steps:

1. Define the **Chapter08** folder in the **Tutorial** folder as a new site. To do this, choose **Site, New Site** from the menu bar to open the Site Setup window. Download the Tutorial folder from www.idiotsguides.com/dreamweaver.

2. In the **Site Name** field, name the site **Chapter08 Travel**. In the Local Site Folder field, navigate to the **Chapter08** folder in the **Tutorial** folder on your desktop.

3. Click the **Advanced Settings** category and select the **Local Info** subcategory. In the **Default Images** field, navigate to the **images** folder in the **Chapter08** folder.

4. Click **Save** to save the new defined site.

DREAMWEAVER DON'T

Make sure you aren't in Live view before working through this tutorial. Click to deselect the Live View option if it's active (highlighted in blue). You can't make edits in Design view if Live view is active.

5. Open the **walkabout.html** page by double-clicking it from the Files panel.

6. Let's add the company logo and a graphical representation of the company name to this page. Click to set your cursor before the first block of text, which reads as follows:

Walkabout Adventure Travel Is Your Group Tour Specialist for Seniors.

7. Create a blank line by pressing **Return** (Mac)/**Enter** (PC) from your keyboard. A blank line is created at the top of the page.

8. This new line has the **Heading 1** document structure applied to it. Set this to a **Paragraph** format by positioning your cursor in this line, clicking the **Format** pop-out menu, and choosing **Paragraph** from the list. Dreamweaver applies **Paragraph** document structure to this new text block by surrounding the text with the <p> tag.

9. Leave your cursor in the new line of text. From the menu bar, choose **Insert, Image** and navigate to the **logo.jpg** file in the images folder. Click **Choose/Select** to select this image.

10. In the Image Tag Accessibility Attributes window, type **Walkabout Logo** in the **Alternate Text** field. Click **OK** to close this window. The logo displays in the web page.

11. Next, let's add a graphical version of the company name as a banner. To add this graphic, first create another blank line of text. Click to set your cursor directly to the right of the logo image and press **Return** (Mac)/**Enter** (PC).

12. With a new line created, go to the Files panel and expand the **images** folder. Locate the **banner.jpg** image and drag it to the new line under the logo image.

13. This opens the Image Tag Accessibility Attributes window. Type **Walkabout Banner** in the **Alternate Text** field. Click **OK** to close this window. The banner image displays in the web page directly under the logo (see Figure 8.25).

Figure 8.25: The two images display at the top of the page.

14. Now let's apply a background color for these two images on the page. Open the CSS Styles panel and click the **New CSS Style** button at the bottom of the panel.

DREAMWEAVER TIP

If your images load slowly, apply a background color to the images that is the same color as the page background. This way the image area doesn't display with a white background (the default) until the image loads.

15. In the New CSS Rule window, set the Selector Type to **Tag (Redefines an HTML Element)**. Type **img** in the **Selector Name** field. Under the Rule Definition section, select **(This document only)** from the pop-out menu. Click **OK** to close this window.

16. This opens the CSS Rule Definition window. Click the **Background** category to select it and, in the **Background-color** field, type **#CCCC99.**

17. Click **OK** to define this rule for the `<img />` tag as an internal style sheet of the walkabout.htm document.

18. Let's create a Class style rule that centers web elements and objects like our logo and banner. In the CSS panel, create a new rule by clicking the **New CSS Rule** button.

19. In the New CSS Rule window, set the Selector Type to **Class (Can Apply to Any HTML Element)**. Type **CenterIt** in the **Selector Name** field. Under the Rule Definition section, make sure you're defining the rule for **This Document Only**. This is an internal style sheet. Click **OK** to close this window.

20. This opens the CSS Rule Definition window. Click the **Block** category to select it. In the **Text-Align** field, click the pop-up menu arrow button and choose **Center.** Click **OK** to close the window and create the new Class rule.

21. As you know, a Class style rule must be applied to an individual HTML element. We're going to use this to center our two images. Click to set your cursor directly to the left of the Walkabout logo image (don't select the logo image itself). Now Shift-click on the second image (Walkabout banner) to select both of them. In the Property Inspector, click the **Class** pop-up menu. Choose **CenterIt** from the list. Both images become centered on the page.

22. Our final step is to add a placeholder for a widget. We'll add this to our page later in the development process on the walkabout.htm page. Click to set your cursor at the end of the line of text that reads "Custom Designed with You in Mind!" and press **Return** (Mac)/**Enter** (PC) to create a new line of text through a paragraph break.

23. From the Insert panel, select the **Common** category and then click the arrows to the right of the **Image** button. From the pop-up menu that opens, choose **Image Placeholder**.

24. This opens the Image Placholder window. In the **Name** field, type **slideshow**. (This is the ID name, so it must be one word, lowercase, and with no special characters except for an underscore). Set **Width** to **425px** and **Height** to **425px.** Set the **Color** field to hexadecimal number **#F0BE4D** (Use a zero, not the letter *O*). Type **Slide Show** in the Alternate text field. Click **OK** to define these settings and close the window.

DREAMWEAVER TIP

The correct way to represent a hexadecimal number in Dreamweaver is to start the number with a pound sign (#). If you forget the #, Dreamweaver automatically adds it to the HTML code.

25. The placeholder displays on your page. Save your document by choosing **File, Save** from the menu bar.

DREAMWEAVER TIP

Firefox version 3.0 and below has trouble understanding the placeholder element and skips this code. If you preview your web pages in Firefox, you might not see the image placeholder.

26. Preview your web pages by choosing **File, Preview in a Browser, "Your Primary Browser"** (see Figure 8.26).

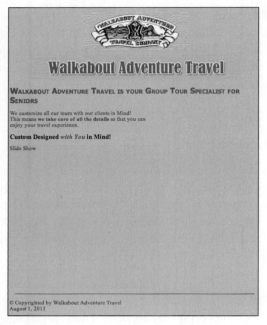

Figure 8.26: Your walkabout.htm page should look similar to this image.

The Least You Need to Know

- Optimize your images to compress them and then convert them to a web graphic format for use in a web page.
- You can insert images through the menu bar by choosing **Insert, Images**.
- You can insert images from other graphic software applications like Photoshop through the **Insert, Image** menu command.
- You can modify and edit web graphics through the Roundtrip editing tool in the Property Inspector.
- You can make quick edits to web images through the Property Inspector and the Quick Edit tools.
- You can insert rollover images through the **Insert, Image Objects, Rollover Image** menu command.
- You can use CSS and style rules to control the appearance and layout of web graphics in your page.

Navigating Your Site with Links

In This Chapter

- Creating hyperlinks, image links, and e-mail links
- Controlling link colors
- Using named anchors to jump around in a web page
- Modifying and deleting a link
- Creating an image map

The user interface makes or breaks your web page. And a good web interface has consistent hyperlinks that are available in the same location on each page throughout the site. If your links and buttons are clearly visible and marked, people have a much easier time navigating through your information. And effective user navigation is key for keeping visitors on your website. If visitors have problems finding what they're looking for, they'll quickly leave.

This chapter is all about the hyperlink, a web feature that lets you jump from one page to another to learn more information about a topic. Hyperlinks don't generate the excitement they used to, but they're still a powerful element of web design. Hyperlinks support the main function of the Internet: to link people, documents, and information. While the concept is simple, making sense of the various types of links can be more complex. This chapter takes you on a tour of the various types of links available on Dreamweaver.

Overview of the Hyperlink

A hyperlink is a reference to another document through a file path that a browser understands; when you click a hyperlink, your browser automatically opens the linked document. The cool thing about linking is that the information can link to a page in your site or to a page on a server halfway around the world.

The HTML code used for linking is the anchor, or <a>, tag, and you can use it to create text links, image links, e-mail links, anchored links, and image maps. Here's a breakdown of each of these types of links:

- **Text link**: A hyperlink applied to text. The link text displays by default with an underline below it indicating the hyperlink.

- **Image link**: A hyperlink applied to an image. When clicked, the image links to another document or web page.

- **E-mail link**: A hyperlink that generates a blank e-mail message with a predetermined e-mail address.

- **Anchored link**: A hyperlink to other locations in the same web page. This type of link is great for very long web pages. You can set up links to different topics or information at the beginning of the document that allow the visitor to jump to a topic later in the web page.

- **Image map**: A hyperlink that creates a hotspot for an area in a web image. These hotspots are clickable and link to other web pages or documents.

Figure 9.1 shows the HTML anchor tag with the required syntax in Code view. It calls out the linked document in a document relative path, and the display text is also included in the code.

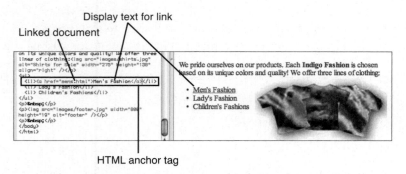

Figure 9.1: This image shows a hyperlink text link. The text "Men's Fashion" links to the mens.htm page.

We first introduced different types of link paths in Chapter 3. The hyperlink can have any of the following link paths:

- **Document relative path:** This form of path is based on the web page (linking document) that's linking to another page/document (linked document).

- **Site root-relative path:** This form of path is based on the root site and always starts the path based on the root folder.

- **Absolute path:** This form of path establishes the complete address to the linked document.

Figure 9.1 shows an example of a link that uses a document relative path. When you defined your site, you established the type of link path for Dreamweaver to use.

Creating Text Hyperlinks

In Dreamweaver, the process for creating a hyperlink is the same whether it's a text link or an image link. You can use three different techniques for creating a link. The first two techniques use the Property Inspector in HTML mode (see Figure 9.2); the third technique uses the Insert Panel.

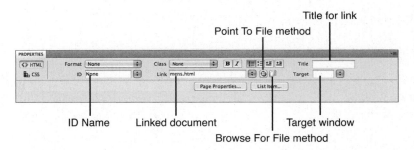

Figure 9.2: *You can choose from two methods for creating a hyperlink in the Property Inspector: the Point To File method and the Browse for File method.*

You can set the various fields in the Property Inspector to adjust the display and functionality of the link. Here's an overview of each field:

- **ID**—Sets a name for your link.

- **Format**—Applies document structure to a link (see Chapter 6).

- **Class**—Applies a Class Style rule to format a link (see Chapter 7).

- **Link**—Establishes the link document.

- **Title**—Sets a title for your link. This is similar to the alternate text of a web graphic and can provide more information about the linked document for visually impaired users.

- **Target**—Sets how the linked document is opened. You can open a linked web page in a new blank window or in the same window as the linking web page. Some of the Target options are only used for Frames (see Appendix E).

The third technique for creating a link is through the Insert panel and the **Common** category **Hyperlink** button, which opens the Hyperlink window (see Figure 9.3). As with the other two methods, you first must select the text or image you want to use to represent the link.

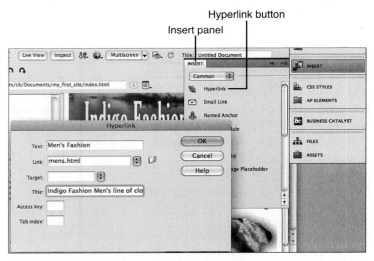

Figure 9.3: *The link you create through the Hyperlink window is inserted into your web page based on where your cursor is located.*

DREAMWEAVER TIP

You can also use the menu bar to add a hyperlink by choosing **Insert, Hyperlink**.

Let's first create a hyperlink using the Browse for File method.

Browse for File Method

The Browse for File method for creating hyperlinks is similar to browsing to locate files. Follow these steps to create a link using the Browse for File method.

1. Select the text on your web page that you want to display as a text link.

2. With the text highlighted on your page, click the HTML mode button of the Property Inspector and then click the **Browse for File** folder icon to the right of the Link field.

3. This opens the Select File window. Navigate to the document you want to link to, and then click **Choose** to close the window. (You can also just type the path in the Link field and click **Choose**.)

4. The highlighted text displays with an underline indicating that it's a link. Look in the HTML code, and you'll see the <a> tag representing the reference to the linked document and the display text.

Point to File Method

To use the **Point to File** method to create a hyperlink, highlight the text on your page that you want to serve as the display text for the link. Open your **Files** panel and make sure you can see the document you want to link to. Click the **Point to File** button to the right of the **Link** field, and drag out a pointer to the file you want to link to in the Files panel (see Figure 9.4).

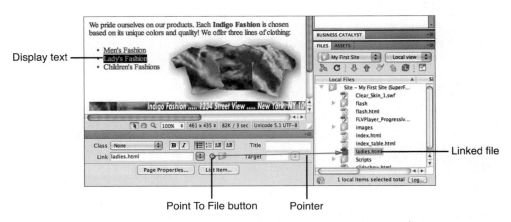

Figure 9.4: *You can link to any file that's in your site with the Point to File method.*

When you let go of your mouse button, the highlighted text displays with a line underneath it indicating that it's linked text. The Property Inspector also displays the linked document in the **Link** field.

You can create a link to a document that resides on another website by typing the URL to the document into the Link field. You must use an absolute link in which the entire URL is referenced, such as **http://www.virtuallyglobal.com/index.html**.

DREAMWEAVER TIP

If you have a second monitor with your computer and have them set up to view side by side with Dreamweaver displayed in the monitor located on the right, the Point to File method will not work correctly. It will be slightly off in its pointing to the linked file. This is a Dreamweaver bug. The Point to File method displays best on a computer with just one monitor.

Setting a Target

The Target attribute is a nice option for more advanced link functionality. This attribute lets you open a linked document in a new window or in a target HTML *frame* of a *frameset*. Frames are a way to present information on a website with multiple documents that are grouped together through a frameset (see Appendix E for more information about frames). By default, this property is set to **_self**, which opens the linked document in the same window as the linking document.

DEFINITION

Frames are a web element that lets you divide a browser window into multiple areas. Each area contains a web page, and the browser displays multiple documents at once.

Framesets are the overall containers for multiple frames. A frameset groups frames together in one window.

The Target attribute is located in the Property Inspector. To set a target, select linked text on your web page and, in the Property Inspector, click the pop-up menu for the **Target** field. Choose the target from the menu list (see Figure 9.5).

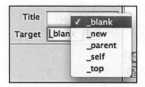

Figure 9.5: *You can link to any file that's in your site, and the linked file opens in the target window you specify in the Target menu.*

Here's an overview of each target attribute:

- **_blank**—Opens the linked document in a blank browser window or Frame

- **_new**—Opens the linked document in a new browser window (The _new value is being phased out in current releases of HTML)

- **_parent**—Opens the linked file into the parent frameset or the window of the frame that contains the link.

- **_self**—Opens the linked document in the same window or frame as the linking document. This is the default value for Target attribute.

- **_top**—Opens the linked document into browser window without any frames.

When you select a target, you'll see the <a> tag in the HTML code reflect the new property of **target,** as shown here:

```
<a href="lady.html" target="_blank">Lady's Fashions</a>
```

Using the Hyperlink Button

The third technique for inserting hyperlinks in your web page is to create a link from scratch using the **Hyperlink** button in the **Common** category of the Insert panel. This process is identical to the process for inserting web graphics. First, position your cursor in the location where you want the link to display on your page, and then click the **Hyperlink** button. This opens the Hyperlink window (see Figure 9.6).

DREAMWEAVER TIP

You can use the Hyperlink button from the Insert panel to add a link to an image or text that exists on your web page. Highlight the text or select the image for the link and then click the **Hyperlink** button in the Insert panel under the Common category.

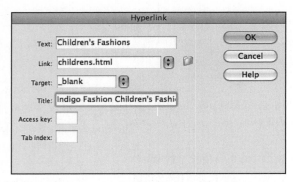

Figure 9.6: The bottom three fields of the Hyperlink window are options used by screen reader programs for low-vision visitors. You may choose to set these accessibility options or not based on the audience for your website.

If you're creating your link from scratch, type the link text to display in the page by typing this text into the Text field. If you want to apply a link to text in your page, highlight it with your cursor to make it display in the Text field. Next, in the Link field, type or navigate to the linked document. Set your target if it's different than the default value of "_self" by clicking the arrows to the right of the Target field and select your link target from the pop-out menu. Type a title into the Title field for the link. Click **OK**, and the link displays in the web page at the location of your cursor.

You can edit or modify the link through the Property Inspector.

Creating Image Links

You can use web images to link to other documents; these are called *image links*, and you can use them to create buttons for navigating your site. To create an image link, select the web graphic in your web page and then, in the Property Inspector or through the **Hyperlink** button in the Insert panel, set the link-related fields to establish the link document and other properties.

The HTML code reflects the image and its associated link.

Controlling Link Colors

When you create a link, it automatically displays in a web page in the default link color set for link states in your browser. Link states are color coded to indicate whether the visitor has already used the link. As you click a link, it briefly displays in a new color. After it has been clicked, the link changes color.

HTML recognizes the following three default link states:

- **Link**—The state of a link when it's first displayed on a web page. The default color is blue.

- **Visited state**—The state of a link that a user has already clicked or visited. The default color for this state is purple.

- **Active state**—The state of a link as it's being clicked; the default color for this state is red. After being clicked, the link quickly changes color.

You can set colors for your link states through either CSS or HTML tags. Let's first look at how to do this in HTML.

Click the **Page Properties** button in the Property Inspector. This opens the Page Properties window; then click the **Appearance (HTML)** category on the left (see Figure 9.7).

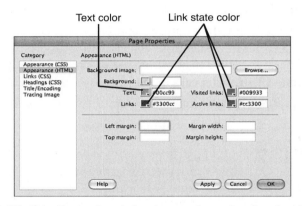

Figure 9.7: The Page Properties window lets you determine the colors for the three states of a link in HMTL.

Click the **Color Palette** button by the link state and select a color from the palette. You can also type a hexadecimal number into the link state color field. Behind the scenes, Dreamweaver creates HTML code that assigns properties for each link state in the web page.

Using CSS for Link Colors

You can also use CSS to set a color for link states. Plus, through CSS, you can assign many more properties and attributes. Just as with style rules for formatting text, you do this by setting formatting properties for your links. You can set the font, color, and font size for displaying your link. You can also apply borders, margins, and cell padding. CSS allows for a fourth link state as well, the hover state. This state displays when the visitor hovers the mouse over a link. The hover state is only available through CSS, and you determine this color when you set up the style rule.

By using style rules, you have a consistent display of your links throughout all pages of your site. The rules control the display of each link state.

To create different styles for the various link states in CSS, use the Compound selector type. See Chapter 15 for a detailed explanation of using the Compound selector type.

DREAMWEAVER TIP

If you try to use a Tag style rule for the <a> tag to format your links, you can't control the link state. Dreamweaver applies properties of this <a> Tag style rule to every link in your site, regardless of their state.

Follow these steps to create a Compound Selector type for your link states:

1. Create a new style rule by clicking the **New CSS Rule** button in the CSS Styles panel.

2. In the New CSS Rule window (see Figure 9.8), set the Selector type to **Compound (Based on Your Selection)**.

3. In the **Selector Name** field, click the arrow icon for the pop-up menu to the right of the field. This displays a menu that lists the four link states: **a:link**, **a:visited, a:hover,** and **a:active**. Choose the link state you want to format.

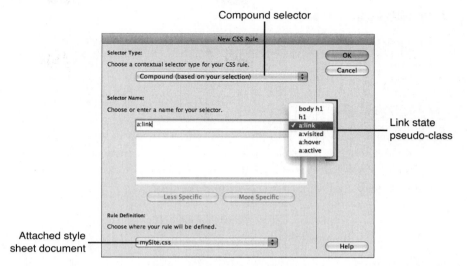

Figure 9.8: The New CSS Rule window showing a Compound selector type for a:link, which is defined in an external style sheet called mySite.css.

4. In the **Rule Definition** section, choose the style sheet where you want your rules to be defined.

5. Click **OK** to display the CSS Rule Definition window. You can use any of the categories and their options to format your link.

This creates a CSS rule for the link state you chose in Step 3 above. To format the other three link states with a CSS rule, repeat the preceding steps and set the Selector Name to each of the remaining three link states.

Using Named Anchors

Named anchors support linking in a web page and are useful in pages with lots of content. Named anchors consist of two objects, an anchor and a linking object. The anchor is a marker; users click on it to go to the linking object. For instance, if you have a web page with information about three types of butterflies, you could use a named anchor for each butterfly name; when users click on the named anchor, it takes them to the linking object, which is information about the butterfly that appears later in the web page. This provides a quick way to jump to specific information in your page.

Creating Named Anchors

Creating a named anchor is a two-step process that involves setting your anchors and then linking to them. In the Insert panel, choose the **Common** category and then click the **Named Anchor** button (see Figure 9.9). You can also access named anchors in the menu bar by choosing **Insert, Named Anchor**.

Figure 9.9: Named Anchors are located in the Common category of the Insert Panel. Your Insert panel may look different based on whether you have Show Labels turned on or off.

Follow these steps to create named anchors:

1. To insert anchors at the location you want to jump to in your web page, click to set your cursor to the left of the text, or web element, and then click the **Named Anchor** button in the **Insert panel**. This opens the Named Anchor window (see Figure 9.10).

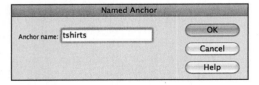

Figure 9.10: The named anchor needs to be one word, with no special characters except an underscore.

2. Type the name for the anchor in the **Anchor Name** field and click **OK**. An anchor icon displays in your web page (see Figure 9.11).

Anchor icon

Figure 9.11: *The named anchor displays at the location of your cursor in the web page.*

DREAMWEAVER TIP

You must have Invisible Elements turned on to see the named anchors in your web page. You can toggle this feature on and off by choosing **View, Visual Aids, Invisible Elements** from the menu bar. If you have **Invisible Elements** turned off, you see only a reference to your named anchors in the HTML code.

3. Repeat steps 1 and 2 to set as many named anchors in your web page as you need.

4. With the named anchors set in your page, you can now link to them. Select either the text or the image that you want to use as the linking object.

5. In the Property Inspector, in the **Link** field, click and drag the **Point To File** button to the named anchor you want to jump to in the web page (see Figure 9.12). The Property Inspector shows the anchor name with a pound sign (#) in front of it; this is the HTML reference to a named anchor (see Figure 9.13).

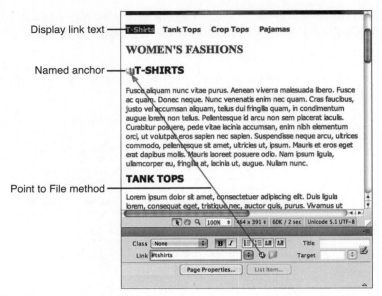

Figure 9.12: Linking to named anchors using the Point To File button in the Property Inspector. You can also just type the name of the anchor preceded by a # in the Link field to create a link to the named anchor.

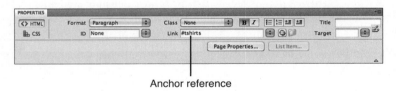

Anchor reference

Figure 9.13: Notice the anchor name preceded by the pound sign. This is the HTML reference to your named anchor.

You can change the name of a named anchor at any time. Follow these steps to modify or edit a named anchor:

1. Select the named anchor by clicking the icon for the named anchor in the web page (see Figure 9.11).

2. In the Property Inspector, change the anchor name in the Name field.

By changing the name of the named anchor, you've broken the link for the linking object. To re-establish the link, you need to change the anchor reference for the linked object. Highlight or select the linking text or object, and in the Property Inspector, change that anchor reference in the Link field to match the new anchor name (see Figure 9.13).

Using ID Names for Linking

You can also use the ID names feature to create links that jump to other areas on your page. Instead of linking to named anchors, you can apply an ID name to a block of text or web element. The process is almost identical to the named anchor two-step process. Instead of setting anchors in the locations on your page that you want to jump to, you set an ID name. You can set the ID name through the Property Inspector (see Figure 9.14).

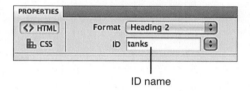

ID name

Figure 9.14: The ID name needs to be one word with no special characters, and it must be a unique word.

You can't see the ID name on your page in Design view, and no icon appears for the ID name. However, you can see the HTML code in Code view. For example, here's an **ID** name of **tanks** applied to the text of **Tank Tops,** which is structured as a Heading 2 block of text:

```
<h2 id="tanks">Tank Tops</h2>
```

You can link to this ID name by selecting your display text or web element and then typing a **#** followed by the ID name you're targeting, such as **#tanks**.

DREAMWEAVER TIP

You must be in Code view to modify or edit an ID name. Find the reference to the ID name in the code, and change the name of the ID there. Next, update the link to this ID by selecting the linking text or web element. Finally, change the link reference in the Property Inspector.

Creating an E-mail Link

E-mail links are a useful communication tool for your website. These links open a new message in the user's e-mail application. The new message is automatically addressed to a recipient, has a subject line relating to the e-mail link, and includes site information.

Dreamweaver makes it easy to create an e-mail link. First, position your cursor where you want the e-mail link to display. Next, in the Insert panel, choose **Common** from the drop-down menu and click the **E-mail Link** button. This opens the E-mail Link window (see Figure 9.15).

Figure 9.15: You can type anything you like in the Text field of the E-mail Link window, but you must type a real e-mail address in the E-mail field.

When you click **OK**, Dreamweaver underlines the e-mail display text to represent a link (see Figure 9.16).

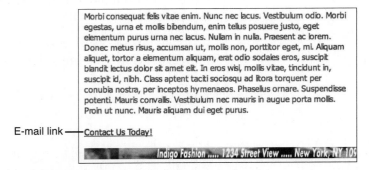

Figure 9.16: When visitors click this link, it opens a new message in the visitor's e-mail application.

You can also use the Property Inspector to create an e-mail link. First, highlight the text or web element that you want to serve as the display link. Next, in the Link field of the Property Inspector type **mailto:** followed by an e-mail address. Here's an example: mailto:info@indigofashion.com.

DREAMWEAVER DON'T

Think twice before using the mailto: form of communication on your site. Spammers sometimes use HTML code to quickly collect e-mail addresses. If you want to avoid having a spammer access your e-mail address in this way, consider adding a form to your website that visitors can use to contact you (see Chapter 19).

Editing and Deleting a Link

Sometimes you need to edit or delete a link because the URL of the linking document has changed or has been removed altogether. To edit a link, first select the linking text or web element. The Property Inspector reflects the link in the Link field. Using either **Browse for File** or **Point to File**, navigate to the new document. You may also type a new URL to a document in the Link field. If you're linking to a new web page outside of your site, you can copy a URL from a browser Address field and paste it into the Link field.

You can also use the menu bar command of **Modify, Change Link** to edit a linked document. This command opens the Select File window. You can then use **Browse for File** to access the new linked document.

If you need to delete a link, select the linking text or object. From the menu bar, choose **Modify, Remove Link**. Dreamweaver deletes the link reference from the page.

Using Image Maps

An image map is a transparent button that you use to create a hotspot on a web image. You can click on a hotspot to access a link to other documents or information. For instance, if you have an image of different types of flowers on a web page, you can make each flower a hot spot; when users click one of the flowers, their browser opens a page with more information about that flower.

To create an image map, you need to have a web image inserted on your page. The image map tools are located on the Property Inspector (see Figure 9.17).

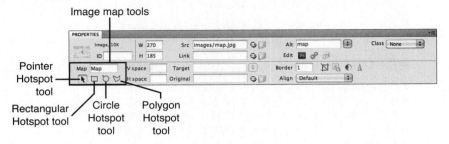

Figure 9.17: You must have a web image selected on your page for the Property Inspector to display the Image Map tools.

You have a choice of the following Image Map tools:

- **Pointer Hotspot tool**—Moves and modifies hotspot areas
- **Rectangle Hotspot tool**—Creates rectangular hotspot areas
- **Circle Hotspot tool**—Creates circular hotspot areas
- **Polygon Hotspot tool**—Creates polygon-shaped or custom hotspot areas

Creating a Rectangle or Circle Hotspot

The Rectangle and Circle Hotspot tools work similarly, creating either a rectangular hotspot or a circular hotspot. Follow these steps for either type of hotspot:

1. Click on the web image that you want to apply a hotspot to.

2. Go to the **Image Map** tools display in the Property Inspector. Select the **Rectangle** or **Circle** tool.

3. Click and drag the tool to designate the hotspot area on the web image (see Figure 9.18).

4. When you've defined the area, release the mouse button. This opens a message window that encourages you to add alternate text to the image. Click **OK** to close the message.

5. Now you can set the link information in the Property Inspector. Make sure you create alternate text in the **Alt** field.

Figure 9.18: The hotspot is a translucent aqua color.

Creating a Polygon Hotspot

The Polygon Hotspot tool creates a polygon shape, which you can use to create any type of polygon shape. It works a little differently than the Circle or Rectangle Hotspot tools. To create a polygon hotspot, follow these steps:

1. Click on the web image that you want to apply a hotspot to.

2. Go to the **Image Map** tools display in the Property Inspector. Select the **Polygon** tool.

3. On the web graphic, click to set a starting control point for the area you want to define as a hot spot (see Figure 9.19). This opens the Alt text message; click **OK** to close the message. Move your mouse to the next location where you want a control point positioned, and click to set another control point. Repeat until you define the area that you want to make a hotspot. (see Figure 9.19).

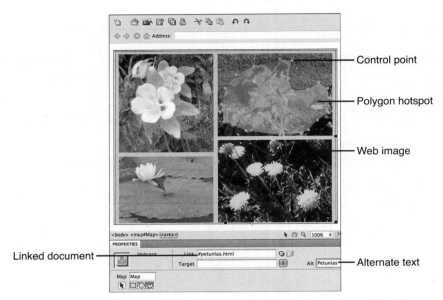

Figure 9.19: *You can click a control point to adjust the shape and size of a polygon hotspot.*

5. Set the Link field in the Property Inspector to a linked document and create alternate text in the **Alt** field.

Modifying Hotspot Areas

To modify an existing hotspot, you need to use the Pointer Hotspot tool. Click this tool and use it to click the hotspot that you want to modify. Click and drag a control point to modify the hotspot. You can resize and reshape the hotspot.

Tutorial: Creating Navigation Links

It's time to create some navigation links for the Walkabout Travel website. In this tutorial, we step you through the process of creating a horizontal menu bar for links to other pages in the Walkabout website. Here's what you do:

1. Define the **Chapter09** folder in the **Tutorial** folder as a new site.

2. Open the **walkabout.html** file and, in Design view, set your cursor to the left of the first paragraph, which says **Walkabout Adventure Travel is Your Group Tour Specialist for Seniors.**

3. Press **Return** (Mac)/**Enter** (PC) to create a new line.

4. Position your cursor in the new line and change the document structure to **Paragraph** by clicking the **Format** pop-out menu in the Property Inspector and choosing **Paragraph** from the menu list.

5. With your cursor in the new line of text, type **Company History**.

6. Press your **spacebar** five times to create five spaces after Company History; then type **Our Philosophy.**

DREAMWEAVER TIP

To create multiple spaces in a row, you need to have a preference setting turned on. In Dreamweaver **Preferences,** in the **General** category, make sure you have the **Allow Multiple Consecutive Spaces** option selected.

7. Add five more spaces and type **Contact Us**. Then add another five spaces and type **Home**. You've created the start for a navigation bar of menu items with just text (see Figure 9.20).

Figure 9.20: These text references will be the links for a navigation bar.

8. Now create a link to the **history.html** page. Highlight the text **Company History** and, in the Property Inspector to the right of the **Link** field, click the **Browse for File** folder icon. Browse to the **history.html** file. Click **Choose** to close the window. The **Company History** text displays, with an underline indicating a link.

9. Let's use the **Point to File** method to link to the **philosophy.html** file. Highlight the text **Our Philosophy** and, in the Property Inspector to the right of the **Link** field, click and drag the **Point to File** tool to the **philosophy.html** document in the Files panel (see Figure 9.21).

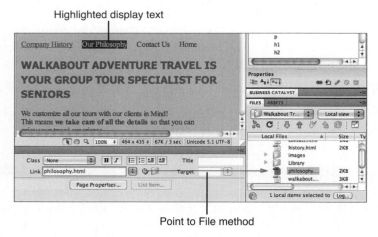

Figure 9.21: By designating the link text to another page in the website, you are creating a menu bar for accessing other pages in the site.

10. At this point in the tutorial, you're creating a link for a file that doesn't exist yet, the **contact.html** file. Again, highlight the text for the link, which in this case is **Contact Us**. In the Property Inspector, type **contact.html** in the **Link** field. You again see the display text underlined, indicating a link, but because there's no linked document, this link won't work when clicked in a browser.

11. Repeat Step 9, but set the **Home** text to link to the **index.html** page. Like the contact.html page, the index.html page doesn't exist. We include steps for creating this web page later in the book.

12. Next let's create a link from the Walkabout logo web image to the **index.html** page. Click the logo web image to make it active.

13. In the Property Inspector, in the **Link** field, type **index.html** to set this image to link to the home page of the Walkabout Travel site.

14. Notice that a blue border displays around the logo image. Dreamweaver automatically inserts this border to indicate the graphic as a link. To delete this border, in the Property Inspector in the Border field type **0** (zero) and then press **Return/Enter** to set this new border attribute (see Figure 9.22).

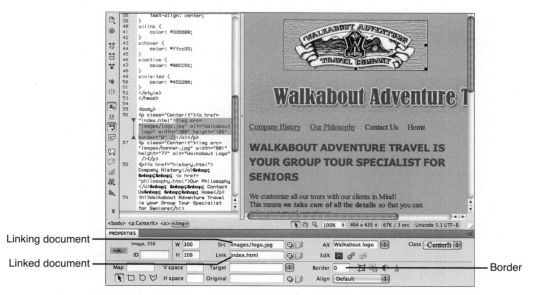

Figure 9.22: You can link an image to any file or URL.

DREAMWEAVER TIP

If you don't designate a border for a table or image, some browsers by default represent these elements with a 1px border. It's a good practice to set borders to a value for all tables and images in your page.

Next, let's format the links using CSS so that they integrate better with the overall design. Follow these steps:

1. Highlight one of the links you created.

2. Click the **New CSS Rule** button in the CSS Styles panel. This opens the New CSS Rule panel (see Figure 9.23). In Selector Type, click the pop-up menu and choose **Compound (Based on Your Selection)**.

3. In the Selector Name section, click the arrows icon to the right of the **Selector Name** field and choose **a:link** from the menu.

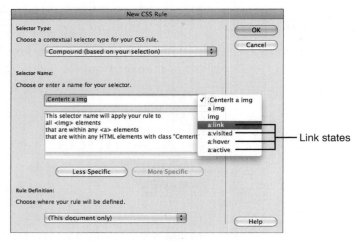

Figure 9.23: *Set up style rules for all four CSS link states.*

4. In the Rule Definition section, set the style sheet for the rule to **This Document Only**.

5. Click **OK** to close the New CSS Rule window. This action also opens the CSS Rule Definition window.

6. In the New CSS Rule window, in the **Type** category, set **Color** to hexadecimal number **#336600**. Click **OK** to close the window. You have set the initial state of the link to match the color of the text used for paragraphs in the document.

7. Notice the new **a:link** rule in the CSS Styles panel. Let's now create a style rule for the visited state. Repeat Steps 1–6, but choose the **a:visited** link state from the pop-up menu and set the hexadecimal color to **#452200**.

DREAMWEAVER TIP

When using hexadecimal colors for setting link colors, always precede the six-digit number with a # (number sign). If you forget to use a #, some browsers won't understand the coding and will skip the color.

8. Instead of using the **New CSS Rule** button to set the remaining two link states, you'll duplicate the existing **a:link** style rule and change the color property to a new color. In the CSS Styles panel make sure the **All** mode is active, then select one of the two style rules that you've created for a link state. Right-click the rule and choose **Duplicate** from the menu.

9. This opens the Duplicate CSS Rule window. In the **Selector Name** section, open the pop-up menu and choose **a:hover** from the list. Click **OK** to close the window.

10. To change the color property to a new color for this rule, in the CSS Styles panel, click the **a:hover** style rule to select it. Then, in the Property pane, change the color to hexadecimal number of **#FFCC33** (see Figure 9.24).

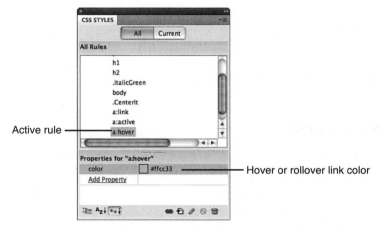

Figure 9.24: Add a new property to this rule by clicking the Add Property link.

11. Repeat steps 8 through 10 and create a rule for the **a:active** state. Set the color to a bright green by using the color palette.

12. The **walkabout.html** page now reflects the new link colors. Save your document and preview it in a browser. Test your links, keeping in mind that some of the links aren't yet linked to an existing document, so they'll display the standard "Can't find the page" default message.

The Least You Need to Know

- Use the Property Inspector to create a hyperlink for linking to other documents or information.

- An image can link to other documents or information through either the Property Inspector or the Insert panel.

- You can control colors for link states through the Compound sector type of CSS.

- You create named anchors for jumping around to different locations in a web page through the Insert panel.

- You can create an e-mail link through the Insert panel or the Property inspector.

- You can modify and delete a hyperlink through the Property Inspector.

- You can create an image map in the Property Inspector and use the Image Map tools to create hotspots on a web image.

Using Tables in Web Design

In This Chapter

- Creating a new table
- Using Extended mode for viewing and working with tables
- Selecting a table to make it active
- Selecting a row, column, or cell in a table
- Formatting and modifying a table, row, column, or cell
- Importing tabular data into a new table in a web page

In the past, designers used tables to structure a whole page layout for their design. Designers used the rows to represent a header, menu bars, and/or a footer. Columns represented sidebars or other vertical page elements. Today, with the growing use of CSS and the Div tag, designers are using tables much less frequently.

Though the W3C no longer recommends using tables to structure your page layout, they're still a valuable web element. For instance, by their very nature, they're ideal for presenting spreadsheet data on a website. Designers also use tables to neatly display many vertical or horizontal elements.

Table cells are diverse elements that you can use creatively in your web design. You can merge cells—either vertically in a column or horizontally in a row—to create structural diversity. You can also merge both vertical and horizontal cells.

How Tables Work

Tables are an element of web design that enable the user to format various web content into controlled fields, or cells. A table in Dreamweaver is similar to tables in other applications. Tables consist of rows and columns; individual cells are located where the row and the column intersect (see Figure 10.1).

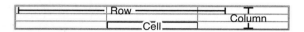

Figure 10.1: You can present your page content in the table cells to provide structure.

DREAMWEAVER DON'T

Don't use a table to create your web page layout. Instead, use Div tags, which create sections or areas for page layout (see Chapter 13).

Creating a New Table

You can insert a table through either the menu bar or the Insert panel. From the menu bar, choose **Insert, Table**. On the Insert panel, choose the **Common** category from the pop-out menu and then click the **Table** button (see Figure 10.2).

Figure 10.2: Click the Table button to insert a table in your web page.

DREAMWEAVER TIP

You don't need to determine a table height. Tables, like web pages, need to be able to adjust in height to the display of the web page in a browser.

When you activate the **Insert Table** command, the Table window opens, enabling you to set up your table structure (see Figure 10.3).

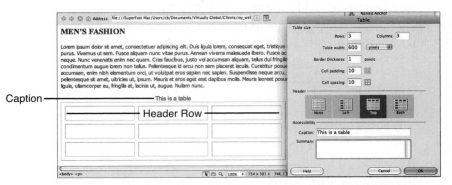

Figure 10.3: *Use the Table window to create a table based on rows and columns as well as other attributes. The table on the right reflects the options that are set in the Table window on the left.*

The Table window lets you define the following attributes for your table:

- **Rows/Columns**—Sets the number of rows/columns for your table.

- **Table Width**—Sets the width of a table. This can be a fixed unit of pixels or a relative unit of percent.

- **Border Thickness**—Sets the thickness of the table border in pixels.

- **Cell Padding**—Sets the space between the cell content and the cell boundary.

- **Cell Spacing**—Sets the space between cells in a table.

- **Header**—Select the row and/or column to be used for row or column headings. Select the format you want from the four Header layout buttons.

- **Caption**—Create a caption or title for the table. This can display below or above the table. This caption is necessary for accessibility and is read by screen readers.

- **Summary**—Create a summary or description of the table. This summary is necessary for accessibility and is read by screen readers.

Examine the HTML code for the table shown in Figure 10.4. This is the HTML code for the table represented in Figure 10.3.

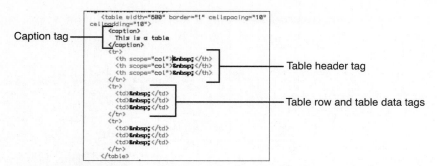

Figure 10.4: *The* `<table>` *tag contains other nested tags for creating the various areas of a table.*

A table in a web page is created through the `<table>` tag and other nested tags that create table elements, such as rows and cells. The `<table>` tag wraps around these other table element tags. The various Table tags are as follows.

- **Table**—`<table>` tag
- **Table header**—`<th>` tag with attributes of scope
- **Table row**—`<tr>` tag
- **Table data**—`<td>` tag

You can control each of these table-related tags with CSS and a Class or Tag style rule for the format of the table tags.

Table Viewing Modes

In Dreamweaver, you can view a table in two ways: Standard mode and Expanded mode. Standard mode is the default view for a table and is somewhat restrictive for selecting tables and table elements like cells, rows, or columns. Expanded mode gives you more control over table view and makes it easier to select table elements. This mode also temporarily inserts additional cell padding and cell spacing while reducing the overall size of the table border, which makes it easier to select various areas of your table. This extra spacing and padding is for display purposes only (see Figure 10.5). At the top of the table is the Table Information bar. Dreamweaver displays the width of the entire table and of each column, including a revised width based on the padding added for display purposes.

Expanded Table mode indicator

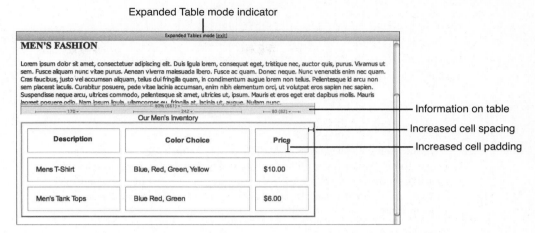

Information on table

Increased cell spacing

Increased cell padding

Figure 10.5: *The inserted extra cell spacing and padding is temporary, for display purposes only. It doesn't alter the set padding and spacing attributes.*

To turn on Expanded mode, from the menu bar, choose **View, Table Mode, Expanded Tables Mode**. Exit Expanded Tables mode by clicking **[Exit]** to the right of Expanded Tables mode, at the top of the document window.

You can also use the **Insert** panel and the **Layout** category to switch between table modes. At the top of the panel are two buttons, the **Standard** and **Expanded** buttons. Click each button to toggle between the two modes.

In Expanded mode, you can easily select the table, rows, and columns, as well as insert elements, text, or images. This can be difficult in Standard mode.

Selecting a Table

Selecting the table can be a tricky task, but like most web elements in Dreamweaver, the key is to know what part to select. To select a table, position your cursor over the outer edge of the table outline and click to select. You can also use the *Tag Selector*. First, click anywhere in your table area; then, in the Tag Selector, click the `<table>` tag to select the table in your document (see Figure 10.6).

Table tag

Figure 10.6: The Tag Selector is located in the bottom left of your Document window. The path of the current item selected is displayed here.

> **DEFINITION**
>
> The **Tag Selector** displays the structure of web elements based on the HTML tags. Some tags are nested in other parent tags. To jump to a specific element, click the representing tag. You can use the Tag Selector to select any page element. Once selected, you can edit this element in either Code or Design view of Dreamweaver.

When you select a table, the Property Inspector displays the table settings (see Figure 10.7).

Figure 10.7: You can change the settings for a table in the Property Inspector.

Through the Property Inspector, you can edit these settings to modify the basic structure of your table.

If you don't establish values for borders, cell padding, and spacing, you're leaving the table open to browser interpretation. Typically, a browser displays borders and cell padding set to a value of 1 pixel, and cell spacing set to 2 pixels, by default. Set these values to zero if you don't want them to have any value.

Selecting Cells, Rows, and Columns

To select an individual cell, just click within the cell box. The Property Inspector displays additional features for cell formatting, and the Tag Inspector displays the selected cell represented by the <td> tag (table data).

To select a row, place your cursor in either the starting cell or the ending cell in the row. Then click and drag your mouse to select the entire row of cells (see Figure 10.8).

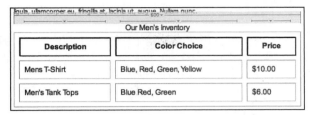

Figure 10.8: You can select groups of cells within a row by selecting just those cells by clicking and dragging. The border of the selected cells turns bold, like the select row at the top of this table.

DREAMWEAVER TIP

Another way to select a row is to position your cursor to the far left of the row. The cursor changes to an arrow pointing right. By clicking with the arrow, you select the entire row.

Selecting columns is a process similar to selecting rows. Place your cursor in either the starting or the ending cell and then click and drag vertically until the column is selected.

You can also select a column by clicking the arrow at the top of each column to the right of the column width information. This opens a pop-out menu that lets you choose the **Select Column** command for an entire column (see Figure 10.9).

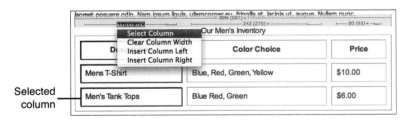

Figure 10.9: The border of a column turns bold to indicate that you've selected it.

You can also select a column by clicking the arrow at the top of each column to the right of the column width information. This opens a pop-out menu that lets you choose the **Select Column** command for an entire column.

Modifying a Table

You can use the Property Inspector to modify many table properties. You can use it to modify the overall table size, width of columns, and row height. You can also modify cell padding and spacing and apply a Class style rule. Finally, you can use the Property Inspector to set the alignment of the table in regard to other web elements on your page.

Manually Resizing a Table

In Design view of Dreamweaver, you can also manually adjust the size of a table by clicking and dragging on the table handles (see Figure 10.10).

Figure 10.10: Click on a handle and drag to adjust the table size.

Manually Adjusting Rows and Columns

To manually adjust the size of rows and columns, position your cursor between two rows or columns to generate the double-arrow tool. Click and drag with the double-arrow tool to adjust the width or height (see Figure 10.11).

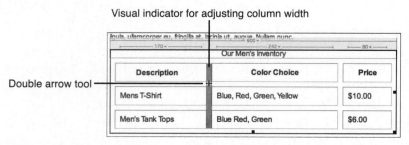

Figure 10.11: The table information at the top of the table display shows the new column or row size.

> **DREAMWEAVER TIP**
>
> Clear a row or column size by clicking the arrow next to the column or row size displayed in the table information. This is located at the top of an active table. From the pop-out menu, choose **Clear Column Width** or **Clear Row Height**.

Using Percentages for Tables, Rows, and Columns

You can set up a table and its rows and columns to be a fixed unit size or a percentage. If you specify a fixed unit size, the table won't change in width based on the size of the browser window. Specifying a percentage unit allows a table to expand and contract based on a percentage of the browser window. If you set the row or column value to a percentage, rows and columns are based on the percentage of the table size. To set a table size to a percentage, click on the table to make it active and then, in the Property Inspector, set the **Width** or **Height Unit** pop-out menu to % (see Figure 10.12). You can also just type a number in the **W** or **H** field, followed by a **%** (percentage) sign.

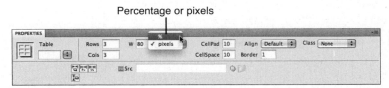

Figure 10.12: Set up a table as a fixed unit size by choosing pixels. To make a table size relative to the browser window, choose the percent option.

Table Alignment

By default, Dreamweaver aligns new tables to the left side of your page. To change the alignment, select the table and, from the Properties Inspector, click the **Align** pop-out menu and select your alignment type (see Figure 10.13).

Figure 10.13: You have a choice of left, center, or right for your table alignment.

Working with Height and Width Values

When you set a row height or column width, this value is set for the first cell in that row or column. All cells in the table conform to this value. If you try to change the value of a cell other than the first cell in a row or column, the first cell's value won't be affected. The first cell of a row or column dictates the size of that row or column, regardless of other sizes you type into other cells.

On a Macintosh, Dreamweaver displays a Table Information bar at the top of all active tables. On a PC, the Table Information bar is located at the bottom of the table. This bar provides information about your table and column widths (see Figure 10.14).

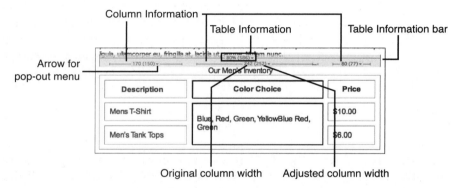

Figure 10.14: The Table Information bar is a useful feature for setting your table and column widths.

In the Table Information bar, when you click the arrow next to the column or table information, a pop-up menu displays a list of options. If you are looking at a Column Information pop-out menu, you'll see the following options:

- **Select Column**—Selects entire column and column data.

- **Clear Column Width**—Clears the set column width.

- **Insert Column Left**—Inserts a column to the left of the active column.

- **Insert Column Right**—Inserts a column to the right of the active column.

If you're looking at the Table Information pop-out menu you'll see the following options:

- **Select Table**—Selects entire table and all data.

- **Clear All Heights**—Clears all row heights determined in the table.

- **Clear All Widths**—Clears all column heights determined in the table.

- **Make All Widths Consistent**—Sets all column widths to a consistent width.

- **Hide Table Widths**—Hides the Table Information bar. To turn it back on, choose **View, Visual Aids, Table Widths** from the menu bar.

If you set your column width to a fixed unit of pixels, and then you add cell padding and spacing, the Table Information bar might show two different sets of values for a column width or table width. You can use this information to set up your table correctly. Remember, the table element is based on the box model (see Chapter 1) so when you add cell spacing or padding, you are actually adding these units to your overall table/column width. Dreamweaver displays the correct value to the right of the value you set. This type of conflict can cause your table to display strangely. To resolve the issue, click the arrow pop-out menu above each column where there's a conflict. Choose **Clear Column Values** to reset your column width to the correct value based on the cell padding and spacing that you added to the table.

Inserting Rows or Columns

After you create a table, you can add or delete rows or columns. You can also merge cells or split cells into two cells. An entire menu is devoted to making modifications to your table. From the menu bar, choose **Modify, Table**. This displays all the sub-menu choices for modifying a table (see Figure 10.15).

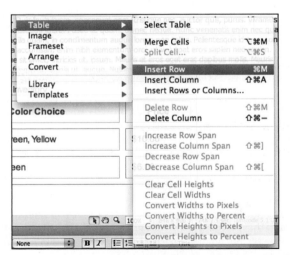

Figure 10.15: Dreamweaver offers three choices for inserting rows or columns into a table: Insert Row, Insert Column, or Insert Rows or Columns.

To insert a row or column, first select a row or a column. From the menu bar, choose **Modify, Table,** and choose from the three insert menu commands listed in the submenu. If you choose **Insert Row** or **Insert Column,** Dreamweaver inserts the new row or column above or to the right of your selected row or column. If you choose **Insert Rows or Columns,** Dreamweaver displays the Insert Rows or Column window (see Figure 10.16).

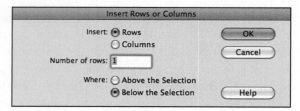

Figure 10.16: This command lets you choose whether you want to insert the column or row before or after the selected row or column.

Deleting Rows or Columns

After you create a table, you can add or delete rows or columns. You can also merge cells or split cells into two cells. An entire menu is devoted to making modifications to your table. First, set your cursor select the cell, row, or column you want to modify. Then, from the menu bar, choose **Modify, Table**. This displays all the submenu choices for modifying a table (see Figure 10.15).

You can't delete an individual cell from a row or column. You must delete the entire row or column.

Merging Cells

As noted at the beginning of this chapter, you can merge cells to create a single cell that spans multiple rows or columns. To do this, first select the cells that you want to merge; then, from the menu bar, choose **Modify, Table, Merge Cells** (see Figure 10.17).

DREAMWEAVER TIP

Keep in mind that merging table cells generates a lot of HTML code. The more code, the slower your web page downloads and displays in a browser.

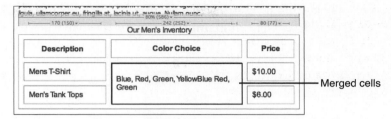

Figure 10.17: Merge any selection of cells, as long as they form a rectangular area in the table.

Splitting Cells

You can split cells into smaller individual cells based on either rows or columns. Start by selecting the cell that you want to split; then choose **Modify, Table, Split Cell**. This opens the Split Cell window (see Figure 10.18).

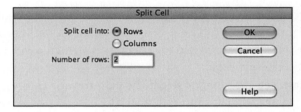

Figure 10.18: You can choose to split any cell into multiple cells based on rows or columns.

In the window, indicate whether you want to split the cell into multiple rows or multiple columns by clicking the bubble next to **Rows/Columns**; then type the number of rows/columns you want to split the cell into.

Using CSS to Format Cells, Rows, and Columns

You can use CSS to create style rules for formatting your tables. Elements that you can format include the font for text display, background colors, and images. You can format the entire table or just individual rows, columns, or cells. Adding background images and colors is a great way to spruce up a table and integrate it with your web page design.

You can even apply custom formatting to a single table on your page by using an ID style rule (see Figure 10.19). For more information on ID style rules see Chapters 13 and 15.

Figure 10.19: You can set an ID name for the table through the ID field. After you name a table with an ID, you can target this ID name with an ID style rule to apply a unique format to just this table.

DREAMWEAVER TIP

You can apply many of the same CSS style rules and properties to tables that you use for other web elements.

To add a background image or a background color to your table, use a CSS style rule and the **Background** category. The process for adding a background color or background image is the same as you use for other web elements (see Chapter 8). Here's a quick refresher on this process:

1. Create a new style rule by clicking the **New CSS Rule** button in the CSS Style panel.

2. In the New CSS Rule window, choose **Tag (Applies to only one HTML element)** as your selector type.

3. Target the <table> tag in the **Selector Name** field.

4. Determine the style sheet for this rule in the **Rule Definition** field. Click **OK** to open the CSS Rule Definition window.

5. In the CSS Rules Definition window, click the **Background** category on the left, choose a background color, or define a background image for the table.

A Tag style rule for the <table> tag applies to all the tables on your page. If you're using an external style sheet (see Chapter 12), the rule then applies to all tables in your site.

You can also set a background color or image to a table header row `<th>` or to the table data tag `<td>`. Create your **Tag** style rule and target the tag that you want to format.

DREAMWEAVER TIP

To format an individual row or column with a background color or image, use a Class style rule. You might want to do this if you want to add a background color to every other row or column. Select the rows you want to format and then apply the Class style rule through the Property Inspector.

If you apply a background color to a table and then apply a new background color to an individual cell, row, or column, CSS formats these based on an established order of precedence. Here's the order of precedence for table elements:

1. Cells

2. Rows/columns

3. Table

Any formatting applied to rows and columns takes precedence over formatting applied to tables; and any formatting applied to cells takes precedence over formatting applied to rows/columns or the table in general.

For example, if a table is formatted with a background image for the entire table, the table displays with this image as a background. If you add a background color to the header row in the table, this color displays on top of the background image because rows/columns take precedence over the table. If you change the font for just one cell in the header row of the table, the font in just that cell displays with the new format, due to cells taking precedence over rows/columns.

Importing Tabular Data

Dreamweaver lets you import tabular data into your web page. This feature makes it easy to control the integration of complex data, no matter how large in size.

Before you import data, you need to make sure it's in text format. Next, set your cursor in the web page where you want the imported data to display and choose **File, Import Tabular Data** from the menu bar. This opens the Import Tabular Data window (see Figure 10.20).

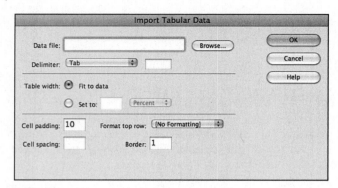

Figure 10.20: In the Import Tabular Data window, you can apply basic formatting to the new table.

Here's an overview of each option in the Import Tabular Data window.

- **Data file:** Determine the file to import. Use the Browse for File folder to navigate to your file or type the path to the file.

- **Delimiter:** Choose the type of *delimiter* your import file uses in the data. This could be Tab, Comma, Semicolon, Colon, or Other (custom character)

DEFINITION

A **delimiter** is a character or sequence of characters used to determine the boundaries between text data. For example, if you export Microsoft Excel spreadsheet data to a Tab delimited file, the data has Tabs in between each column of data in each row, separating the individual cells of data.

- **Table width:** Set how the data is imported into a Dreamweaver table. The Fit to data option sets the column width to the longest string of text in a column. The Set to option sets a fixed or relative unit for the table width.

- **Cell padding:** Set the number of pixels to display between a cell's content and the cell's boundary.

- **Cell spacing:** Set the number of pixels to display between adjacent table cells.

- **Format top row:** Determine the format of the table's top row.

- **Border:** Set the border width in pixels for the table.

In the Import Tabular Data window, first select a source file to import in the **Data file** field. This file needs to be in tabular format to properly import. Dreamweaver doesn't recognize Excel files. Choose the type of delimiter that your data uses. A popular choice is **Tab delimited** but you can choose **Comma**, **Semicolon**, or **Colon** as the delimiter. You can even specify any other character through the **Other** option.

Next, set the other options, including Cell Padding, Cell Spacing, Border, and Format Top row, based on the display you want for your imported table. Click **OK** to import the data into a new table in your web page.

 # Tutorial: Creating a Table

You're planning to add a form that visitors can fill out and submit on the Contact Us page of the Walkabout Travel site. (For details on forms, see Chapter 19.) A table is an ideal way to structure a form, because you can create columns and rows to serve as the fields in the table. Here's what you do:

1. Define the **Chapter10** folder in the **Tutorial** folder as a new site.

2. Open **contact.html** from the Files panel. This is a new page that has been partly developed for this tutorial.

3. To begin creating a form, you first need to insert a table into the web page to hold the form fields and text. Click to set your cursor under the two web images on the page.

4. Insert a table by choosing **Insert, Table** from the menu bar. This opens the Table window.

5. Set your table settings identical to those in Figure 10.21. Click **OK** to insert a table into your page.

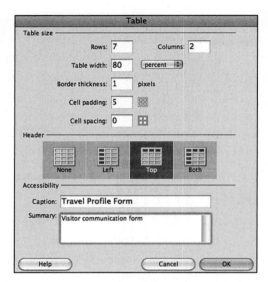

Figure 10.21: *This table is seven rows by two columns, with a caption and a table header row. The border is set to 1px, cell padding is set to 5px, and there's no cell spacing.*

DREAMWEAVER TIP

The Caption and Summary fields are accessibility features for visually impaired users. Anything you type into these two fields is accessible to a screen reader. The Caption displays at the top of the table and is visible in a browser, but the Summary will not display in a browser.

6. Now set the column widths. Click in the first cell of the left column. In the Property Inspector, set the **w** field to 30 percent of the table by typing **30%** in the field. You need to type the % (percentage sign) immediately after the number for the column width field.

7. Click in the first cell of the right column. In the Property Inspector, set this column **w** to **70%**.

8. Click and drag across the first row of the table to select both cells. This is the table header row; in Code view, look at the HTML code. You see the `<th>` tag for the table header.

9. Merge these cells by choosing **Modify, Table, Merge Cells** from the menu bar. The first row of this table is now all one cell (see Figure 10.22).

Figure 10.22: This header row is now one long cell that expands the width of the table.

10. Click in the second cell in the left column under the table header row and type **Name:**. This is a text label for the form's first input field.

11. Click in the next cell under the **Name:** cell in the same column and type a second text label of **Address:**. Repeat this process to add **City:, State:, E-mail Address:,** and **Comments & Questions** into the cells in the first column. Your table should look like the table in Figure 10.23.

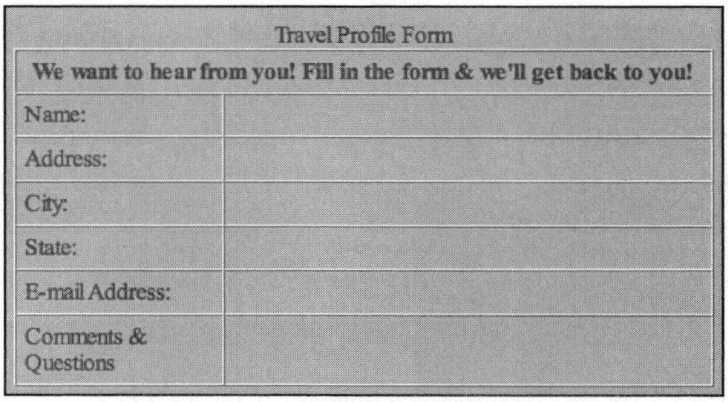

Figure 10.23: The cell padding you applied adds 5 pixels of space on the inside of each cell, so the text labels aren't flush with the borders of the cell.

12. Click in the first row of the table that's just one cell and type the following sentence:

    We want to hear from you! Fill in the form & we'll get back to you!

13. You need to split the cell next to the **State:** label in the second column so that you can add the **Zip:** text label. You also need to leave a blank cell for the text field. This requires you to split the cell into three cells. Click in the cell to the right of the cell containing the **State:** text label.

14. Choose **Modify, Table, Split Cell** from the menu bar. In the Split Cell window, select **Columns** for the **Split Cell Into** Option and set **Number** to **3** (see Figure 10.24).

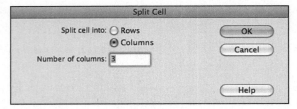

Figure 10.24: *Your goal is to split one cell into three cells, so use columns to split this cell.*

15. The cell splits into three cells. Click in the middle cell of the three split cells. Type **Zip:**.

16. Set a column width for each of these three new cells to **30%**, **30%**, and **40%** by clicking in each cell and setting the **w** field in the Property Inspector.

17. Save your file by clicking the **Save** button in the Standard toolbar. Now preview the Contact Us page in a browser by choosing **File, Preview in Browser** from the menu bar. Figure 10.25 shows how your page should look in a browser.

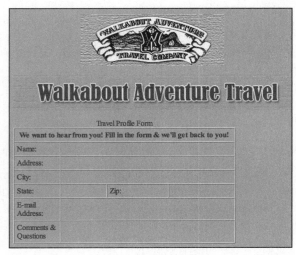

Figure 10.25: *Your Contact Us page has the beginning structure for a form.*

The Least You Need to Know

- You can use the Extended mode for a table to make viewing and working with tables easier.

- When you click a table border, it becomes the active element on the page. You can also click the `<table>` tag in the Tag selector to make a table active.

- You can select a row, column, or cell in a table by clicking and dragging across the cells, rows, or columns that you want to select.

- You can modify a row or column of a table by positioning your cursor on a border between a row or column and dragging to create a new width or height for the row or column.

- You can modify a table by making the table active and then clicking and dragging one of the handles that display on the table border.

- You can apply formatting to a Header row when you create a table through **Insert, Table** in the menu bar.

- You can import tabular data into a new table in a web page through **File, Import, Tabular Data** in the menu bar.

Building a Website

This part focuses on building a website using many of the Dreamweaver tools and features that make the design process a little easier. You find out how to develop page layouts that work with many types of screen sizes and how to use the all-powerful <div> tag to add more structure to your site.

You also explore more uses of CSS for page layout and design, create templates for consistent site layout and structure, and test and maintain your site before posting it to the web. Hands-on practice is provided for building a website and is invaluable for understanding the Dreamweaver website building features and tools.

Helpful Tools of the Trade

In This Chapter

- Using the Find and Replace features
- Viewing multiple displays of your web page using Multiscreen Preview
- Targeting specific browsers with Media Query
- Streamlining HTML and JavaScript programming
- Creating and using Library items

Dreamweaver CS5.5 offers several tools that make your job as a web designer easier. You can locate and change particular text, HTML tags, tag attributes, and web documents using the Find and Replace command. Multiscreen Preview displays your web pages in many different sizes. The Quick Tag Editor, the Inspect mode, and the all-powerful Code toolbar help you work with HTML coding. Other useful features include the Dreamweaver Library and the Reference panel.

In this chapter, you learn how to harness Dreamweaver's powerful tools to refine and streamline your site.

Find and Replace

You can use Dreamweaver's Find and Replace command to find and replace information in a single web page or a group of web pages. You can search for any text, HTML tags and their attributes, or a document or set of documents. You find this tool in the menu bar under the **Edit** menu. Choose the **Find and Replace** command to open the Find and Replace window (see Figure 11.1).

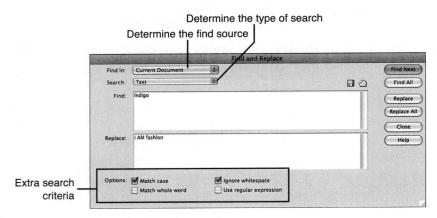

Figure 11.1: The Find and Replace window.

The Find and Replace feature functions the same whether you want to find and replace words, documents, or source code. First, determine the source for the find by clicking the **Find In** pop-out menu and choosing the source you want to use for your search. You can choose from the following menu options to determine the source document(s):

- **Selected Text:** Performs the Find and Replace on the highlighted text on a web page

- **Current Document:** Performs the Find and Replace on the opened web page in Dreamweaver

- **Open Documents:** Performs the Find and Replace on all open documents in Dreamweaver

- **Folder:** Performs the Find and Replace on all documents in the identified folder.

- **Selected Files in Site:** Performs the Find and Replace on a group of selected files in the site.

- **Entire Current Local Site:** Performs the Find and Replace on all pages in a site.

Next, you set the type of search by clicking the **Search** pop-out menu and choosing the search type. You can choose from among the following search criteria:

- **Source Code:** Search only for code.

- **Text:** Search only for text.

- **Text Advanced:** Search for text either inside or outside of HTML tags.
- **Special Tag:** Search for a specific HTML tag, attribute, or attribute property.

With the search source and type determined, type the information that you want to find in the **Find** field and type the information that you want to replace it with in the **Replace** field. Notice that you can apply other search criteria settings to your search below the **Replace** field. When you click these options, you further define your search. Here's an overview of each of these settings:

- **Match Case:** Turn this on if you want your search to be case sensitive.
- **Match Whole Word:** Turn this on if you don't want to find partial word matches, like "book" in "bookkeeper."
- **Ignore White Space:** Used for finding HTML code. Turn this on to ignore a space or multiple spaces used between code pieces.
- **Use Regular Expression:** A regular expression is a way to represent complex patterns in text. You can use this option to create text patterns from certain characters or short strings of text, such as *, \w, or ?.

DREAMWEAVER TIP

If you select the **Use Regular Expression** option, the **Ignore White Space** option isn't available.

Click the **Find Next** or **Find All** buttons to initiate the find. **Find Next** jumps from an exact match to the next exact match in the document. **Find All** finds all occurrences of the match throughout your document. When you have a match, click **Replace** to replace just that match or **Replace All** to replace all occurrences of the match throughout the document.

DREAMWEAVER TIP

If you're working in Code view of Dreamweaver and use the **Find and Replace** command to find anything other than source code, such as the company name in the document, Dreamweaver needs to synchronize Code view with Design view. This syncs up the tags with the visual display of content in the Design view so you can search both code and content. You'll see a message display indicating that this synchronization is occurring.

Multiscreen Preview

Multiscreen Preview helps you address how multiple screen types and sizes affect the display of your web page. To access this feature, click the **Multiscreen** button in the Document toolbar. You can also access the Multiscreen Preview command through the menu bar by choosing **Window, Multiscreen Preview**.

This feature lets you see multiple displays of your page based on certain devices and the dimension of their screen. The screen settings of 320 × 300, 768 × 300, and 1,126 × 210 are used by default (see Figure 11.2).

Figure 11.2: Using Multiscreen Preview, you can set the screen sizes to any dimensions that you need, to see how your web page will look on various browsers.

The Multiscreen button isn't accessible in Code view. Design view must be active to access this button.

Other Window Sizes

To view a page in a different window size or screen display than the default sizes, click the small triangle to the right of the Multiscreen button to generate a pop-up menu (see Figure 11.3).

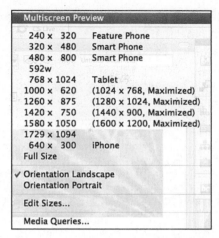

Figure 11.3: From the pop-out menu of Multiscreen Preview, you can choose any of these common window sizes.

From this menu, choose a new window size; Multiscreen Preview displays your web page based on the screen dimensions you choose (see Figure 11.4).

Figure 11.4: The screen dimension of 240 ×320 pixels is a standard display size for feature phones.

You can add or delete the screens listed in the Multiscreen Preview menu by going to your Dreamweaver Preferences. Under the Window Sizes category on the left, you can add or delete window sizes (see Figure 11.5).

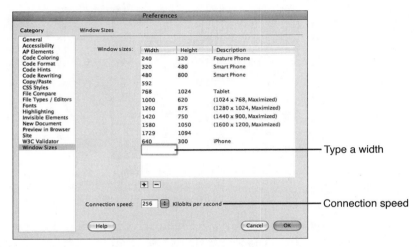

Figure 11.5: You can preview any custom window size by setting those width and height dimensions in the Window Sizes category of Dreamweaver Preferences.

To add a new custom window size, follow these steps:

1. Click the **+** button. This sets your cursor in the next new line in the list of window sizes.

2. Type a width in the **Width** field, and then click in the adjacent **Height** field and type a height.

3. Click in the **Description** field and type a name for the new custom window size.

4. Set the connection speed that you are targeting by clicking in the **Connection Speed** field and either typing the new speed in the field or clicking the pop-out menu and choosing a speed from the list.

5. Click **OK** to save the new custom window size.

DREAMWEAVER TIP

You can also click below the list of window sizes in the **Width** field to create a new screen dimension.

Applying a New Window Size

To preview your web document in the new custom window size, open the **Multiscreen Preview** pop-out menu and choose the window size option you want from the list (see Figure 11.6).

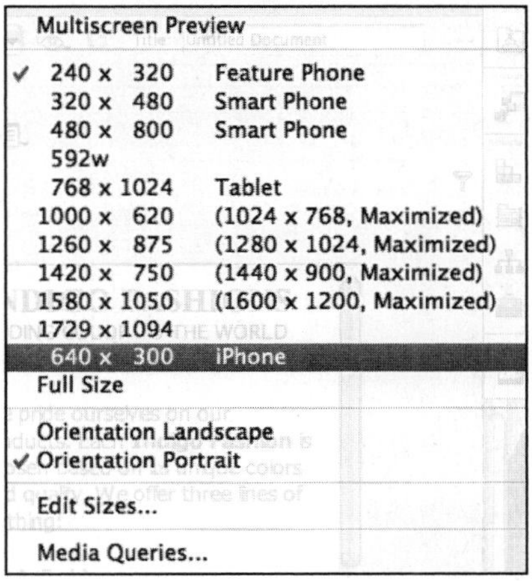

Figure 11.6: You can create as many custom window sizes as you need. After you do, they appear on the Multiscreen Preview pop-out menu.

Media Queries

Media queries are a new feature of CS5.5 that enable you to target certain devices that your website is viewed on. When you create a media query for your site, you're instructing your site to communicate with the user's media device to find out the device's screen dimension. Here's the really neat part: you can create a style sheet that formats your web page to fit that screen dimension. The style sheet is created just for this screen size and adjusts your web page to ensure that it looks great. Media queries take some of the guesswork out of web page design.

You'll find the **Media Queries** button in the Multiscreen Preview popout menu or in the upper-right corner of the Multiscreen Preview window. Click this button to open the Media Queries window (see Figure 11.7).

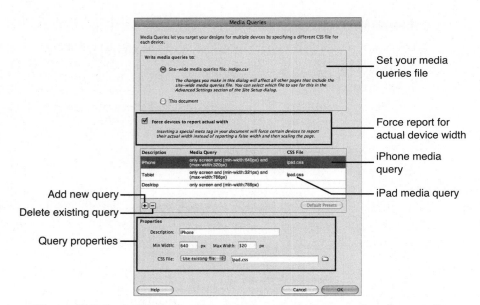

The labels around the figure read:
- Set your media queries file
- Force report for actual device width
- iPhone media query
- iPad media query
- Add new query
- Delete existing query
- Query properties

Figure 11.7: *In the Media Queries window, you can set any number of new media queries.*

You can set a site-wide media query for all files in your site or for just one document on your site. When you create a media query, Dreamweaver inserts HTML code that questions the device that's serving up the page on its screen dimensions. Figure 11.8 shows a sample of this code.

```
charset-utf-8 />
<meta name="viewport" content="width=device-width" />
<title>Untitled Document</title>
```

Figure 11.8: *This HTML code communicates with the device and requests it to return its screen size.*

Based on the window dimensions of the device, Media Query creates and inserts additional code into the HTML of the web document; this code instructs the device browser to use a certain style sheet for the page content display (see Figure 11.9).

```
<link href="iPhone.css" rel="stylesheet" type="text/css" media="handheld" />
```

Figure 11.9: *This code is calling the style sheet named iPhone.css.*

> **DREAMWEAVER TIP**
>
> To ensure that your site is developed for optimum viewing on multiple devices, you should set up several media queries and style sheets. Each media query is focused on a specific device and is associated with a specific style sheet (see Figure 11.9). So if you target an iPhone and an iPad, you need two media queries that identify two style sheets, one that is developed for a screen display of the iPhone and another that's developed for a screen display of the iPad.

The Magical Quick Tag Editor

The Quick Tag Editor enables beginners and pros alike to quickly edit HTML tags. Better yet, you can use it both in Design mode and Code view. To access the Quick Tag Editor, press **Cmd/Ctrl+T** (see Figure 11.10).

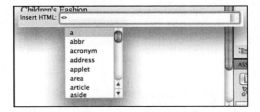

Figure 11.10: The Quick Tag Editor.

The Quick Tag Editor is great for beginning programmers because you can scroll through the list of tags to start learning them and their use in HTML. For instance, if you want to create a table in your page, you can access the Quick Tag Editor and select the `<table>` tag from the list. The Editor inserts this tag into the HTML code for you and inserts a table into your page.

To use this tool, do the following:

1. Select the text or element of your web document, or position your cursor where you want to place the new tag.

2. Press **Cmd/Ctrl+T** to activate the Quick Tag Editor.

3. Scroll through the list of tags and choose the one you want. This tag is inserted into your page code, and the Design mode updates to display the tag you inserted.

The Quick Tag Editor creates both the opening and closing tags in the HTML code.

Inspect Mode

Inspect mode of Dreamweaver is a powerful feature for understanding document structure and formatting. It works hand in hand with Live view. Turn on Inspect mode by either clicking the **Inspect** button in the Document toolbar or choosing **View, Inspect** in the menu bar.

You might see a message at the top of the document workspace indicating that, to get the best results from Inspect mode, you must switch to a different workspace (see Figure 11.11).

— Inspect mode

Figure 11.11: Click the **Switch Now** *link to switch to a supporting Dreamweaver Workspace or click the* **More Info** *link to learn more about the Inspect Mode tool and the optimum workspace layout.*

Click the **Switch Workspace** link to switch to Split view, which shows both the code and the page design. Inspect mode begins to inspect the page elements that you hover your mouse over in Design view (see Figure 11.12). The page element you're inspecting is highlighted in a yellow outline, and the supporting source code is highlighted in Code view. Inspect mode also shows any CSS format that might be applied in the CSS panel, as well as gives a visual representation of the box model for tables (see Chapter 10) and Div tags (see Chapter 13). The box model shows cell padding, cell spacing, margins, and border widths. To freeze this feature on an element, click to set your cursor in the page. To exit Inspect mode, double-click in a blank area of your web document or click the **Inspect** button in the Document toolbar to toggle this feature off.

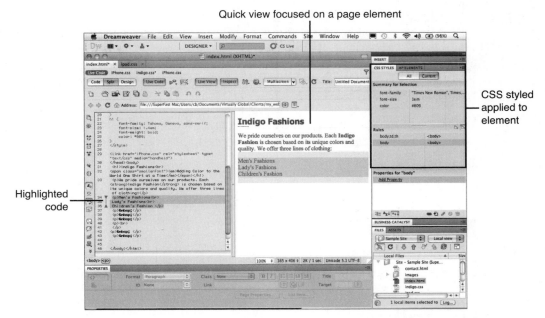

Figure 11.12: As you hover your mouse over page elements in Design view, Code view and the CSS panel change to reflect the code and CSS style rules applied to that element.

Reference Panel

The Reference panel is a handy tool for referencing HTML, CSS styles, and specific tags. It provides information about a specific tag so you can correctly use the tag in your page. The Reference panel works only in Code view or the Code Inspector. To use this tool, select a tag and then right-click the tag and choose **Reference** from the pop-out menu. This opens the Reference panel as the active tab in a panel group (see Figure 11.13).

Reference tab

The <strong>
tag is being
referenced

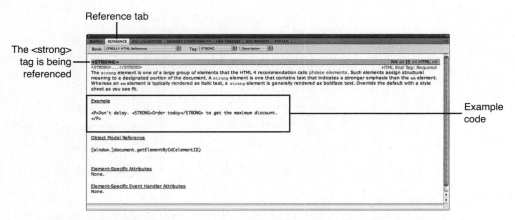

Example
code

Figure 11.13: The Reference panel provides information about the selected tag and gives example code as well.

The Reference panel is another useful tool for learning HTML source code and tags.

Coding Toolbar

The Coding toolbar contains tools that help with programming in HTML. It displays only when Code view is active. You'll find it to the left of Code view (see Figure 11.14); it's a vertical toolbar. You can also access the Coding toolbar by choosing **View, Toolbars, Coding** from the menu bar.

Coding toolbar

More Tools arrow

Additional tools

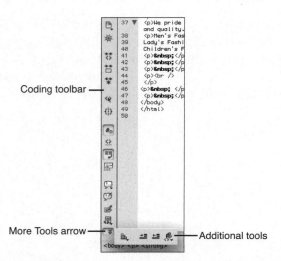

Figure 11.14: The Coding toolbar. The More Tools arrow displays buttons that can't be shown in the toolbar due to space restrictions of the Workspace layout.

You can hover your mouse over the button to see the button name. You can open a document with this toolbar, as well as collapse and expand a tag or lines of code. You can also select specific tags and balance your braces {}, brackets [], and parentheses () in your source code. When you balance braces, brackets, and parentheses, Dreamweaver checks to make sure your code has the correct syntax—in other words, all braces, brackets, and parentheses have an opening and closing reference. You can add comments and delete comments, and perform other coding processes and techniques.

Code Hints

Code hints are another useful feature for creating code. As you type your code in Code view, code hints display, listing the possible tags, functions, and methods that might complete your code (see Figure 11.15). Code hints also list tag attributes, function parameters, and object methods. Select from the list the code that creates your desired functionality. Code hints help developers avoid mistakes by providing the correct code syntax.

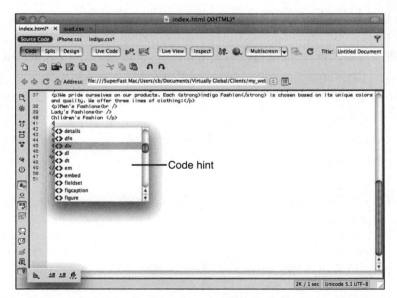

Figure 11.15: Select from the list to insert code from the list of code hints into your document.

JavaScript Code Hints

JavaScript is a popular web programming language that brings a wide variety of functionality and interactivity to web pages. Code hints in Dreamweaver have been upgraded to handle JavaScript programming. Now this feature includes JavaScript code to help support the popular jQuery JavaScript functionality. Code hints display when you're working in a JavaScript file.

DREAMWEAVER TIP

In JavaScript, you create custom classes for advanced functionality. The beefed-up code hints feature recognizes these custom classes and also includes them in the hints list.

Dreamweaver Library

Dreamweaver has a Library that holds frequently used page assets such as a company's logo, copyright information, or any page element that you might reuse often or update regularly on your site. These Library assets are referred to as *Library items* and are accessible in the Assets panel in the Library category. Library items are available to all pages in your site (see Figure 11.16).

To view the Library, open the **Assets** panel. You'll find the Assets panel in the same panel group as the Files panel. You can also open this panel from the menu bar by choosing **Window, Assets** panel.

In the Assets panel, click the **Library** button located in the category list on the left at the bottom of the panel (see Figure 11.16).

DREAMWEAVER TIP

In Dreamweaver, every defined site (see Chapter 3) has a Library associated with it by default. When you create a Library item, Dreamweaver stores it in the site's Library. A Library folder becomes visible in the Files panel after a Library item has been created. All Library items have an .lbi extension.

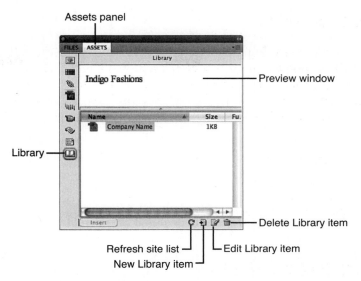

Figure 11.16: The Library of the assets panel. The Preview window displays a visual preview of the selected Library item.

The Library makes it easy to insert Library items into your web documents. The inserted Library item maintains a link or reference back to the original Library item. When you update or edit a Library item, you can update all occurrences of that item on your site with the click of a button.

Creating Library Items

You can use any of the following techniques to create a Library item:

- Highlight or select text or page objects and, from the menu bar, choose **Modify, Library, Add Object to Library**.

- Highlight or select text or page objects and click the **New Item** button in the **Library** category of the Assets panel. You can also use this button to create a blank Library item and then develop the Library item later.

- Drag a selection into the **Library** category of the Assets panel by dropping it in either the Preview window or the Library item area.

You must name the Library item. No restrictions limit Library item names. After you name the item, it appears in the Library. Select it to see a preview of the item in the Preview window of the Library category in the Assets panel. The Library item is now available for all pages of your site.

Placing Library Items on a Page

To add a Library item to your page, drag the Library item from the Assets panel to the location you want it on your web document. In Design view, you'll see the library item inserted on your page with a yellow highlight (see Figure 11.17).

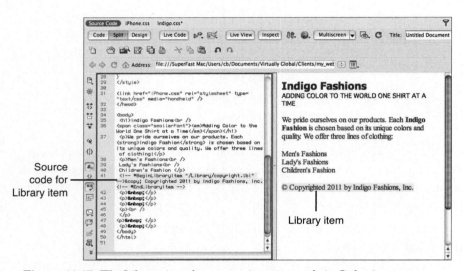

Source code for Library item

Library item

Figure 11.17: The Library item has supporting source code in Code view.

Whenever you make changes to your Library item, all linked page items get updated, too.

Modifying a Library Item

The power of the Library Item is that you can update it and then easily update all references throughout your website. To update an existing Library item, use the **Edit Library item** button and follow these steps:

1. Select the Library item in the Assets panel.

2. Click the **Edit Library item** button (see Figure 11.18).

LBI document for the blank Library item

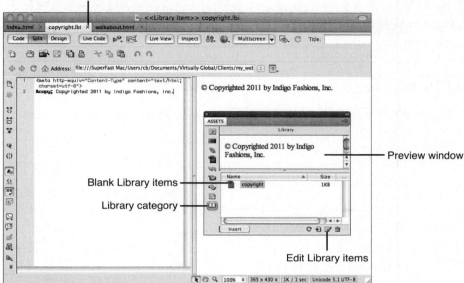

Figure 11.18: The Preview window provides instructions for adding content to your a blank Library item.

3. This creates a Library item file with an .lbi extension that opens in Dreamweaver. Add the necessary content and functionality to the page and click **Save**. Click **Close** to close the .lbi file.

DREAMWEAVER TIP

Each Library item is its own file with a file extension of .lbi. These files are automatically created in the Library folder of the local root folder.

Tutorial: Creating a Library Object for the Travel Site Logo

Walkabout Adventure Travel needs to update the copyright area of its site every year. In this tutorial, you make the copyright a Library item so that you can easily update it. Follow these steps:

1. Define the **Chapter11** folder in the **Tutorial** folder as a new site.

2. Open the walkabout.html file by double-clicking it in the Files panel.

3. Open or access your Assets panel. Click the **Library Category** button on the left to access the Dreamweaver Library.

4. On the **walkabout.html** page in Design view, highlight the copyright information at the bottom of the page.

5. Drag this to the Assets panel. You can drop it in either the Preview window or the Library item area.

6. Name your Library item **Copyright** by typing this into the Name field.

7. Press **Return/Enter** to set the Library item name. You have created a Library item for copyright information.

8. Access the Files panel, and open the new Library folder and view your .lbi file (see Figure 11.19).

Figure 11.19: Your new library item. Note the code for the item in Code view.

DREAMWEAVER TIP

After you create a Library, the Library folder appears in the Files panel. You can use the Files panel to delete the Library folder or an individual Library item by selecting the folder/file in the Files panel and pressing the **Delete** key.

The Least You Need to Know

- Dreamweaver has many tools and features to make your job as a web designer easier.
- Find and Replace helps you find text, documents, and HTML source code.
- Multiscreen Preview lets you see multiple displays based on the window size of your web documents.
- Dreamweaver's many programming and code-related tools streamline and make the coding process more accurate.
- Dreamweaver's Library is useful for holding frequently used items or page elements that you update regularly.

Working with CSS Style Sheets

In This Chapter

- Exporting your defined rules to an external style sheet
- Creating a new CSS style sheet
- Attaching external style sheets to other documents in your site
- Moving style rules between style sheets
- Deleting a style sheet

Up to this point, you've learned how to create various style rules using an internal style sheet. An internal style sheet is part of the active document, and the style rules are located in the `<head>` area of the document (see Chapter 7). All style rules apply to the active document only. If you want to apply those same style rules to another document in your site, you need to re-create them as an internal style sheet for that document. Fortunately, you have another option: you can create external style sheets to hold your style rules, and then attach these style sheets to other pages in your site.

This chapter is all about using an external style sheet to create consistent formatting throughout your site. You can create as many external style sheets as you need for displaying your information. In fact, you can use style sheets to target specific media, like printers, mobile devices, and even Braille readers. This means you can set up style rules that present your website in the best format for a particular medium. For instance, you can target a printer to set the format for all printed pages of your site; to do this, you set up a style sheet that formats your site using points (fixed unit for print) for all fonts and that's structured to fit on an 8.5-x-11-inch sheet of paper. Working with style sheets is all about making style sheets work for you.

The Power of CSS

So far, you've seen how you can use CSS to format text blocks, HTML tags, images, and links. This in itself makes CSS a great tool for web design, but the power of CSS really shines when you link an external style sheet to pages in your site (see Figure 12.1).

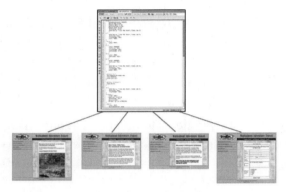

Figure 12.1: An external style sheet linked to multiple pages in a site. The format for the pages in this site is consistent due to the linking CSS document.

You can link the external style sheet to any or all of the pages of your site. All your style rules are then accessible to other pages that are linked to the external style sheet. This gives you a pretty powerful tool for creating a consistent design throughout a site. By using a style sheet that's linked to all pages, when you change a property for an individual style rule, that change is reflected in all pages linked to your style sheet. CSS gives web designers a great deal of precision, flexibility, and control over their sites.

All About Cascading

The "Cascading" in Cascading Style Sheets has to do with the order of style rules and a feature called *inheritance*. The order of your rules, or the cascade, plays a big part in how the browser interprets the code. If you have a <p> tag that has a Tag style rule applied to it through an internal style sheet, making it blue, and then you import another style sheet with a <p> tag applied to color the text red, the browser needs to know which style takes precedence so that it can correctly apply either red or blue to the text.

The order of precedence for style sheets is as follows, from highest level of precedence to lowest:

- External Style Sheet (highest level of precedence)

- Internal Style Sheet

- Inline Style (lowest level of precedence)

In the `<p>` tag example above, the internal style sheet makes the font color blue. When the external style sheet is attached, and it sets the color of red for the font, this takes precedence over the internal style sheet so the font for the `<p>` tag is displayed red. The external style sheet takes precedence over the internal style sheet.

Understanding Inheritance

Inheritance is a feature of CSS that involves the passing down of properties in a certain order. All tags in an HTML document are presented in a tree structure. An HTML document begins with the `<html>` tag, and all other tags are nested or enclosed in this tag. A nested tag is called a *child element* of the enclosing parent element. In an HTML document, all other tags, except the initial `<html>` tag, have a parent tag that encloses it. Due to inheritance, when a style is applied to the parent tag, that style is inherited by the child tags unless you specify otherwise.

For instance, if you set your `<body>` tag to have a font-family of Times New Roman, Times, Serif, then all other tags within the `<body>` tag will inherit this font unless you specify otherwise by creating a new style rule for that child element.

DREAMWEAVER TIP

CSS is constantly being updated, and older browsers may not be able to interpret all of the new coding. The only way to know if a browser correctly interprets your web page and the CSS is to preview it in many browsers.

Creating a New Style Sheet

Up to this point, you've been working with an internal style sheet that embeds the CSS code in the `<head>` area of the active HTML document. External style sheets are separate documents that you attach to HTML pages in your site.

You create a new CSS style sheet using the **File, New** command. From the New Document window that opens, select **Blank Page** (far-left category) and then select **CSS** from the **Page Type** category (see Figure 12.2). Click **Create** to generate the new external style sheet with a **.css** extension.

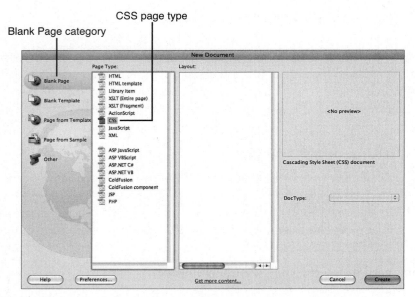

Figure 12.2: *Use the New Document window to create a new CSS external style sheet.*

Save the new external style sheet with a one-word name by choosing **File, Save** from the menu bar. In the Save window, type the name for your external style sheet in the **Save As** field. Notice the **.css** extension indicating that this is a Cascading Style Sheet.

By default, the style sheet is set to save in the site root folder. You can navigate to another location to save the style sheet if you need through the **Browse for File** folder. Click the **Save** button to save your file. The new external style sheet appears in the Files panel for the active site.

Exporting CSS Rule Definitions

If you have style rules as part of an internal style sheet, you can export them into an external style sheet you've created for your site. To do so, follow these steps:

1. In the **CSS Styles** panel, select the style rule(s) you want to export. Use the Shift-click technique to select multiple rules.

2. From the **More Options** pop-out menu in the upper-right corner of the **CSS Styles** panel, choose **Move CSS Rules**. This opens the Move to External Style Sheet window (see Figure 12.3).

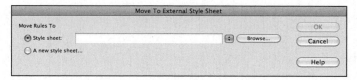

Figure 12.3: *You can create a new style sheet if you click the New Style Sheet option on the Move to External Style Sheet window.*

3. You have two options in this window: you can move your style rules to a new style sheet or to an existing style sheet. If you want to create a new style sheet, click the **A new style sheet** option and type the name of the new style sheet. If you want to use an existing style sheet, select the **Style sheet** option and click the **Browse for File** button to open the Select Style Sheet File window. In this window, select an existing style sheet and click **Choose**. The Select Style Sheet File window closes, and the Move to External Style Sheet window shows the selected style sheet.

4. Click **OK** to close the Move to External Style Sheet window. You've moved your style rules from your internal style sheet to the external style sheet. Notice the external style sheet with your exported style rules in the CSS Styles panel (see Figure 12.4).

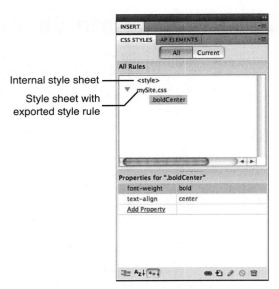

Figure 12.4: *The new external style sheet is named mySite.css. The* <style> *internal style sheet is still visible, but it doesn't contain any style rules so it can't be expanded.*

In the CSS Styles panel, you can also move style rules between internal and external style sheets by selecting a rule and dragging it to another style sheet (see Figure 12.5).

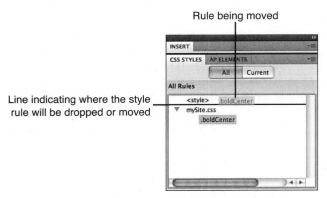

Figure 12.5: *You can drag and drop style rules between attached style sheets. This figures shows the **boldCenter** style rule being moved from the **mySite.css** external style sheet to the internal style sheet **<style>**.*

Attaching an External Style Sheet

Now that you know how to create a new external style sheet, take advantage of the power of CSS by attaching that style sheet to a web page in your document. On the CSS Styles panel, click the **Attach Style Sheet** button located at the bottom of the panel (see Figure 7.4).

When you click the **Attach Style Sheet** button, you open the Attach External Style Sheet window (see Figure 12.6).

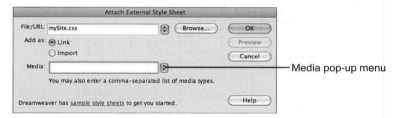

Figure 12.6: *The Attach External Style Sheet window. Click the sample style sheets link to use pre-created style sheets that are included in Dreamweaver.*

Follow these steps to attach an external style sheet and determine the media type for the display:

1. In the **File/URL** field, type the file path to the file, or click the **Browse for File** folder and navigate to your file.

2. You have two options to select from in the **Add as** section of the Attach External Style Sheet window. Select **Link** to attach the external style sheet document to the active page. Select **Import** to import all the style rules of the identified external style sheet into the active page internal style sheet. Typically, Link is the option you'll use for your site design.

3. In the **Media** field, click the arrows to access the pop-up menu. Select the media type you're targeting for your web page from the menu (see Figure 12.7).

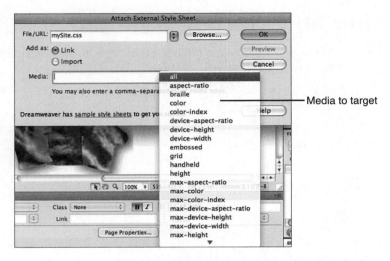

Figure 12.7: You can create as many style sheets as you need and set them each to target a different media type.

4. Click **OK** to attach the external style sheet.

Targeting Media Types

When you set a media type for your external style sheet, you're targeting that media for the display of your page. For example, if you want to have your web page print with point measurements for your fonts (points are an exact measurement, so your page will appear consistent in its font usage), attach an external style sheet that's set up for printing. Such a sheet would have style rules that apply point measurements for all your fonts, along with a page layout that fits 8.5-x-11-inch paper. To do this, set the **Media** field in the Attach External Style Sheet window to **Print**.

When a website visitor initiates the Print command to print your web page, the browser automatically knows to access the Print media external style sheet and prints the web page with the appropriate point settings and layout.

Style Rendering Toolbar

You can preview your web page and the CSS style rules based on the media you're targeting through the **Style Rendering** toolbar. To open this toolbar, choose **View, Toolbars, Style Rendering** from the menu bar (see Figure 12.8).

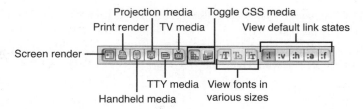

Figure 12.8: View various settings for font size display and the various states of links.

Click a **Media Type** button to view your web page with the style rules of the associated and attached external style sheet.

> **DREAMWEAVER TIP**
>
> When your page is viewed by a certain device that matches a media type you're targeting with an external style sheet, this style sheet and all its rules are automatically applied to the page display.

Detaching an External Style Sheet

You can also easily detach an external style sheet. In the CSS Styles panel, click the **All** mode so you can see all your style rules and attached style sheets. Next, right-click the style sheet name you want to detach. This displays a pop-out menu; choose **Delete** from this menu. The style sheet and all its style rules are removed from the CSS Styles panel. This process doesn't actually delete the external style sheet, but it does detach the link between the external style sheet and the active web page.

 # Tutorial: Create and Attach an External Style Sheet to the Walkabout Travel Site

With a few style rules defined, you can export these rules to an external style sheet so you can use this style sheet with other documents in your website.

1. Define the **Chapter12** folder in the **Tutorial** folder as a new site root folder.

2. Open the **walkabout.html** file by double-clicking it in the Files panel.

3. Open the CSS Style panel and click the **All** mode to display all the style rules in the **walkabut.html** page. Also, click the **Show Just Current Style Rule** button in the lower-left corner of the CSS Styles panel to show only the set properties of each active rule. Expand the <style> internal style sheet by clicking the arrow to the right of <style>. Notice that the internal style sheet has all the rules we have defined up to this point in the Walkabout Travel site development (see Figure 12.9).

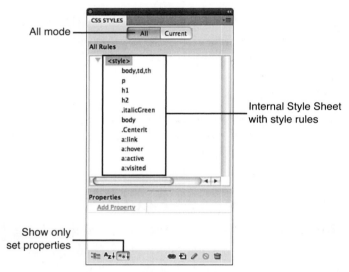

Figure 12.9: *You must be in the **All** mode of the CSS panel to see all the style rules for a web page.*

4. Let's move the style rules to an external style sheet. First, select all the style rules in the internal style sheet. To do this, click on the style rule at the top of the list and then Shift-click on the last rule. This selects all the style rules in the internal style sheet.

5. To move these selected rules to a new external style sheet, right-click anywhere in one of the highlighted rules. This displays a pop-out menu; choose **Move CSS Rules** from the menu.

6. From the Move to External Style Sheet window, click **A New Style Sheet** and then click **OK**.

7. In the Save Style Sheet File As window, name the style sheet **walkabout.css.** Click the **Site Root** button to make sure you're creating this style sheet for the defined Walkabout Travel site. Keep the other settings as they are, and click **Save**.

8. Look in the CSS Styles panel. The internal style sheet named **styles** now has no style rules, and the new **walkabout.css** style sheet is now listed. Click the arrow next to the style sheet name so you can see all the style rules that are now in the external style sheet (see Figure 12.10).

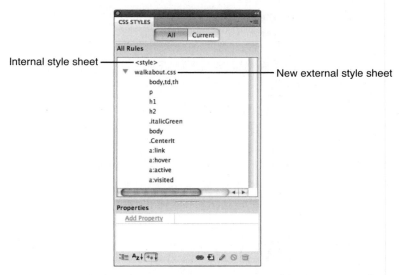

Internal style sheet

New external style sheet

Figure 12.10: All style rules have been exported to the walkabout.css style sheet, and this new style sheet is attached to your walkabout.html page.

9. Next, let's attach our **walkabout.css** style sheet to other pages in the site. In the Files panel, open **history.html**, **philosophy.html** and **contact.html**. Make **philosophy.html** the active document by clicking the tab at the top of the Document window.

10. In the CSS Styles panel, click the **Attach Style Sheet** button at the bottom of the panel.

11. This opens the Attach External Style Sheet window (see Figure 12.11). Click the **Browse** button to the right of the **File/URL** field and browse to the **walkabout.css** file. If you need to, click the **Site Root** button to go to the root directory of your site. Select the file and click the **Choose** button.

12. Keep the **Add As** option set to **Link**.

13. For the **Media** option, scroll down to choose **screen** from the list (see Figure 12.11).

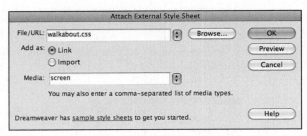

Figure 12.11: The Screen setting indicates to browsers that this style sheet is the one to use for computer screen display.

14. Click **OK** to attach the **walkabout.css** style sheet to your **philosophy.html** document. The philosophy web page reflects the new settings and formats that you set for the style sheet.

15. Open the **history.html** and **contact.html** web pages and repeat steps 10 through 13 to attach the **walkabout.css** external style sheet to both web pages.

16. You have a little cleanup to do with the **history.html**, **philosophy.html**, and **contact.html** web pages. Make **Philosophy.html** active and in the CSS Styles panel, notice that the `<style>` internal style sheet still has a style rule, **CenterIt**. Right-click this style rule and from the pop-out menu choose **Delete**. Delete the internal style rules for the other two web pages as well.

DREAMWEAVER TIP

When you delete multiple style rules, a message appears asking you to confirm your action. Click **Yes** to delete multiple rules.

17 Now let's make a change to a style rule in the **walkabout.css** style sheet. If needed, in the CSS Styles panel, click the **walkabout.css** (screen) external style sheet to expand the list of rules.

16. Click the **P** style rule in the CSS Styles panel to make it active. The properties for this style rule display below in the Properties pane of this panel.

17. Next, let's add a property to change the font-family to a sans-serif type. In the Properties pane of the CSS panel, you'll see the properties section with the `<p>` tag properties. Click the **Add Property** link below the defined font color. This adds a new property below the font size (see Figure 12.12).

18. Click the **Property** pop-out menu and choose **Font-Family** from the list.

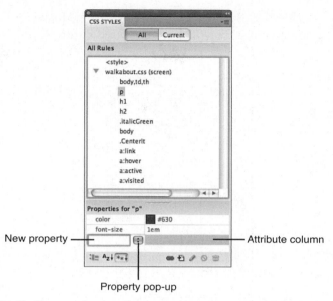

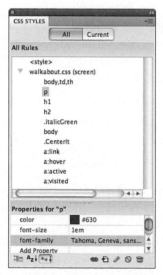

New property — Property pop-up

Attribute column

Figure 12.12: *You can also type the property name instead of choosing it from the Property pop-out menu.*

19. Click to set your cursor in the **Attribute** column for the Font-Family attribute. This displays the pop-out menu arrows. Choose **Tahoma, Geneva, sans-serif** from the list (see Figure 12.13).

Figure 12.13: *You can change this property and attribute by selecting a new property or attribute. You can also add another property by clicking the **Add Property** link again.*

20. Save your files by choosing **File, Save All** from the menu bar to save the change you just made to your web page (see Figure 12.14).

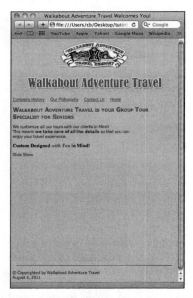

Figure 12.14: Your walkabout.html page should now look like this.

The Least You Need to Know

- You can export your defined rules to an external style sheet.
- You can create a new CSS style sheet.
- You can attach external style sheets to other documents in your site.
- You can move style rules between style sheets, both internal and external.
- You can delete a style sheet.

Creating Page Layouts

In This Chapter

- Using predeveloped page layouts
- Creating your own page layout
- Working with Div tags
- Editing style properties

Designing for the web is a lot different than designing for print. Print allows for overlapping images, wrapping text around those images, and using layers to create transparencies and blends of images and text. In web design, you're far more restricted. The table had its day, but today there's a better way to create page layout in web design, and that way is through the all-powerful Div tag.

You can use the `<div>` tag of HTML (commonly referred to as the Div tag), to create divisions, or boxed areas, on web pages. After you've established your divisions, you can format them with CSS. This chapter delves into using the Div tag to create a page layout.

Overview of Page Layout for Web Design

Page layout in web design can be structured in different ways. Typically, you structure your layout into distinct areas. For instance, most sites have a menu bar in the same area on every page in the site so users can easily navigate the site. Another common feature is a sidebar with other useful links. Web designs usually have a main content area, a header area, and/or a footer area. See Figure 13.1 for examples of popular layouts for structuring web content.

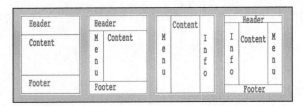

Figure 13.1: Each of these layouts has distinct areas for structuring your web page content.

DREAMWEAVER TIP

English-speaking audiences are used to reading a page of text from left to right and from top to bottom. As a result, our eyes naturally look first for information on the top-left side of the page. So that's where you should put your most important information, such as your company logo or company name.

Dreamweaver makes it easy for the novice web designer to create a CSS-driven page layout. Notice that when you create a new HTML page, you have a choice of preset layouts. You can select from among these layouts for your site (see Figure 13.2).

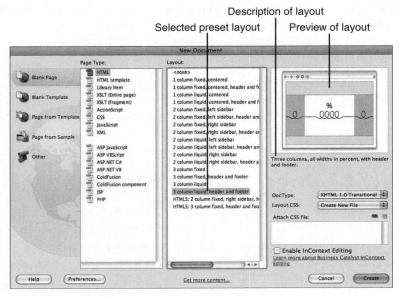

Figure 13.2: You can choose from 19 layouts in the Layout category of the New Document window.

When you click a layout option, a preview appears in the Preview window on the right. Notice that you can select the following ways to display the content areas:

- **Fixed layout**—A layout that has a set page width for displaying information
- **Liquid layout**—A layout that expands and shrinks in width based on the display area of the user's browser window

Each layout type, fixed or liquid, has its advantages and disadvantages. For instance, if you set a fixed page size of 900 pixels in width, people with older monitors and screen resolutions of 800×600 pixels will need to scroll to the right to see your entire web page.

And designing with a liquid layout can be a challenge because you have to design a site that still looks good when it's shrunk or expanded.

DREAMWEAVER TIP

Based on data gathered from W3 schools, in 2009, 57 percent of all monitors used to access the Internet had resolutions higher than 1,024×768. This opens web designs to a much wider page width area than in the past.

The following sections walk you through some sample sites to give you a better grasp of fixed and liquid layout types and how to design for each type.

Website Examples

Take a look at some website designs to see how others in the business are using fixed and liquid layouts. The following examples show websites that make use of different layouts of the content areas.

Figure 13.3 shows Adobe's website, which has a fixed-width layout and a page that's centered in the browser window. It makes for a nicely balanced layout, with a set width for the content of the design.

Fixed width

Page layout boundary

Figure 13.3: This layout is a fixed-width layout centered in the browser window.

Fixed width

Liquid area - expands or shrinks based on the size of the browser window

Figure 13.4: This layout is also a fixed-width layout, but it's presented flush left in the browser window. The far-right column can be any size based on the browser window.

Figure 13.4 shows a design using a fixed-width layout that's aligned left in the browser window. This allows an area to the right of the page layout to be expandable or liquid. As the browser window gets bigger, this area expands to fit the browser window, while the rest of the page design stays the same width.

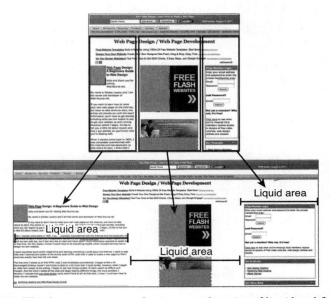

Figure 13.5: This layout is structured using a combination of liquid and fixed areas.

Figure 13.5 shows a website as it displays in two different size browser windows. This helps to show the liquid areas of this page. It has three distinct areas: the left sidebar area, the middle content area, and the right sidebar area. Each of these areas is set to a percentage of the browser window size. This allows them to expand or contract based on this window size.

Mixing liquid and fixed areas of page layout can result in a clean and creative design.

Using Predeveloped Page Layouts

You can quickly create a new page for your site based on one of Dreamweaver's predeveloped page layouts. To create a new page from a predeveloped layout, follow these steps:

1. From the menu bar, choose **File, New**. This opens the New Document window.

2. From the far-left category, select **Blank Page**. In the **Page Type** category, select **HTML**. In the **Layout** category, select the layout you want to use for your web page.

3. Determine your HTML version for your page by clicking the **DocType** pop-out menu and choosing the document type. Click **Create**.

4. The **Save Style Sheet File As** window opens and asks where you want to save the external style sheet. By default, it's set to display the active site. Click **Save**, saving the file in your active site. A new, preformatted page opens in layout and design (see Figure 13.6).

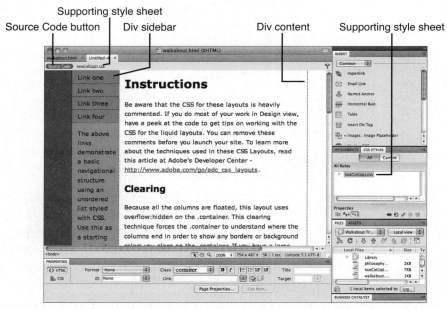

Figure 13.6: This preformatted page is a two-column liquid layout.

You can learn a lot from the pre-developed page layouts in Dreamweaver. Exploring how the page was created can be an eye-opening experience. These pages use Div tags for the different page areas and then attach CSS style rules to format the Div tags areas.

In Figure 13.6, notice the two buttons at the top left of the page. The button on the left is the **Source Code** button. The button on the right is the supporting CSS style sheet, which, in this example, is **twoColLiqLt.css.** You can jump between the code of the HTML document and the supporting style sheet by clicking these buttons.

To see the divisions on the HTML page, click on a word on the page. At the bottom-left corner of the Document window, in the Tag Selector, you can see the nesting of tags and any CSS style rules that are applied to a tag (see Figure 13.7).

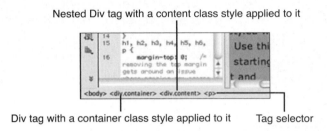

Figure 13.7: This example shows the nesting of tags starting with the parent tag of <body>, *and then lists the nested* <div.continter>, *which nests the* <div.content>; *inside of* <div.content> *is the selected* <p> *tag.*

When you click one of the tags displayed in the Tag Selector, you highlight the content contained in that tag in Design and Code view (see Figure 13.8).

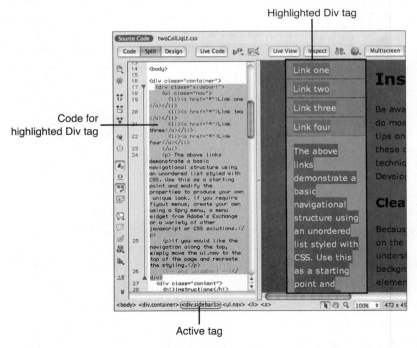

Figure 13.8: This example shows the <div.sidebar> *tag nested inside the* <div.container> *tag.*

Design view shows the Div tag in a bold outline. It also highlights the text and web elements contained in the Div tag. Code view highlights all the code used to create the Div tag and the contained web elements.

The CSS Styles panel reflects the controlling CSS style rules. In the two-column liquid page example, the Files panel reflects all the style rules of the twoColLiqLt. css style sheet. In Chapters 7 through 9, you learned how to change style rule properties, as well as how to add new properties. To modify and customize a predeveloped layout, simply change and edit properties of existing style rules and/or add new properties to the existing rules.

DREAMWEAVER TIP

You can even add your own rules to the supporting style sheet. Just make sure you select that style sheet when defining the rule.

Creating a Page from a Sample

When you create a new HTML page, one of the category options is the **Page from Sample** category (see Figure 13.2). You can use this category to create a predefined CSS style sheet and style rules. Click **Page from Sample** category; then click the **CSS Style Sheet** option in the **Sample Folder** category and select one of the listed sample pages under the Sample Page category. A preview of this style sheet and style rules appears in the Preview window (see Figure 13.9).

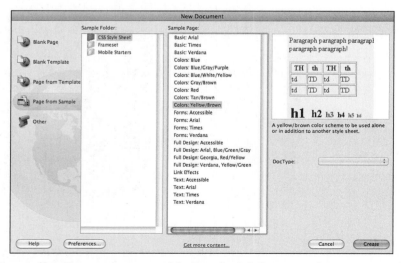

Figure 13.9: You can choose any of the Page Sample Layouts and see a preview of the style rule in the Preview window.

Click **Create** to create a new style sheet from the sample. This style sheet displays the CSS code for all style rules. You may edit and modify the code directly to customize your style rules. You also can attach this document to a page in your site and then use the CSS Styles panel to modify the style rules and properties.

DREAMWEAVER TIP

When you create a CSS Style Sheet from the Page Sample category, you are creating a style sheet only, not the actual HTML page. You can attach this style sheet to any web page in your site.

Creating a Custom Page Layout

To get the design you're striving for, you might need to create your own custom page layout and control it with your own CSS style rules. In fact, most designers create their own page layouts.

About Div Tags

You already know that a Div tag creates a division in your web page for different content areas. You structure a page layout by positioning your Div tags where you want specific content to be displayed. You can give those tags a fixed layout, which results in absolute positioning, or a liquid layout, which floats your Div tags relative to the browser window.

DREAMWEAVER TIP

CSS is supported by newer releases of popular browsers, including Internet Explorer 6.0+, Firefox 2.0+, Safari 2.0+, Chrome 1.0, and Opera 2.0+. Due to this extensive support, the Div tag has become the element of choice for web page layout.

You can also use Div tags to control the formatting of many elements of your site using CSS style rules. This allows you to set the font, font size, style, cell padding, background colors and images, margins, and borders for individual areas within your design. This feature gives you much greater control of your content.

Inserting a Div Tag

Adding a Div tag is similar to inserting an image in your page. Div tags are by default stacked vertically on the page. After you create the first Div tag, others are created below or above the defined Div tag on the page. You can use CSS to format and control this stacking of Div tags.

To insert a Div tag on the page, first position your cursor in the document where you want your Div tag to be located. Next, use one of the following techniques to insert the Div tag:

- Menu bar: Choose **Insert, Layout Objects, Div tag**.

- Insert panel: In the **Common** (or **Layout**) category, click **Insert Div Tag** (see Figure 13.10).

*Figure 13.10: Click the **Insert Div Tag** button in the Common or Layout category of the Insert panel to add a Div tag to your document.*

Either technique opens the Insert Div Tag window (see Figure 13.11), where you can name the Div tag, set its position, and define style rules for it.

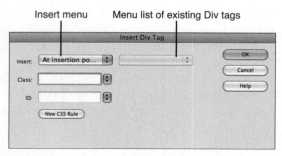

Figure 13.11: The Insert menu lets you choose where to create a Div tag based on other Div tags on the page.

The **Insert** option is set through two pop-out menus. The first menu lets you position your Div tag on the page. The second menu establishes this position in relation to other Div tags that you've already created on your page. Click the first **Insert** pop-out menu, and you can choose various options for positioning your Div tag (see Figure 13.12).

Figure 13.12: After you create a Div tag, this menu reflects more menu options in relation to existing Div tags on the page.

You have the following choices for inserting a Div tag:

- **At insertion point:** Creates a Div tag based on where your cursor is on the web page.

- **Before tag:** Creates a Div tag before another Div tag on the page.

- **After start of tag:** Creates a Div tag nested inside another Div tag but right at the start of the other Div tag.

- **Before end of tag:** Creates a Div tag nested inside another Div tag but at the very end of the other Div tag.

- **After tag:** Creates a Div tag after another Div tag on the page.

If you choose the **At insertion point** menu choice for the Insert option, Dreamweaver inserts the Div into your page at the location of your cursor. The other four menu choices create a Div tag in relation to other Div tags on your page. When you choose one of these four menu choices, you need to set the pop-out menu to the right in the Insert option. This menu lists all existing Div tags on the page.

Next, you need to assign a Class style rule in the **Class** field. If you have Class style rules defined, you can assign a Class style rule to your Div tag by clicking the **Class** pop-out menu and choosing the style rule from the list. This menu lists all defined Class style rules in the pop-out menu.

Create a name, or ID, for your Div tag by typing it into the **ID** field. Like other IDs, this name needs to be unique on the page and must be a single word, with no special characters except for the underscore.

New CSS Rules button lets you assign style rules to apply format to your Div tag.

To create a Div tag, follow these steps:

1. From the menu bar, either choose **Insert, Layout Objects, Div** or click the **Insert Div Tag** button in the **Common** or **Layout** categories of the Insert panel.

2. In the Insert Div Tag window, set the location of your Div tag with the **Insert** option (see Figure 13.12).

3. Click the **New CSS Rule** button to open the New CSS Rule window.

4. Set your **Selector Type**. You have two choices for Selector types of a Div tag. Choose either a **Class** or an **ID**.

> **DREAMWEAVER TIP**
>
> You can also use the Tag Selector type for a Div tag. When you use this type of selector, you apply your style rules to all Div tags in your page. To have variety in your format, you should use the Class or ID Selector type style rules.

5. Set the selector name by typing it in the **Selector Name** field. If you're creating a Class style rule, start the name with a period, as in **.navigation**. If you're creating an ID name, start the name with a number sign, as in **#header**.

6. In **Rule Definition**, determine where to store the new style rules.

7. Click **OK** to close this window and open the CSS Rule Definition window. Set your rule properties based on the categories and formatting you want to apply.

8. When you're done, click the **OK** button to close the CSS Rule Definition window. This returns you to the Insert Div Tag window (see Figure 13.13).

9. Click **OK** to close the Insert Div Tag window. The Div tag you just created appears in your page.

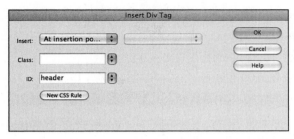

Figure 13.13: *The Class name or ID name is reflected in the associated field of this window. This window is a confirmation window of your Div tag set up; click OK to proceed with the set up.*

You can create any style rule for your Div tags. The Box, Background, Positioning, and Extensions categories for style rules let you apply borders, cell padding, margins, and other properties directly to the Div tag. Web designers use the Box category to create the layout and formatting of Div tags; it is discussed in the following section. The categories of Background, Positioning, and Extensions are discussed in Chapter 15.

Controlling Layout with the Box Category

The Box category of the CSS Rule definition window controls the layout of elements and tags on your web page (see Figure 13.14); for a discussion of the Background, Positioning, and Extensions categories, see Chapter 15. You can precisely place elements on your page or use relative properties that position an element based on the location of another element.

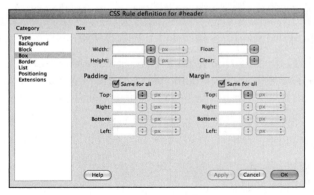

Figure 13.14: *Designers make frequent use of the Box category to control the layout of elements and tags on web pages.*

Here's an overview of the settings in the Box category:

- **Width/Height**—Sets the width and height for an object or element of your web page, such as a `<div>` tag.

DREAMWEAVER DON'T

Any content area that has lots of textual data shouldn't be any wider than 400px. Research has found that the human eye has trouble reading text in areas larger than 400px.

- **Float**—Positions an element to float to the left or right of another element. This is a commonly used feature for positioning `<div>` tags on the page. (For more on this feature, see "Floating Div Tags," later in this chapter.)

- **Clear**—Sets certain sides of elements to not allow other *AP elements*. If an element has Clear applied to it on the right and an AP element is created on the Clear side, it displays below the element rather than beside it.

DEFINITION

AP element stands for an *Absolute Positioning element*; it's a type of Div tag that's positioned in a set x and y coordinate on your page. AP elements can contain text, images, and other HTML objects, although images work best for this type of element (see Chapter 14).

- **Padding**—Sets the cell padding around an object. You can apply padding to the top, bottom, left, and right edges of an object. Click the **Same for All** option to set the same amount of padding for all sides of an object. Turn off this option to set different padding properties for each side of an object.

- **Margins**—Sets the value for the margins of an object like a `<div>` tag. Margins can be applied to all sides of an object. Click the **Same for All** option to set the same value for all margins. Turn off this option to set different values for the objects margins.

Adding Content to Div Tags

When you create a new Div tag, Dreamweaver automatically adds generic description text in the Div tag content area. You can highlight this text and replace it with new text, and you can add document structure tags and other web elements to the information that you put inside the Div tag. Any web element you can add to a web page, you can also add in the content area of the Div tag.

Editing Div Tags

After you've created a Div tag, you can edit it through the CSS style rules. First, click the outline of the Div tag in the Document window to focus on this Div tag (see Figure 13.15). It highlights the outline of the Div tag, and the Property Inspector provides a CSS Panel button for accessing the style rules. You can also access the CSS Styles panel directly and modify the style rules applied to the active Div tag.

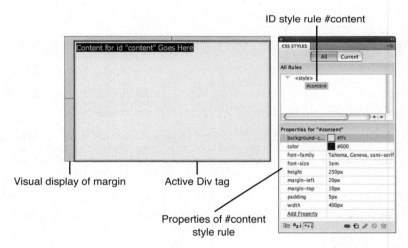

Figure 13.15: This Div tag is formatted based on the rules and properties displayed in the CSS Styles panel.

As you make your modifications, the Div tag reflects the new formatting.

Floating Div Tags

We touched upon the **Float** property of CSS earlier in this chapter, so you should already have a basic understanding of the concept of floating Div tags. Floats can be set to create some variety to the Div tag stacking order by allowing you to float a Div tag to the left or right.

The CSS Float property is in the **Box** category of the CSS Rule Definition window (see Figure 13.16).

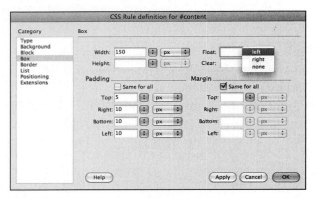

Figure 13.16: You can choose to float a Div tag left or right. To turn off an existing float, choose **None**.

For instance, if you have a Div tag for a sidebar, you can float a new Div tag for a content area to the right of the sidebar bar Div tag. Here's how:

1. Create a new Div tag by choosing **Insert, Layout Objects, Div Tag** from the menu bar for the sidebar. Set the **Insert** field in the Insert Div Tag window to **At Insertion Point**. This Div is the sidebar Div tag.

2. In the Insert Div Tag window, in the **Insert** field, choose **After Tag** from the pop-up menu. This inserts a new Div tag after the Div tag that already exists on the page.

3. Click the menu directly to the right of the **Insert** field menu. This menu lists all existing Div tags in your web page. Choose the name of the Div tag that the new Div is to be based upon (see Figure 13.17). In this example, we want the new Div tag to be based on the <div id="sidebar"> Div tag.

4. Click the **New CSS Rule** button to open the New CSS Rule window. Create the type of CSS rule by selecting **Selector Type, Selector Name,** and the appropriate style sheet. Since the new area is going to be a content area, set the Selector Type to **ID** style and name the Div **content**.

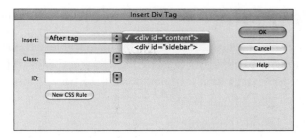

Figure 13.17: When you create a new Div tag, you position it based on the position of other Div tags on your page.

5. Click **OK** to open the CSS Rule Definition window. Click the **Box** category and, in the **Float** field, click the pop-out menu arrow button. Now choose a **Float** property of **Right**. Click **OK** to set the CSS properties. This returns you to the Insert Div Tag window. Confirm the fields in the window and click **OK** to close this window.

6. Next you need to float the **Sidebar** Div tag to the left of the **Content** Div tag. In the CSS Styles panel, double-click the style rule for **Sidebar**. In our example, this is **#sidebar**. This opens the CSS Rule Definition window.

7. Select the **Box** category and, in the **Float** option, set this to **Left**. Dreamweaver floats the new Div tag to the left of the existing Div tag (see Figure 13.18). (Your screen may not be wide enough to show the Div tags next to each other. If that's the case, Dreamweaver places the new Div tag to the right and underneath of the Div tag that's floated to the left. Always preview your web page in a browser to truly test your layout.)

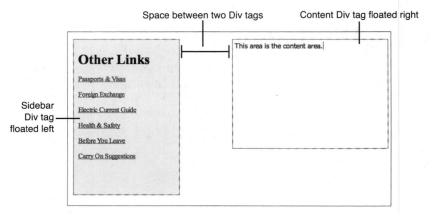

Figure 13.18: Based on the size of the browser window, the space between the two floating Div tags gets larger or smaller.

Clearing a Float

When you float Div tags left and right, you need to clear the float for other Div tags that are positioned after the floated Div tags. If you forget to do this, any Div tags after the floated Div tags won't display borders or background images or position correctly on the page.

To clear a float, follow these steps:

1. Insert a Div tag after the floated Div tags on the page by clicking the **Insert Div Tag** button in the Insert panel and the **Common** category.

2. In the Insert Div Tag window, set the first **Insert** pop-out menu to **After Tag**. To the right of this pop-out menu is a second pop-out menu. Click to select a floated Div tag.

3. Click the **New CSS Rule** button to open the New CSS Rule window.

4. Create an **ID** or **Class** style rule for the Div tag in the New CSS Rule window. Click **OK** when you have your settings determined (see earlier instruction in this chapter for this process or see Chapter 7).

5. This opens the CSS Rule Definition window. Select the **Box** category on the left and in the **Clear** field, click the pop-out menu and select the one of the four menu choices, **Left**, **Right**, **Both**, or **None**.

6. Click **OK** to close the CSS Rule Definition window and return to the Insert Div Tag window. Confirm your setting in this window and then click **OK**. The Div tag is inserted into the page after the floated Div tag(s) and the float property is cleared.

Wrapping Div Tags

To create a fixed-width layout, you need to wrap a containing Div tag around the other Div tags. This confines them to a set area (see Figure 13.19).

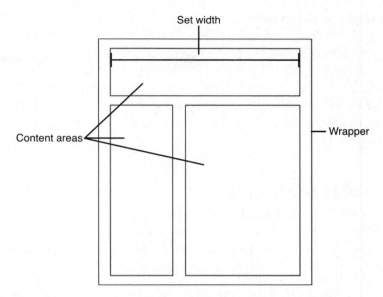

Figure 13.19: You can set the width of the wrapper Div tag through CSS and constrain the content areas to a fixed width.

When you create your Div tags, work either from the outside in or from the inside out. If you work from the outside in, create a wrapper Div tag first and then create and position your other Div tags inside the wrapper. If you work from the inside out, create your content area Div tags first and then wrap a div tag around the content areas.

When you create a Div tag, Insert option in the Insert Div Tag window lets you position your Div tag based on other existing Div tags (see Figure 13.20).

Figure 13.20: You can set the width of the wrapper Div tag through CSS and constrain the content areas to a fixed width.

It's possible to wrap a Div tag around any existing web element, or a group of elements. In fact, it's a good idea to wrap a container or wrapper Div tag around the entire page content. The <body> tag contains all the web elements for the display of a web page, so a quick way to select all the content on the page is to click the <body> tag in the Tag Selector. This selects the page content. Open the Insert Div Tag window and set the Insert option to **Wrap Around Selection**. Now you can apply your CSS properties for controlling the appearance of the entire page, which is in this containing or wrapping Div tag.

Deleting a Div Tag

To delete a Div tag, you first need to select it. Click the **Div tag** in the Tag Selector bar or click a border of the Div tag in the Design view. This focuses Dreamweaver on that Div tag, and the code for the Div tag becomes highlighted in the Code view. Now you can do one of two actions to delete the Div tag:

- In the Design view with the Div tag selected in the Document window, press **Delete/Backspace** on your keyboard.

- In the Code View, click and drag to highlight just the starting tag of <div> and delete it by pressing **Delete/Backspace** from your keyboard. Then find the ending tag </div> and delete that tag. This deletes just the Div tag, not the content or the style rule.

 ## Tutorial: Creating Page Layout with CSS

In this tutorial, you create the basic design of the page layout for the Walkabout Travel site. This layout is based on Div tags (see Figure 13.21).

Figure 13.21 shows the finalized Walkabout Travel site. This tutorial begins the process for establishing the page layout of this finalized site. As you progress through the other chapters of this book, you develop the entire site.

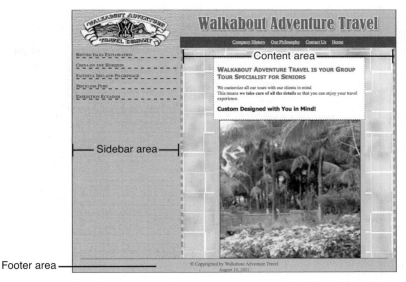

Figure 13.21: *The Walkabout site has distinct divisions, including a left sidebar, a content area, and a footer.*

1. Define the **Chapter13** folder in the **Tutorial** folder as a new site root folder. You'll use this defined site for the tutorial.

2. Open **walkabout.html**. This page is similar to what you've created up to this point, with the Walkabout logo on the top followed by the banner, and then the menu bar and content area.

3. Click the Walkabout logo at the top of the page to select this image. You'll create the left sidebar area first by wrapping a Div tag around this image to use for this area. Choose **Insert, Layout Objects, Div Tag** from the menu bar.

5. In the Insert Div Tag window, set the **Insert** option to **Wrap Around Selection**. Than click the **New CSS Rule** button.

6. This opens the New CSS Rule window. Set the **Selector Type** to **ID (Applies to Only One HTML Element)** and, in the **Selector Name** field, type **leftSide**. In the **Rule Definition**, make sure you're targeting the **walkabout.css** style sheet (see Figure 13.22). Click **OK**.

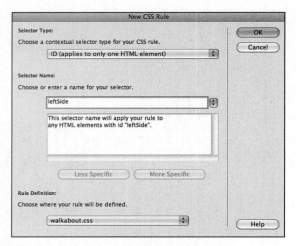

Figure 13.22: The ID name for this Div tag is leftSide.

7. In the CSS New Rule window, click the **Box** category and set the width to **300** pixels. Click the arrows to the right of the **Float** field and choose **Left** to set this Div to float to the left. Click **OK** to close the window. This returns you to the Insert Div Tag window (see Figure 13.23).

Figure 13.23: Make sure you see leftSide in the ID field.

8. Confirm that you see **leftSide** in the **ID** field. Click **OK** to close this window and create a Div tag for the left sidebar with the Walkabout Logo image already in it.

9. The next step is to create a **content** Div tag for the page layout. This area holds the content of the page. For the content of this Div tag, you're going to use existing page content from the banner down to the placeholder. Click in front of the Walkabout banner image (not the Walkabout logo image) and drag a highlight that includes the placeholder (see Figure 13.24).

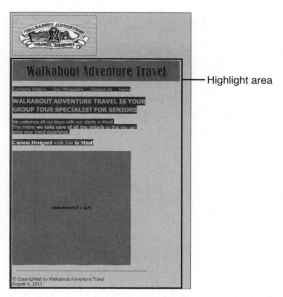

Highlight area

Figure 13.24: You can also use the Shift-click technique to highlight this area.

10. With the material highlighted, in the Insert panel, select the **Favorites** category and then click the **Insert Div Tag** button.

11. In the Insert Div Tag window, set the **Insert** option to **Wrap Around Selection**. Click the **New CSS Rule** button.

12. In the New CSS Rule window, set the **Selector Type** to **ID** and type **content** in the **Selector Name** field. In the **Rule Definition**, make sure you're targeting the **walkabout.css** style sheet. Click **OK**.

13. In the CSS Rule Definition window, click the **Box** category and set **Width** to **600** pixels. Set the **Float** field to **Right**. This floats the **content** Div tag to the right of the **leftSide** Div tag. Click **OK**, and you return to the Insert Div Tag window (see Figure 13.25).

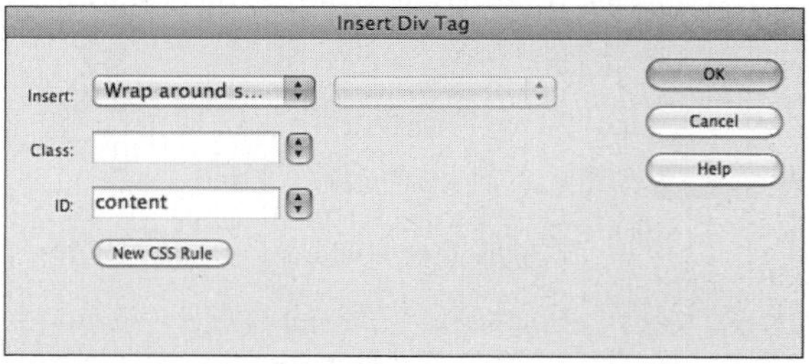

Figure 13.25: Your Insert Div Tag window should look like this figure.

14. Confirm that **content** is in the **ID** field and click **OK** to close this window and create the Div tag for the page content.

15. Save the page and then preview it in the browser. A message appears indicating that other files need to be saved for an accurate preview of the page. This is a common message and indicates that the **walkabout.css** external style sheet also needs to be saved. Click **Yes** to save the style sheet. In the browser, the two Div tags float to each side of the browser window. Based on your browser this footer area displays differently, but we are going to fix that next.

DREAMWEAVER TIP

If you're using Firefox, Opera, or Safari, the footer displays between the two Div tags. If you're using Chrome or Internet Explorer, the footer is displayed at the bottom of these two Div tags.

16. Now it's time to position the footer at the bottom of the page. Highlight the footer information on the page. Be sure to include the Horizontal Rule with the Library item. You might want to highlight the HTML code for both these items (see Figure 13.26).

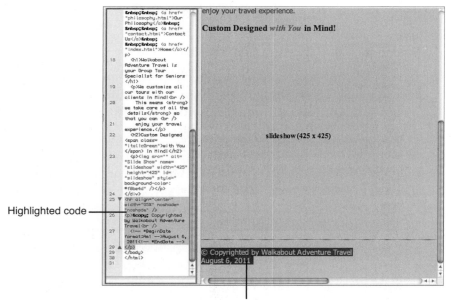

Highlighted code

Highlighted Footer Information

Figure 13.26: Make sure you include in your highlight the ending `</p>` *tag for this footer selection in the code as shown in this figure.*

17. With the footer information highlighted, insert a new Div tag using any of the techniques described in this chapter. Set the Insert to **Wrap Around Selection** and click the **New CSS Rule** button.

18. In the New CSS Rule window, set **Selector Type** to **ID** and, in the **Selector Name** field, type **footer**. Set the Rule Definition to target **walkabout.css**. Click **OK**. This opens the CSS Rule Definition window.

19. Click the Box category and set the width to **900** pixels.

20. Now clear the float of the other two Div tags. With the Box category selected, in the **Clear** field, click the arrows and choose **Both** from the menu.

DREAMWEAVER TIP

You must clear the floats in order for your background images and borders to show in your other page Div tags.

21. Click the **Background** category, and set the **Background-color** field to **#cccc99**. Click **OK** to close the window. In the Insert Div Tag window, click **OK** to close this window.

22. Save and preview your page in a browser. The footer displays below the other two tags, but they're still flush with the sides of the browser window.

23. Notice the gap at the bottom of the footer. This is because the **Paragraph** format is applied to this block of text. Click after the library item to set your cursor in the line of text and, in the Property Inspector, set Format to **None**.

24. Now let's wrap a Div tag around the **leftSide, content,** and **footer** Div tags. Click the <body> tag in the Tag Selector or choose **Select All** from the **Edit** menu. This selects everything on the page.

25. Insert another Div tag using the insert method you like. In the Insert Div Tag window, set the **Insert** field to **Wrap Around Selection** and click the **New CSS Rule**.

26. In the New CSS Rule window, set the **Selector Type** to **ID (Applies to only one HTML element)**. In the **Selector Name** field, name this **wrapper**. Confirm that this rule is defined in the **walkabout.css** external style sheet in Rule Definition. Click **OK** to close this window and open the CSS Rule Definition window.

27. Click the Background category to select it. Set the **Background-color** field to **#cc9** (shorthand for **#cccc99**). Then define a background image in the **Background-image** field by clicking the **Browse for File** button. Browse to the **background.jpg** in the **images** folder. Click **Choose** to select this image as the background for the wrapper Div tag.

28. Now set the background to repeat. Click the arrows to the right of the **Background-repeat** field and choose **Repeat** from the pop-out menu (see Figure 13.27).

29. Click the **Box** category and set **Width** to **900px**. This creates a 900px width Div tag that wraps around the **leftSide**, **content**, and **footer** Div tags. By not setting a Height, the Div tag adjusts to the height required to hold the tag content and elements.

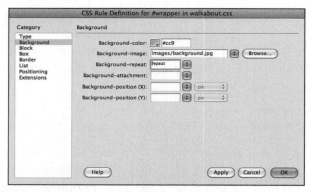

Figure 13.27: Your CSS Rule Definition window for the Background category should look like this figure.

30. Let's add a border for this Div tag. Click the **Border** category and make sure the **Same for All** option is selected for all three border attributes areas. Under the **Style** attribute, click the arrows to the right of **Top** and select **Solid**. In the **Width** attribute, set **Top** to **1** pixel by clicking in the field and typing **1**. Set the **Color** attribute to **#630** (see Figure 13.28). Click **OK** to close this window and set these properties for the wrapper ID style rule.

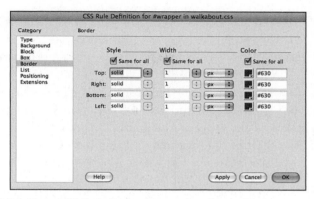

Figure 13.28: *Your CSS Rule Definition window for the Border category should look like this figure.*

31. This returns you to the Insert Div Tag window. Make sure that your ID field displays **wrapper** and that the **Insert** field is set to **Wrap Around Selection**. Click **OK** to create this Div tag.

32. Preview your page in a browser. The footer should display below the other two Div tags, with the wrapper holding them all together (see Figure 13.29).

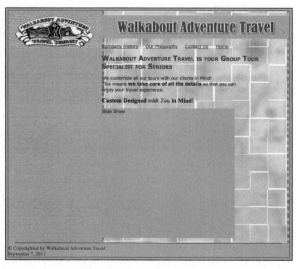

Figure 13.29: *Your web page should look like this figure.*

33. Now add more content to the **leftSidebar** Div. In the Design view, click the Walkabout logo in the **leftSidebar** Div tag to make it active, and then press the **right arrow** key on your keyboard. This moves the cursor into the text block to the right of the logo image. Press **Return/Enter** to create a new line of text. Type the following tours with a paragraph return between each line.

> **British Isles Exploration**
>
> **Faithful Ireland**
>
> **Priceless Peru**
>
> **Expedition Ecuador**
>
> **China on the Horizon**

34. Notice that these tours are all centered. This is due to the **CenterIt** class style rule you applied to the Logo in Chapter 8. This class style rule carries down to all new lines that you create from the block of text that the Walkabout logo is inserted. To remove the **CenterIt** class style rule, highlight the tours and click the **Class** pop-out menu in the Property Inspector; choose **None** from the list. The class rule is removed and the text moves to flush left.

35. Notice that the Walkabout logo is not flush with the top of the **leftSidebar** Div tag. The **Paragraph** format is applied to the information in the leftSidebar Div tag, which includes the logo. This creates an automatic space before and after block level elements, like the Paragraph document structure tag. To fix this, you need to turn off the **Paragraph** document structure for this line. Set your cursor either before or after the logo image by clicking the image so that it's active, and then press the right or left arrow key from your keyboard to move your cursor into this line of text. In the Property Inspector, set the format to **None**.

36. Repeat step 35 for the Walkabout banner, so that it displays flush with the top of the page. You might see a funny display of the page design in the Design view of Dreamweaver but don't worry about this.

37. Save your page and preview it in a browser (see Figure 13.30).

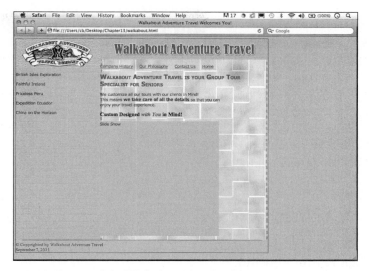

Figure 13.30: *Layout of the Walkabout Travel website up to this point.*

The site layout is defined. The next chapter shows you how to improve the look of this layout.

The Least You Need to Know

- Through New Document window, you can create a page based on a predeveloped page layout.

- You can create your own page layout through Div tags that you insert into your web page.

- You can create a Div tag either through the menu command of **Insert, Layout Objects, Div Tag** or by clicking the **Div Tag** button in the **Common** category of the Insert panel.

- CSS style rules are used to format and control Div tags.

- You can float a Div tag to the left or right on a page but you must clear the float for other Div tags that are inserted after the floated Div tags for them to display correctly in a browser.

- A Div tag can be wrapped around one or more page elements to create a container or area for their display.

Using Absolute Positioning (AP) Elements

In This Chapter

- Assigning an absolute position to any web element to make it an AP element
- Learning uses and limitations of AP elements.
- Inserting or drawing an AP Div tag
- Resizing and moving AP Div tags in the Document window
- Managing AP elements in the AP Elements panel
- Using CSS style rules to control format and positioning of AP elements
- Converting AP Div tags into a table

Absolute Positioning (AP) is a type of web page element that has an absolute position assigned to it. In other words, it has a set x and y coordinate on the page that never changes. You can assign an ID to most web elements and then set an absolute position to that element.

AP elements can create visual effects that enhance your design. You can place AP elements in front of or behind other elements. Using these elements is the only way you can create overlapping elements on the page. Combined with the use of background images, you can achieve certain effects with AP elements that would be difficult to achieve any other way.

Overview of AP Elements

An AP element is any type of web element with an absolute position applied to it. An AP web element can be an image, Div tag, or a table that you want to precisely position on the page. The most popular use is the AP Div tag. Similar to regular Div tags, AP Div tags are block elements, but they are set to an absolute position on the page. You set the position of AP elements in the Position category of the CSS Rule Definition window (see Figure 14.1).

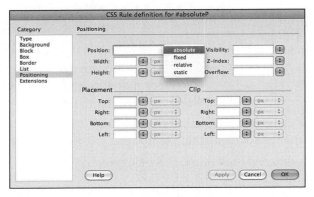

Figure 14.1: Four types of positions are used for web elements: absolute, fixed, relative, and static.

AP Elements are based on a parent element. This could be the <body> tag of the page or a <table> tag. Based on the parent element for the AP element, you can choose between four types of positioning. To creat an AP element, you set the Position option to **Absolute**. This removes the AP element from the flow of the HTML code for the page. The AP element no longer influences the size or position of any other page element excluding any elements it contains. It virtually floats above the rest of the page content in an absolute position that you determine. More is covered on the other types of Position options later in this chapter.

You can set an absolute position based on four placement options: Top, Bottom, Left, and Right. These placement options determine where to place the AP element in regards to the browser window. For instance, if you set the Top field to 10px, the AP element is positioned 10 pixels below the top of the browser window.

AP Div vs. Div Tags

Both AP Div tags and Div tags are used for page layout, and both have structural behavior you can control with CSS. AP Div tags require exact coordinates and can be overlaid on top of each other. The position is based on the browser window. They have a z coordinate as well as x and y coordinates. Div tags, on the other hand, are based on other Div tags and are stacked on top of one another on a page vertically. They are based on the elements before or after them.

AP Element Limitations

Since the AP element is based on a fixed position on the page, getting this element to behave with normal document flow can be a challenge. Another limitation in its use is browser support for this tag. Browsers interpret this tag differently, relying on default settings for the display. To use the AP element effectively in your design, you need to use CSS for formatting and page layout.

Uses for AP Elements

A common use for an AP element is to overlay it with other elements. By default, it has a transparent background, so you can position it over other elements and even overlap them. When you insert your content, it displays on top of the other web element. You can also apply behaviors to an AP element to create interesting effects for your website, such as showing or hiding elements based on user interaction. You can even move an AP element across the screen.

DREAMWEAVER TIP

Many designers avoid the AP element as if it were a plague. Because AP elements are absolutely positioned, they don't flow with the rest of the web page.

Inserting AP Div Tags

To insert an AP Div tag, position your cursor in the document where you want the AP Div tag to reside. Next, from the **Insert** menu, choose **Layout Objects, AP Div**.

You can also draw an AP element directly on your document in Design view. Click the **Draw AP Div** button on the Insert panel in the **Layout** category (see Figure 14.2).

Figure 14.2: *The Draw AP Div button creates the AP Div tag.*

You draw AP Div tags directly in the Document window. To use this feature, you must be in Design or Split view. Click where you want the AP Div tag, and drag a rectangular shape (see Figure 14.3).

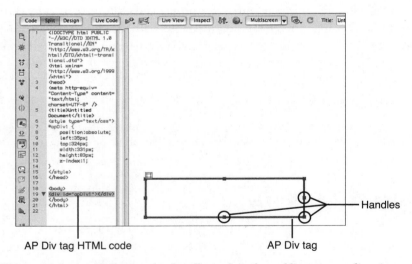

AP Div tag HTML code   AP Div tag

Figure 14.3: *An AP Div tag has handles and a tab, enabling you to adjust its location and size.*

To move an AP Div tag, click and drag the tab. You can adjust the size of the AP Div tag by dragging the handles.

To draw multiple AP Div tags, one after another, hold down the **Cmd** (Mac)/**Ctrl** (PC) key and drag multiple AP Div tags in different locations on your page.

Managing AP Div Tags

To select an AP Div tag, simply click the border of the AP Div tag in the Design view. The Property Inspector displays the properties of the AP Div tag (see Figure 14.4).

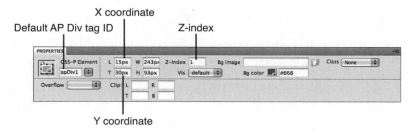

Figure 14.4: *You can adjust the size of the AP Div tag by setting new coordinates for the L/T fields or setting new W/H values in the Property Inspector.*

If you want to move the AP Div tag to a different location, type in a new value for the **T** (Top) and **L** (Left) fields in the Property Inspector. The Dreamweaver Document window has a gridlike setup, with the upper-left corner equating to the coordinates of x = 0 and y = 0. The **T** value equates to the y coordinate, and the **L** value equates to the x coordinate. The *registration point* for an AP element is the upper-left corner of the box shape.

DEFINITION

A **registration point** is a point or location on an element that adheres to x and y coordinates. All web elements take up a rectangular area in a page. This rectangular area displays as a box outline for the element. The box outline has a registration point in the upper-left corner. If an x and y coordinate are set for the element, the element is located at this coordinate based on the upper-left corner (the registration point) of its box outline.

Manually Resizing AP Div Tags

When you select the border of an AP Div tag, handles display around the box outline. Click and drag any handle to resize vertically or horizontally. On a Macintosh you can adjust the box proportionally by selecting any corner handle while holding the **Shift** key and dragging it. The AP Div tag resizes but maintains its original shape. PCs don't allow for this proportional resizing so you must adjust each of the handles to get the size and shape you want.

Manually Moving AP Div Tags

A tab is located in the upper-left corner of an AP Div tag. When you hover over this tab, the cursor changes to a hand icon (Mac)/four-headed arrow tool (PC). Click with this cursor tool and drag the element to a new location. The Property Inspector reflects the new **T** (Top) and **L** (Left) coordinates.

You can also use the arrow keys on your keyboard to move the selected AP Div tag to 1 pixel at a time. If you hold down the **Shift** key while using the arrow keys, the AP element moves 10 pixels at a time.

Using the AP Elements Panel

AP elements have their own panel in which they can be managed. This panel lists all the AP elements in your document (see Figure 14.5).

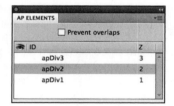

Figure 14.5: When you select an AP Div tag from the list in the panel, it becomes active in the Document window.

You can also use the **Modify, Arrange** menu command to rearrange the stacking order of AP Div tags. You can choose **Send to Back** or **Bring to Front.** When an AP element overlaps another AP element, the hidden portion is represented by a dashed line.

Stacking Order

The AP Elements panel represents your AP Div tags based on their stacking order in the web page. This stacking order is based on a Z-index. The z-index can be equated to the z-axis, which is the axis that extends out from the x-axis and y-axis, making a three-dimensional space. The z-index for AP Elements represents their arrangement on the page. They are stacked or arranged based on the order that they were created. This order is called the z-index. You can manage this order. Open the AP Element panel and click the number in the z-index column. Change the number and then repeat this process to create the stacking order that you need for the AP Div tags on your page. The AP element on the page rearranges to the z-index of the stacking order.

Overlapping AP Elements

You can overlap AP elements in your page design. No limit applies to how many you can overlap, but if you overlap too many, you'll have a hard time keeping track of all the AP Divs and knowing which ones to manipulate.

To overlap an AP Div tag with another, select the AP Div tag to be the parent element and then draw an overlapping AP Div inside the parent element.

DREAMWEAVER TIP

The **Prevent Overlaps** option in the AP Elements panel doesn't allow AP elements to have any overlapping features. If this option is turned on, you must deselect it to overlap an AP Div tag with another AP element.

Show and Hide AP Elements

In the AP Elements panel, the first column controls the visibility of the AP element. To hide individual AP elements, click in the column to the left of the AP element name. An icon with a closed eye displays, indicating that this element is hidden. The AP element on the page becomes invisible, too. It still exists in the document—it's just not visible. Now take a look at the code for the hidden AP Div tag. The visibility property for the CSS style rule for this element has been set to **hidden**. Click the closed eye icon to toggle and make the AP Div tag visible.

Renaming AP Elements

You can use the AP Elements panel to rename an AP element. Double-click the name of any AP element in the list. This provides access to the name field. Then type the new name.

You can rename an AP Div tag through the Property Inspector, too. Select the AP element in the Document window and then, in the Property Inspector, change the name in the ID name field. You must use a one-word unique name with no special characters except for the underscore.

Using CSS to Format and Position AP Elements

When you insert an AP Div tag into your page, Dreamweaver automatically creates an ID selector type style rule named the same as the name you set in the AP Element panel. You can modify this style rule. Simply double-click the style rule in the CSS Styles panel to access the CSS Rule Definition window and add, edit, or modify the properties for this element (see Figure 14.6).

The **Positioning** category of the CSS Rules Definition window works hand-in-hand with AP elements.

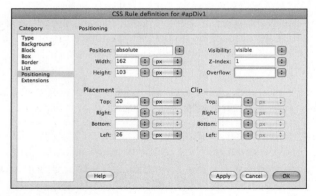

Figure 14.6: You can use the Positioning category to assign any web element to an absolute position.

Here's an overview of the options available in the Positioning category:

- **Position**—Sets the position type for an element. **Absolute** sets the element position to a set x/y coordinate. **Fixed** locks the element to that location in the document. **Relative** sets the AP element relative to an HTML tag. **Static** is the normal behavior of HTML and places the element based on where it's used within the HTML code.

- **Width/Height**—Determines the width and height of the element.

- **Visibility**—Same as the eye icon option in the AP Element panel. Use this to make an element visible or hidden.

- **Z-index**—Sets the stacking order for elements. A z-index of 1 always indicates the element that's at the bottom of the stack. A z-index of 2 displays on top of the z-index of 1 element.

- **Overflow**—Determines how the AP element handles content that extends past the Height setting. **Visible** adjusts the height attribute to accommodate the content, keeping everything visible. **Hidden** doesn't show any overflow content. **Scrollbar** displays a scrollbar for scrolling through any overflow content. **Auto** also displays a scrollbar, but only when there's overflow.

- **Placement**—Establishes the Top, Right, Bottom, and Left coordinates for an element. These are used in reference with the document grid.

- **Clip**—Sets clipping region for an AP element. You can then access the clipping region with JavaScript and, through CSS style rules and properties, create special transition effects such as wipes and pushes.

Set your options in the Positioning category and click **OK** to create your style rule.

DREAMWEAVER TIP

Many of the properties in the Positioning category aren't supported in Design view or Live view of Dreamweaver. The best way to view these properties is through a browser; however, not all browsers support the Positioning category, either.

Converting AP Div Tags to Tables

Some older browsers have difficulty displaying AP Div tags. You can convert your AP Div tags to a table to ensure that your layout is consistent in older browsers (see Figure 14.7). To convert AP Div tags to a table, select all the AP Div tag elements by Shift-clicking them in the Design view. Then choose **Modify, Convert, AP Divs to Tables** from the menu bar.

You can also convert a table to AP Div tags by selecting the table to convert and then choosing **Modify, Convert, Tables to AP Divs** from the menu bar.

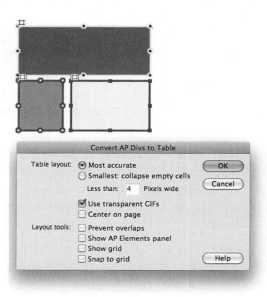

Figure 14.7: You can set many options to control the look of the converted table.

Dreamweaver converts your AP Div tags and displays the new table in the Document window (see Figure 14.8).

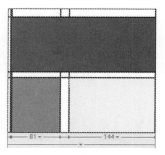

Figure 14.8: If you don't have your AP Div tags aligned exactly, the converted table reflects these spaces with columns and rows.

DREAMWEAVER TIP

AP elements are difficult to control in liquid layouts due to the document fluidity. Although AP elements do have value, they can be challenging to work with, and most designers avoid using them.

The Least You Need to Know

- Any web element can be assigned an absolute position; it then becomes an AP element.
- AP Div tags can be used for advanced interactivity in a Web page, but because they're an absolutely positioned element on your page, they are difficult to use with a fluid layout design.
- You can insert an AP Div tag by choosing **Insert, Layout Objects, AP Element** from the menu bar.
- In the Design view, you can manually resize and move AP Div tags to different locations in your page.
- The AP Elements panel manages AP elements.
- CSS style rules control format and positioning of AP elements.
- You can convert AP Div tags into a table, and you can convert a table into AP Div tags.

Making It Pretty with CSS

In This Chapter

- Getting acquainted with the principles of design
- Creating and using the Compound selector style rule
- Saving time with CSS tips and tricks
- Using the Code Navigator

CSS is an amazing addition to HTML for controlling your page layout, format, and design. This chapter takes a deeper look at CSS and how you can use it to design your web page. You need to follow some fundamental design principles to achieve an aesthetically pleasing site. These principles, addressing issues of color theory, texture, and typography, help you create a website that really stands out and communicates a message. This chapter introduces you to these design principles and shows you how to use CSS to apply them to your site.

Principles of Design 101

If you've had any classes in design, you know that you need to follow some basic principles to create an effective overall visual appearance for your website. For instance, you need to lay out web page features such as the header, content area, menu bar, sidebar, and footers in consistent areas that divide the page layout in a nice balance of those elements.

You want to choose colors that support and communicate the site's message. Certain colors, by their nature, communicate feelings. For instance, blue invokes the feeling of calmness, and red is associated with love or anger.

Texture in your background images and other web images adds visual interest, which encourages visitors to stick around and explore the site. Using textures in table header rows and buttons can help provide unity in your page design, tying it all together.

The font you use further communicates a message or feeling. A bold large font stands out on the page and almost shouts the message of the text. Flowery and fun fonts create a playful feeling for the site content.

Here's a brief overview of the major principles of design:

- **Rule of thirds**—Also called the Golden Ratio, this principle dictates that, when dividing your page, you should do so in thirds—both vertically and horizontally—so that the design is more pleasing.

- **Color**—Color theory is a science in itself and is based on how colors make us feel, what different colors communicate, and what color combinations work well together or clash. You can create color schemes to set the mood for your site.

- **Balance**—All elements in a design have weight, similar to physical elements. You need to balance the weight of each element in your design so that the visitor's eye explores your entire page.

- **Unity**—Unity is based on how all the different elements on your page fit together. A good layout presents all elements as a unified composition. Consistent colors, layout, highlights, and text format all help create unity.

- **Emphasis**—Use emphasis to make certain elements on your page really stand out. Use emphasis to draw your visitor's eye to the key point or message on your page.

You can apply these principles of design to the web or print media. When used together, they help you create an aesthetically pleasing design.

Keep these design principles in mind as you create your page layout and site design. Doing so will help your websites stand out and really communicate a message.

And that's what web design is all about: communicating a message, whether it's information about a new product or service, a sales policy, technical information, a process, or a plan.

Using Compound Selectors

To apply these design principles to your website, you can use CSS. Previous chapters introduced the CSS Tag, ID, and Class selector types. In this chapter, we show you how to use the *Compound selector*, which is a type of style rule that targets two or more tags.

The Compound selector style lets you really focus your formatting on individual elements in your site. For instance, if you wanted to format all images with a purple 1px border in a Div tag, you'd create a Compound style rule based on the combination of these two tags, <div> <img>. To take this concept further, you can target a specific Div tag and any images in that particular Div tag by identifying the ID of the Div tag, as in <div#content><img>. This way, the style rule applies only to the content Div tag and any images in it.

The process for creating a Compound selector rule is basically the same as for the other selector types except you should select a web element on your page first. Follow these steps to create a Compound Selector style rule:

1. Select an element by clicking or highlighting it on your page.

2. Create a new style rule by clicking the **New CSS Rule** button in the CSS Styles panel. This displays the New CSS Rule window.

3. In the New CSS Rule window, set the Selector Type to **Compound (based on your selection)** (see Figure 15.1).

4. The tags for the object that you selected on your page display in the **Selector Name** field preceded by the **#** (pound sign). Click the **Less Specific** or **More Specific** buttons to make the list of tags more specific or less specific in their reference.

5. Choose the style sheet that you want your Compound rule to be in, and then click **OK** to set the properties of this style rule.

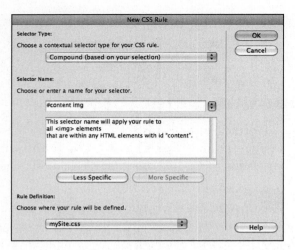

Figure 15.1: The Selector Name field reflects these tags based on your selection of the web element on the page.

Focusing the CSS Styles Panel

The CSS Styles panel has two modes: **All** and **Current**. Both modes help you create and modify style rules and their properties.

All Mode

To access **All** mode, click the **All** button at the top of the CSS Styles panel (see Figure 15.2).

This mode shows all the style rules for all style sheets attached to the active document. You can move style rules to different locations in the list by dragging them to a new location and then dropping them in the new location, which is represented by a bold horizontal line (see Figure 15.3).

DREAMWEAVER TIP

You can move style rules between style sheets, too. To do so, the style sheet must be attached and visible in the CSS Styles panel.

All mode

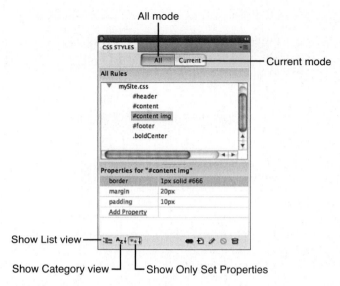

Current mode

Show List view

Show Category view   Show Only Set Properties

Figure 15.2: *All mode is the default display for the CSS Styles panel when it first opens.*

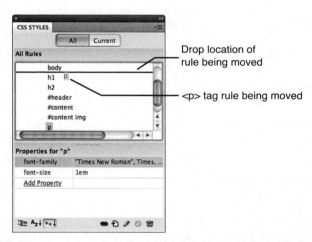

Drop location of rule being moved

<p> tag rule being moved

Figure 15.3: *You can rearrange style sheets by clicking and dragging them to a new location in the list. You can collapse them for ease of moving.*

Current Mode

Current mode of the CSS Styles panel provides a summary of the active rule that you've selected in the **All** mode of the CSS or a web element that you've selected on your page (see Figure 15.4).

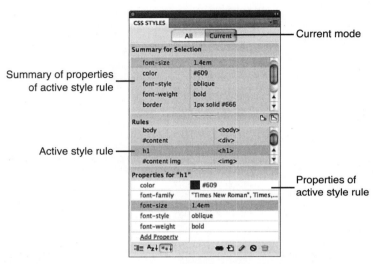

Figure 15.4: Current mode shows detailed information about properties and attributes of an individual style rule.

You can choose a different style by clicking a new style rule in the middle section of this panel. The top section of this panel provides summary information about a style rule. The bottom area lists all properties for the style rule and lets you modify, delete, and add properties.

DREAMWEAVER TIP

Use the **Current** mode of the CSS Styles panel for an at-a-glance overview of what rules are applied to your page content. As you click different elements on your page, the panel shows the style rules and properties applied to those elements.

Style Rule Categories

Up to this point, you've learned how to use some basic properties to create style rules and apply formatting to your web elements. The following sections offer a more detailed look at the eight categories of the Define Style Rules window (see Figure 15.5).

Figure 15.5: The rule definition categories present properties and attributes for your style rules.

Type Category

You learned about the font settings for the **Type** category in Chapter 7, but now let's look at the text-decoration properties, which are as follows:

- **Underline**—Creates an underline under text. Because a text link by default has an underline, this property is rarely used in a web page.

- **Overline**—Creates a line that displays over text.

- **Line Through**—Creates a line that runs through text.

- **Blink**—Makes text blink.

- **None**—Removes the line that automatically displays underneath text links.

You can use this eclectic list of properties to create interesting effects for text in your web page. In Dreamweaver, only some of the available CSS properties display in Design view and Live View (see Figure 15.6); you need to preview your site in a browser to see all the properties you've applied.

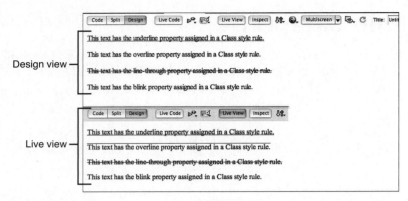

Figure 15.6: Neither Design view nor Live View can display the Blink property. But if you preview this feature in a browser, the line of text blinks.

DREAMWEAVER DON'T

Use the Blink property sparingly, as it can be annoying to have something blinking at you on a web page. Also, keep in mind that very few browsers, and no versions of Internet Explorer, support Blink. It was created by the now-defunct Netscape in an effort to compete with Internet Explorer back in the early days of web design.

Background Category

The Background category of the CSS Rule Definition window offers options for defining your background color and image, as well as different ways to repeat or tile the background image you assign to a web element (see Figure 15.7).

Figure 15.7: You can position a background image to set x and y coordinate through the Background-position (X)/(Y) options.

You can set the following background options for controlling the display of your background image:

- **Background-color**—Enables you to choose a background color for web elements on your page.

- **Background-image**—Lets you add a background image to display behind a web element.

- **Background-repeat**—Offers a choice of the following four options for tiling (repeating) and displaying a background image:

  Repeat—Tiles a background image along both the x- and y-axes, repeating the image both horizontally and vertically as necessary to fill area.

  Repeat-x—Tiles a background image horizontally to fit the element.

  Repeat-y—Tiles a background image vertically to fit the element.

  No Repeat—No tiling of background image. The image displays just once at the beginning of the element.

- **Background-attachment**—Controls how a background attaches to an element. You can set the image to always display even while the page is scrolling or to make it scroll with the page content as the user scrolls down the page.

- **Background-position (x) & (y)**—Sets precise coordinates for displaying your background image in an element.

Here are a couple of creative uses for backgrounds:

- You can add a background color to a block of text through a Class style rule for applying backgrounds.

- You can add a background image to a Div tag and then add text on top of the image. To create a button, simply add a link to the text (see Figure 15.8; refer to Chapter 9 for details on adding links and Chapter 8 for details on adding images).

Figure 15.8: This button was created through a Div tag with a background image applied. The text isn't part of the background image; instead, it was typed into the Div tag.

Block Category

We covered the Block category in Chapter 7. This category applies formatting properties to the area surrounding an object or a block of text (see Figure 15.9).

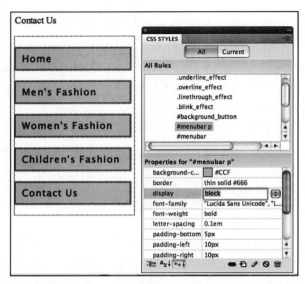

Figure 15.9: You can create a block area around a web element by setting the Display property to Block.

A neat trick to use with this category is to transform a list into a menu bar. Let's look at this process to give you a better sense of how to use this category:

1. Type in a menu name and press **Return/Enter** to create a paragraph block of text. Repeat this with four other menu names.

Figure 15.10: These five blocks of text are created through the <p> tag.

2. Highlight all five blocks of text and then wrap a Div tag around them (see Chapter 13 for instructions on working with Div tags). Name the Div tag and then create a style rule that sets the width of the Div tag to a width that accommodates the width of your text blocks (see Figure 15.10).

3. Create a Compound selector style rule that targets the <p> tag of the Div tag you just created (see Figure 15.11).

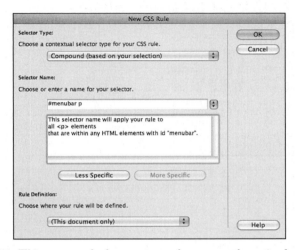

Figure 15.11: This compound selector targets the paragraph tag in the #menubar Div tag.

4. In the CSS Rule Definition window, click the **Block** category and set **Display** to **Block**. This creates a block around all paragraph tags in the **#menubar p** Div tag.

5. Click the **Background** category and add a background color for the text blocks. Click the **Box** category and set some cell padding to display around the <p> tag text. Finally, add a border by clicking the **Border** category and setting your border type, size, and color (see Figure 15.12).

Figure 15.12: The text has a block around it so that you can apply background and border properties to give text blocks the appearance of buttons or menu items.

Box and Border Categories

You can use the Box and Border categories to set cell padding, margins, and borders (see Figure 15.13).

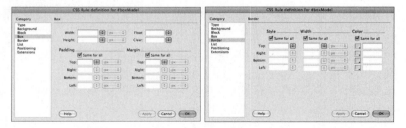

*Figure 15.13: Each of these categories makes use of the **Same for All** option for setting the width and height of the border and properties.*

New with Dreamweaver CS5.5 is a better visual representation of the box model. As discussed in Chapter 1, the box model is the rectangular area around a web element. Working from the inside out, you can add padding, a border, and a margin to each web element. Each setting affects the web element's size, placement, and layout.

The settings for both the Box and Border categories are based on the box model (see Figure 15.14). By default, all web elements are enclosed in a rectangular shape. You can format these elements with cell padding, margins, and borders for the rectangular area. Each of these properties adds width and height to the element's dimensions. For instance, if you have a table in a page that's 400 pixels wide, and you set a border of 2 pixels, the table becomes 404 pixels wide. If you add a margin of 20 pixels on just the left side of the table, it changes to 424 pixels wide.

You need to have the Box Model Visual Aid turned on to see a visual representation of the margins, cell padding, cell spacing, and borders. Choose **View, Visual Aids, Box Model** to turn on this setting. Now when you click on any box web element, you'll see a visual representation of the properties applied to the element.

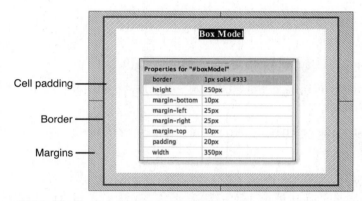

Figure 15.14: The Box Model showing the border, margins, and cell padding applied to the Div tag box outline.

List Category

Use the **List** category to format your lists in a web page. You can customize the appearance of unordered (bulleted), ordered, and definition lists. You can even set your own bullet to be used with an unordered list, as well as define the bullet size and type (see Figure 15.15).

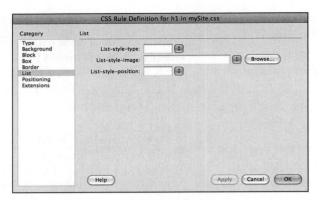

Figure 15.15: Control how a list item text wraps and indents the list with the List style position.

Here is an overview of the List category properties:

- **List-style-type:** Define the display of bullets or numbers.
- **List-style-image:** Set a custom image to be used for a bullet in the unordered list.
- **List-style-position:** Determine how list item text wraps and indents.

Positioning Category

The **Positioning** category (see Figure 15.16) is covered in Chapter 14, in reference to the AP element. You can use this category to define how any web element is positioned on your web page.

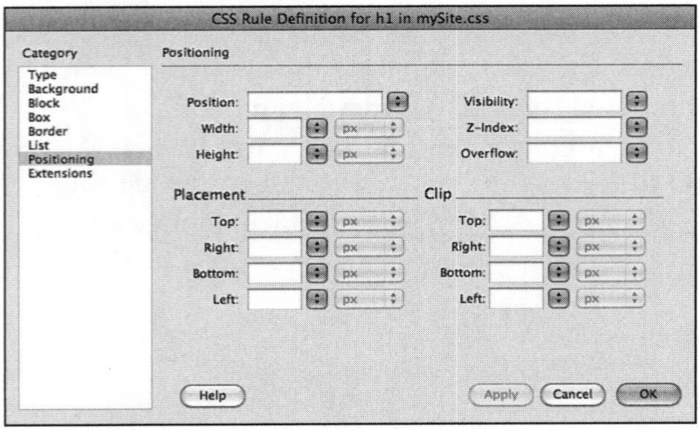

Figure 15.16: The Width and Height options work with the Position type you select.

> **DREAMWEAVER TIP**
>
> The CSS Rule Definition window displays only some of the popular properties for each category. To see all the properties available, use the CSS Styles panel.

Extensions Category

The Extensions category in CSS defines page breaks, pointer options, and filters (see Figure 15.17). You can use the page breaks to create breaks in a web page for printing. You can use the cursor option of the Extensions category to change the user's cursor to something else when it hovers over an object.

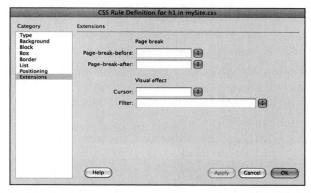

Figure 15.17: *Use the Filter option to set blurs and other special effects for the controlled object.*

The filters in the Extensions category are specific to Internet Explorer; some of them are even specific to certain versions of Internet Browser. They will not display properly in most browsers.

Using the Code Navigator

Dreamweaver's Code Navigator lets you see a list of code sources, such as style sheets or JavaScript files that are attached to your document (see Figure 15.18).

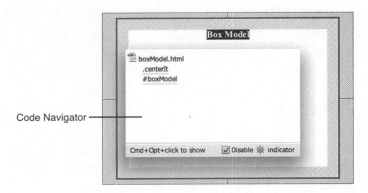

Figure 15.18: The Code Navigator works in Design view, Split view, and Code view.

The Code Navigator lists all the code applied to a web element. If you click one of the list items, Dreamweaver takes you to the code in Code view by either highlighting the code in Code view or opening the attached source code document. For instance, if you have an external style sheet attached to your document and you click a CSS rule in the Code Navigator, Dreamweaver opens the external style sheet and highlights the supporting code.

Opening the Code Navigator

To display the Code Navigator, use one of the following techniques:

- **Command-Option-click** (Mac) or **Alt-click** (PC) on the web element that has other code sources attached.

- **Right-click** on a web element and choose **Code Navigator** from the pop-out menu.

- Click on the **Code Navigator** indicator icon (looks like a ship's steering wheel) that displays temporarily on the active web element (see Figure 15.19).

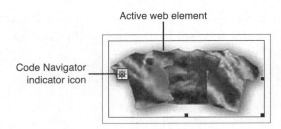

Figure 15.19: The Code Navigator indicator icon displays whenever you have an element selected and there's code applied or attached to the element.

Disabling the Code Navigator

The Code Navigator indicator icon can be a little annoying when you're working on a web page and it keeps appearing. To disable the icon, select the **Disable Indicator** option in the lower-right corner of the Code Navigator and then click outside the Code Navigator to close it. The Disable Indicator option is a toggle button; click it again to re-enable the indicator.

Tutorial: Controlling the Page Format with CSS

In Chapter 13, you created the page layout for the site. Although your website now has structure, you need to fine-tune the design. This tutorial steps you through the process of adding borders, cell padding, and margins to make the design shine. Let's get started:

1. Define the **Chapter15** folder in the Tutorial folder as a new site root folder. You'll use this defined site for the tutorial.

2. Open the **walkabout.htm** page. You'll see that this page has been developed a little more with Div tags, and the paragraph tag has been set to the font-family of **Times New Roman, Times, Serif**. The following new Div tags have been added: menubar, sideMenu, pageContent, and display (see Figure 15.20).

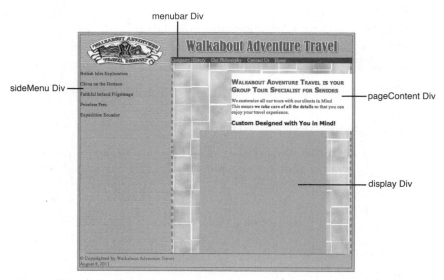

Figure 15.20: The layout shows evidence of further development, with the addition of a few more Div tags.

3. First, let's work on the **menubar** Div and center the menus. Click in the **menubar** Div and highlight all the links. In the Property Inspector, click the **Class** pop-out menu and apply **centerIt**. The group of links center in the Div tag.

4. In this step, you set cell padding to help balance the text with the bar area. In the CSS Styles panel, double-click the **menubar** style rule. This opens the CSS Rule Definition window. Click the **Box** category and, in the **Padding** area, click the **Same for All** option to **deselect** it. Then set your **Top** and **Bottom** cell padding to **8** pixels. Click **OK** to set this padding and close the window.

5. Now let's work with the **pageContent** Div to get that looking nicer. In the CSS Styles panel, double-click the **pageContent** style rule. Click the **Box** category and set a consistent cell padding of 10 pixels for all fields. To do this, under Padding, make sure the **Same for All** option is selected, click in the **Top** field, and type **10**. Set the unit field to **pixel**. This populates the value of 10 pixels for all padding fields.

6. To add a margin to help center the Div tag, in the **Margin** settings, deselect the **Same for All** option. Click in the **Right** field and type **85**. Make sure the unit is **pixels**.

7. Set a border for the Div. Click the **Border** category. Keep the **Same for All** option selected for all three property areas. In the **Style** property, click the arrows to the right of the **Top** field and choose **Dashed** from the pop-out menu. In the **Width** attribute area, in the **Top** field, type **1**; keep the unit set to pixels. In the **Color** attribute area, click in the field and type **#663300**. Click **OK** to set these new properties for the **pageContent** Div tag.

8. Save your page and test it by previewing in a browser (see Figure 15.21).

DREAMWEAVER TIP

Firefox doesn't understand the image placeholder and will skip this rule. If you are previewing your page in Firefox, you will not see the image placeholder.

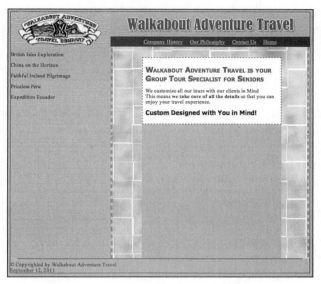

Figure 15.21: The pageContent Div is centered in the Content Div, with padding applied to the left and right, as well as a dashed border around the Div tag.

9. Now let's focus on the sidebar menus of the current tours. You're going to develop the menu to act more like buttons in a menu bar, with highlights of background and text for the different link states. First, though, you need to make these tour links by adding link placeholders. Highlight **British Isles Exploration** and, in the Property Inspector, type **british.html** into the **Link** field. This links to a document that you haven't created yet.

10. Repeat Step 9 for all other tours by selecting the entire tour name in the Design view and creating links to the following documents: **ireland.html, peru.html, ecuador.html, china.html** (see Figure 15.22).

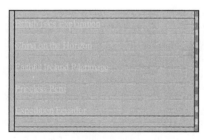

Figure 15.22: Yuck, the display of these links in the sideMenu Div tag looks awful—we'll fix that next.

11. So that you don't affect the other links in the document, you need to use Compound selector style rules. Highlight the first link in the new **sideMenu** Div tag.

12. Create a new style rule by clicking the **New CSS Rule** button in the CSS Styles panel.

13. Set Selector Type to **Compound (Based on Your Selection).** Click in the **Selector Name** field to focus Dreamweaver on this field. Make the rule less specific by clicking the **Less Specific** button twice so that the field displays **#sidemenu p a.** Then set your cursor after the **a** and type **:link** to target the static link state (see Chapter 9). Now the Selector Name field should contain **#sidemenu p a:link**. Make sure you're targeting the walkabout.css style sheet (see Figure 15.23). Click **OK** to move to the CSS Rule Definition window.

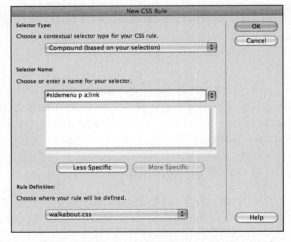

Figure 15.23: Your New CSS Rule window should look like this figure.

14. In the CSS Rule Definition window, click the **Type** category. Set your settings to match Figure 15.24.

15. Click the **Background** category and set **Background-color** to **#cccc99**.

16. Click the **Block** category and set **Display** to **Block**.

17. Click the **Border** category and deselect all the **Same for All** options for all three properties. Set your border settings to match those displayed in Figure 15.25.

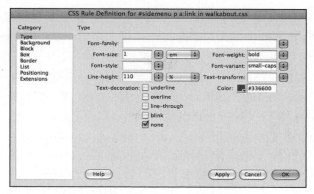

Figure 15.24: Under the Text-decoration area, the None setting causes the underline that is associated with links to not display.

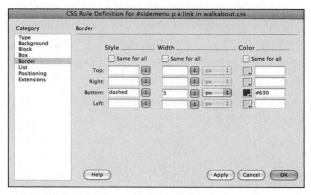

Figure 15.25: These settings create a dashed bottom border of 3px width and a color of #630 for each menu link.

18. Click **OK** to set the properties for the Compound style rule. The links in the sideMenu now look more like buttons (see Figure 15.26).

Figure 15.26: The links in the sideMenu look more like buttons, but they extend to the left and right borders of the sidebar area.

19. Let's make the links a little narrower. To do this, you need to add cell padding to the parent Div of **sideMenu** Div. In the CSS Styles panel, double-click the **sideMenu** ID style rule to open the CSS Rule Definition.

20. Click the **Box** category and in the **Padding** area, deselect the **Same for All** option and, in the **Right** and **Left** fields, type **10**. Make sure the unit is **px**. Click **OK** to set the new properties.

21. In the CSS Styles panel, click the **All** mode button at the top of the panel. Also, click the **Show only set properties** button in the bottom left of the panel to turn on this feature.

22. Now let's add some other link states to the tour buttons. You've already developed the static state so you can simply duplicate that rule for the other three link states. In the CSS Styles panel, click the **#sidemenu p a:link**. Then right-click it and from the pop-out menu choose **Duplicate**.

23. This opens the Duplicate CSS Rule window. In the Selector Name field, change the link portion of the selector name, **a:link**, to **a:active** (see Figure 15.27). Click **OK** to duplicate the rule as an **a:active** rule.

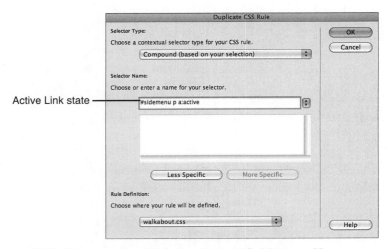

*Figure 15.27: You can target a link state in a specified Div tag. Here we are targeting **#sidemenu**.*

24. With the rule duplicated, you can now modify a property to make this link state look different than the static link state. Click the new **#sidemenu p a:active** rule in the CSS Styles panel to make it active.

25. In the Properties pane of the CSS Styles panel, click the **color** property and change it to **#006633** (see Figure 15.28). This changes the color of the font for this link state.

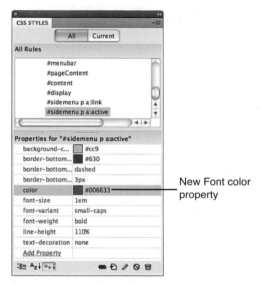

New Font color property

Figure 15.28: By duplicating an existing style rule, *all the properties set for that rule are also included in the duplicated style rule.*

26. Repeat steps 22 through 25 to duplicate the **#sidemenu p a:link** style rule for the other two link states, **a:visited** and **a:hover**. After you've duplicated these style rules, set the Properties panes as indicated in Figure 15.29.

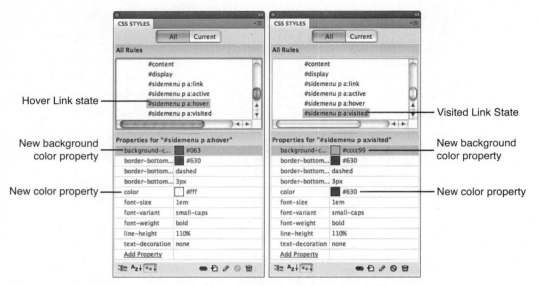

Figure 15.29: *Set up a style rule for both the a:hover and a:visited link through the Properties pane of the CSS Styles panel.*

27. Save your page and preview it in a browser. Test your links to see the new functionality. (If you click the link you'll get a "Page Missing..." message because these pages don't exist yet in the site.)

28. You have one final modification to make for your page: you need to center it in a browser window. To do this, click the **#wrapper** style rule in the CSS Styles panel to select it.

29. In the Properties pane of the CSS Styles panel, click the **Add Property** link at the bottom of the list. Type **margin**. Then click in the field to the right and type **auto** (see Figure 15.30).

30. Click the **New Property** link; this time, click the arrows to display the pop-out menu and select **Position** from the menu list. Click in the field to the right, which displays the field with the pop-out menu arrows. Next, click the arrows to display the pop-out menu and select **Relative** from the menu list.

23. Save your file and preview it in a browser (see Figure 15.31).

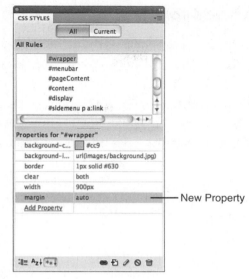

*Figure 15.30: You can set properties for existing style rules by clicking the **Add Property** link.*

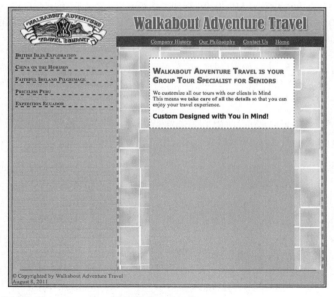

Figure 15.31: Your page should look like this figure.

The Least You Need to Know

- The principles of design can enhance the visual appeal of your website.
- Compound selector style rules let you focus on a combination of tags for applying your CSS style rules.
- The CSS Styles panel has two modes: All mode and Current mode. Each mode lets you see specific and helpful information about your style rules.
- You can use CSS to create the appearance of a menu bar and button functionality from text blocks
- You can turn the Code Navigator on by using **Command-Option-click** (Mac) or **Alt-click** (PC) on a web element to see the code that was used to create and format that element.

Building Your Website with Templates

In This Chapter

* Creating templates for site design
* Making tag attributes editable
* Creating new pages with a template design
* Applying a template design to existing pages
* Updating all pages based on a template
* Detaching a template from a page

Another powerful feature that Dreamweaver brings to web design is the template. You can create a template for your website and then create new pages based on the template. This ensures consistency of your design in all pages throughout your site. You experience another nice feature of templates when you want to update your site. You make the edits in the template file, and when you save the template, you update all pages in your site with the changes.

Overview of a Template

The template in Dreamweaver is a versatile tool. You can create as many templates as you need for your site. Then you can either create a new page from your template or attach a template to an existing page. This gives you a great deal of flexibility when creating and controlling your site.

Before templates were introduced in web design, when you needed to update a feature of your page design, you had to open all existing pages of your site and then make the change to each page. If your site was large, this was a long and laborious process.

Creating a Template

Two processes exist for creating a template. You can convert an existing page to a template, or you can create a template from scratch. I like to create a page design first and then, when I have everything set the way I want, convert the file to a template. This allows me to develop the design and test the page functionality before I convert it to a template.

DREAMWEAVER TIP

Dreamweaver templates are a little different than templates in other applications in that they're not editable by default. You need to set up fields that make certain areas of your page editable, which you find out how to do in this chapter.

Converting a Web Page to a Template

You can convert an existing web page to a template through the Dreamweaver menu bar command **File, Save As Template**. This opens the Save As Template window (see Figure 16.1).

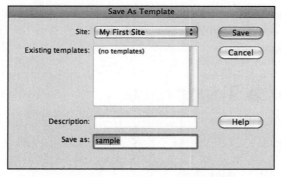

Figure 16.1: The Save As Template window lets you establish the connection between your template and the website to which it is associated.

The Save As Template window lets you establish a name for your template and where to save the file. By default, the **Site** pop-out menu lists the site that you have active when you create a template. Type a name for your template in the **Save As** field, and then click **OK**.

This opens a message window asking whether you want to update the document links. These are any links and attached style sheets that you have for your document. Click **Yes** to update the links.

You have just created a template. In the Files panel, you now see a new folder labeled **Templates**. Open the folder to see your new template document (see Figure 16.2).

DREAMWEAVER DON'T

Don't rename or move the template folder that Dreamweaver creates; if you do, the template files you create may not work properly. This folder needs to be on the root level of your site and labeled **Templates**.

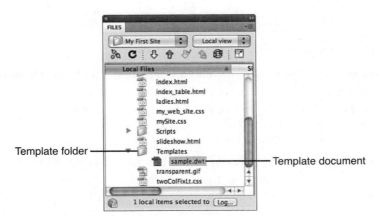

Template folder —————

————— Template document

Figure 16.2: As you create more templates for your site, they are saved in the Template folder.

Notice that the template document has a .dwt extension. This indicates that it's a Dreamweaver template.

You can also choose **Insert, Template Object, Make Template** from the menu bar to convert a document to a template. Or you can click the **Make Template** command in the Insert panel pop-out menu, **Common** category. Click the arrow next to the **Template** button and choose **Make Template** from the menu list.

Creating a Template from Scratch

You can also create a template from scratch. As with creating a new HTML or CSS document, you choose **File, New** from the menu bar. This opens the New Document window (see Figure 16.3).

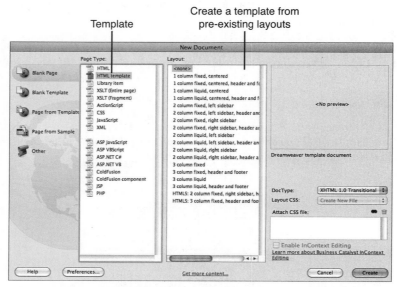

Figure 16.3: *You can choose from any of the 19 different preset layouts for your template document, or you can create a blank file and develop your own page layout.*

In the **Blank Page** category, select **HTML Template** under the **Page Type** category. At this point, you can choose from any of the 19 predesigned layouts or choose **None** to create a blank page. Set your desired document type and click OK. This opens a blank document in the Dreamweaver Document window, which is ready for your creative touch.

You can also select the **Page from Template** category on the far left of the New Document window and select **HTML Template** from the **Page Type** category. The **Page from Template** category only contains templates you have already made.

Using Template Regions

By default, a Dreamweaver template isn't editable. You need to create editable areas or regions on your page for any content area that you want to reflect different information. But other areas on the page, like menu bars, sidebars, and header or footer areas, shouldn't be editable; they should stay the same on each page.

Creating an Editable Region

Dreamweaver makes it easy to create an Editable region on your template page. When you create editable areas, you can add any web elements to these areas. Follow these steps to create an Editable region in a template:

1. Select the area that you want to make an Editable region. This could be a Div tag, an image, or just a highlight of text that you have on the page.

2. From the menu bar, choose **Insert, Template Objects, Editable Region** (see Figure 16.4).

Figure 16.4: *Dreamweaver offers this submenu of commands focused on templates and template objects.*

3. The New Editable Region window opens (see Figure 16.5). Type a name for your Editable region in the **Name** field. Click **OK**.

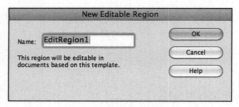

Figure 16.5: *You can name an Editable region any name you like as long as it's one word, and doesn't use any special characters except for the underscore.*

Dreamweaver displays your Editable region with an outline defining the area on the page. Notice that it has a tab in the upper-left corner labeled with the Editable region name. This area is editable (see Figure 16.6).

Editable region name

Figure 16.6: *You can select an editable region by clicking the label tab or the outline of the region.*

Creating a Repeating Region

You can also create a Repeating region in Dreamweaver. This is a region that can be repeated as often as necessary to accommodate the information. For instance, you can set up a web page to import XML data for records of authors, with each record containing the author name, a brief author biography, and an author photo. To create such a site, you would use a Repeating region for the name, one for the author photo, and another for the biography. When a browser renders the page, it pulls in all the records that are in the XML document. Then all this data adheres to the template design and format for presenting the page.

Setting up a template with Repeating Regions is a bit different than setting up normal Editable areas. First, you need to define what will repeat, and then you define what portion of that area is Editable. Follow these steps to create a Repeating region:

1. Select the text or content for the Repeating regions or insert your cursor where you want the region to be located.

2. Choose **Insert, Template Objects, Repeating Region** from the menu bar. Dreamweaver inserts a Repeating region into the web page (see Figure 16.7).

Figure 16.7: The Repeating region looks just like an Editable region, but the tab label reflects that this template object is a Repeating region.

3. The New Repeating Region window displays. Type a name for the Repeating region in the Name field. This name must be unique for the page (it must be distinct from other page element ID names, too). Click **OK** to close the window and create the region.

4. Now with the Repeating region created, add Editable regions for containing the records of the data you are importing (see earlier in this chapter for instructions for creating Editable regions).

DREAMWEAVER TIP

If you don't add Editable regions to a Repeating Region, you can't change the information in it. It repeats the first record of data over and over again.

Creating Repeating Tables

Repeating Tables are Editable regions laid out in table format. This is a nice way to display tabular data. To create a Repeating Table, choose **Insert, Template Objects, Repeating Table** from the menu bar. This opens the Insert Repeating Table window (see Figure 16.8).

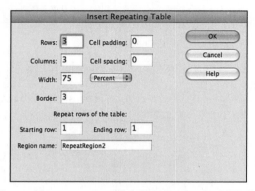

Figure 16.8: *These table options are coded directly into the HTML code, just like when you create a table.*

Set the Repeating Table options just like you would with a regular table (see Chapter 10). Click **OK**, and Dreamweaver creates the table from the options that you set in a Repeating Table region. The repeating table displays in a template region (see Figure 16.9).

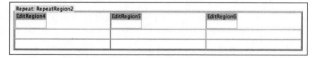

Figure 16.9: *Notice that the Repeating Table automatically creates Editable regions for the table.*

DREAMWEAVER TIP

A fourth region that you can create for a template is the Optional region. You can set the Optional region to display or hide, depending on conditional statements based on user interaction with the website. The conditional statements are **If-Else** statements or **True/False** operations.

Making Tag Attributes Editable

You can use templates to control the tag attributes of a property in a style rule, and you can set these attributes so that they're editable. This feature might come in handy if, for example, you're working with a group of web designers. You can create a template for controlling the site and then set certain property attributes that can be changed, like the color of a border for an image. This gives the other designers a bit of creative freedom when creating their pages.

To make tag attributes editable, follow these steps:

1. In the template, select the web element that you want to make editable.

2. From the menu bar, choose **Modify, Templates, Make Attribute Editable**. This opens the Editable Tag Attributes window (see Figure 16.10).

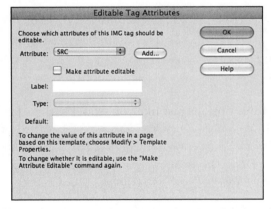

Figure 16.10: *The options presented in this window vary based on the type of web element you selected.*

3. From the **Attribute** pop-out menu, select the attribute that you want to make editable. If the attribute you want to make editable isn't listed in the **Attribute** pop-out menu, click the **Add** button and type the attribute there.

4. Check the **Make Attribute Editable** option to make this attribute editable.

5. Dreamweaver automatically populates the remaining fields with the appropriate attribute information. In the **Label** field, type a name for the editable attribute. The name must be a single word with no special characters. Define a default value in the **Default** field.

6. Click **OK** to close the window and set the editable attribute.

Creating New Web Pages from a Template

Now that you have the basics of creating a template and Editable regions under your belt, it's time to create a new web page from a template. Dreamweaver makes this process effortless. In the **New Document** window, choose **Page from Template.** In the **Site** category a list displays of all sites you've defined that have a template. Click the site you want and, in the **Template for site** category, select the template to use for your new page (see Figure 16.11).

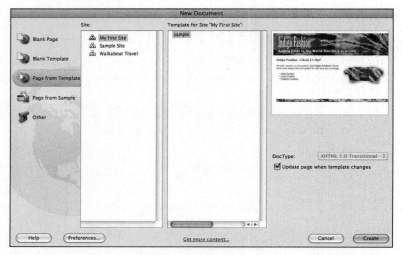

Figure 16.11: *The Template for Site category displays all templates that you have set up for the site you selected in the Site category.*

Click **Create**. Dreamweaver generates a new page based on your template. Any of the Editable regions can be modified, but the rest of the design on the page is not editable.

Applying a Template to an Existing Page

You can also apply a template to an existing web page. This is a useful feature for website redesigns or for converting web pages to the template site design. To do this, follow these steps:

1. Open the web page to which you want to apply the template. Figure 16.12 shows a basic web page with little document structure.

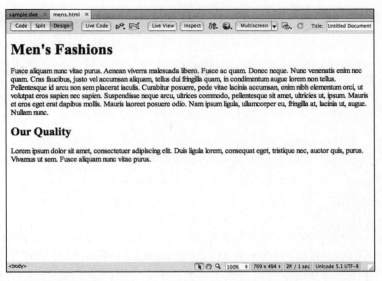

Figure 16.12: This is just a basic web page with a little document structure applied to it.

2. From the menu bar, choose **Modify, Templates, Apply Template to Page**. This opens the Select Template window (see Figure 16.13).

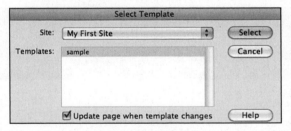

Figure 16.13: When you select a site from the **Site** *pop-out menu, the Template field displays a list of templates that have been created for the site.*

3. From the **Site** pop-out menu, choose the site of the template to be applied and then select the template from the **Templates** list field. Click **Select**.

4. If Dreamweaver doesn't find any conflicts between web elements that exist on the web page when compared to the template, it formats the web page with the template design. (These conflicts occur based on tags used for regions of content. Many times a conflict occurs between Document `<head>` and/or `<body>` tags in the web page and the template.) If Dreamweaver identifies a conflict, the Inconsistent Region Names window displays (see Figure 16.14).

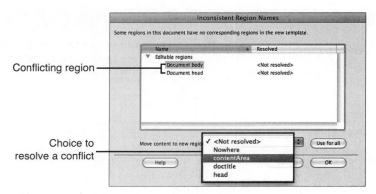

Figure 16.14: The Inconsistent Region Names window.

5. If Dreamweaver identifies a conflict, in the Inconsistent Region Names window, select a conflicting area and, in the **Move Content to New Region** pop-out menu, choose the region in the template design you want to move the data into. (If you choose **Nowhere**, the conflicting region on the original web page isn't brought into the template design.)

6. After you've resolved your conflicting regions, click **OK**. Dreamweaver formats the web page with the template design (see Figure 16.15).

Figure 16.15: The original page (shown in Figure 16.12) is transformed and fitted into the template design.

7. Save your page with the template design by choosing **File, Save** from the menu bar.

If your template has style sheets attached to it, these style sheets are also attached to any page you create from the template and any page to which you apply the template. This includes internal style sheets, too.

Updating a Template-Based Site

You can update an entire site by modifying the template that's applied to the pages of the site. This is a powerful tool for maintaining and updating your website. To do this, you need to modify the template with your changes. When you save the modified template, Dreamweaver updates all pages that have the template applied and then displays the Update Template Files window (see Figure 16.16).

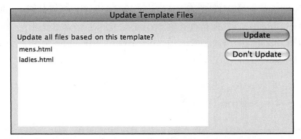

Figure 16.16: All files with the template applied display in the list titled "Update all files based on this template?"

You can choose to update all the files listed by clicking **Update**. If you want to update individual files, select them from the list and then click **Update**.

All pages that have the template applied are updated with the changes made to the template. Your site design is consistent and controlled.

Click the **Don't Update** button if you don't want to update any pages that have the template applied. For instance, if you're working on the functionality of the template, you might not want to update any other page until you're satisfied with the functionality.

You can manually update a page based on the template that's applied to it. From the menu bar, choose **Modify, Templates, Update Current Page**. To manually update an entire site, choose **Modify, Templates, Update Pages**. Both of these commands reapply the template.

Detaching a Template from a Page

You can detach a template and its design from a page. To do this, open or make active the page with the template attached. Then, from the menu bar, choose **Modify, Template, Detach Template**. You can also use the **Insert** panel, **Common** category, and click the **Templates** button on the pop-out menu. In this menu, choose the **Detach Template** command. The template is removed and the page returns to its basic format.

 # Tutorial: Creating a Template for the Travel Site

It's hard to beat the power of a template for creating a site. You have a well-developed page for Walkabout Travel at this point. Now let's turn it into a template and apply it to other pages in the site. Using templates creates a consistent page layout and design while also allowing you to create unique content for each page. Follow these steps to create a template:

1. Define the **Chapter16** folder in the Tutorial folder as a new site root folder. You'll use this defined site for the tutorial.

2. Open the **walkabout.html** page. You're going to convert this page to a template.

3. From the menu bar, choose **File, Save As a Template**. This opens the Save As Template window (see Figure 16.17).

4. Make sure **Walkabout16** is the folder identified in the **Site** field. Type **wat_site** for the name of your template in the **Save As** field. You can type a description of the template to provide more information about its functionality in the **Description** field. Click **Save** to save the template.

5. Dreamweaver converts your document to a template. A message displays asking if you want to update the document links. Click **Yes** to update the template document links.

Figure 16.17: If you have other templates defined, they display in the Existing Template field.

6. Open the **Files** panel. You'll see a new folder named **Template**; inside the folder is the new template file. (See Figure 16.18.)

Figure 16.18: Dreamweaver automatically creates a new Template folder and places the new site template in the folder.

DREAMWEAVER TIP

Dreamweaver always creates the Template folder at the root level of your defined site. If you don't define a site, the template might not work properly.

7. Next, you need to create some editable fields in the template to allow for each page's content. The overall design needs to stay consistent, so you should keep areas like the menu bars, page layout, and footer noneditable. The text in the **pageContent** Div tag needs to be editable, as does the Placeholder element in the **display** Div tag. Highlight all the text in the **pageContent** Div tag to make it active.

DREAMWEAVER DON'T

Use a unique, one-word name for the Editable Region. If you use a name that you've applied to other web elements, your web page might not function properly.

8. From the menu bar, choose **Insert, Template Objects, Editable Region** (see Figure 16.19). This opens the New Editable Region window. Type **content_area** in the **Name** field. Click **OK** to create the editable area.

Figure 16.19: An Editable Region is an outline around the text area in the pageContent Div tag and a tab indicating the name of the Editable Region.

9. Repeat steps 7 and 8 to create an Editable Region around the Placeholder element in the **display** Div tag. Name this Editable region **display_area**. Now you can use two areas on the page to create each individual page of the site. Save the template document by choosing **File, Save**.

10. Let's create the home page for the Walkabout site using use the **wat_site** template. From the menu bar, choose **File, New**. This opens the New Document window (see Figure 16.20). Click the **Page from Template** category on the far left. Then click the **Walkabout16** site in the Site category.

Select **wat_site.** Click **Create** to create a new page that's based on the template.

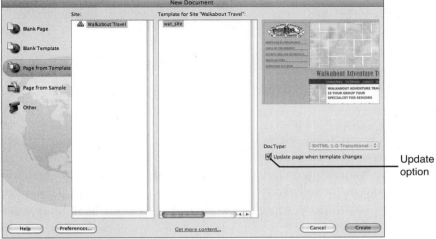

Figure 16.20: Make sure the Update Page When Template Changes option is selected so that any updates to your template are reflected in all files attached to the template.

11. A new document opens, with all the template layout and design. This page will be the home page for the site. (The preview window for the template might look odd, but this is due to limited size of the display area in the New Document window.) You'll see a typo in the **content_area** Editable region. In the second paragraph, fix the first line of text to read:

    We customize all our tours with our clients in mind!

12. Save the page as **index.html** by choosing **File, Save.** This is our home page for the site.

13. Now let's attach the template to the existing pages of the site. Open the **history.html** document. Choose **Modify, Template, Apply Template to Page** from the menu bar.

14. This opens the Select Template window (see Figure 16.21). Click the **wat_site** template in the Templates field. Click **Select.**

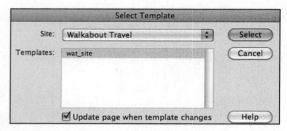

Figure 16.21: Make sure the Update page when template changes option is selected.

15. This applies the template to the **history.html** page. The Inconsistent Region Names window displays, listing conflicting regions between the template and the **history.html** page (see Figure 16.22). Click the **Document body** region in the Name column, and then click the **Move Content to New Region** pop-out menu and choose **content_area**. Click **Document head** from the Name column and, again in the **Move Content to New Region** menu, set this to **Nowhere**.

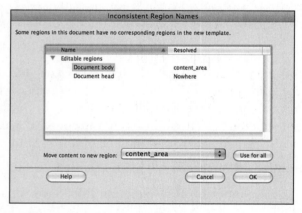

Figure 16.22: This window sets the information in the <body> tag of the history. html document to go to the template region content_area and sets the information in the <head> tag to go nowhere.

DREAMWEAVER TIP

The template document has the **walkabout.css** style sheet attached to it. All the style rules are applied to any document to which the template is attached.

16. Click **OK** to apply the template. The **history.html** document is formatted with the template elements and design. But some issues arise with the transfer of the `<body>` tag content. The web graphics don't fit in the **pageContent** Div width. Let's fix this.

17. Click the **Walkabout** logo web graphic and delete it. Delete the Walkabout banner. Then delete any blank lines of text to move the heading to the top of the text area (see Figure 16.23). Save the page by choosing **File, Save**.

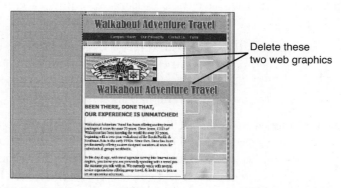

Delete these two web graphics

Figure 16.23: Based on the existing page content, you might need to modify contents in the Editable regions to fit the new page layout.

17. Open **philosophy.html** and **contact.html**, and repeat steps 13 through 17 to apply the template to each of these pages. Delete extra graphics and lines of text. In the Contact Us page, adjust the table to 400 pixels in width. To do this, first click in the table to make it active and then, in the Tag Selector, click the `<table>` tag to select the table. Next, in the Property Inspector, change the **W** field to **400** pixels.

18. Save all files by choosing **File, Save All**.

19. Now let's make a change to the template and update that change to all pages of our site. In the Files panel, Double-click the **wat_site.dwt** file in the **Template** folder to open it.

20. Let's fix the footer to look a little nicer with the design. Click the **Library object** of the Walkabout copyright info in the footer to select it. Press the **right/back arrow** key to position your cursor in front of the Library object. In the Property Inspector, click the **Class** pop-out menu and choose **CenterIt**. This centers the footer information (see Figure 16.24).

Library object

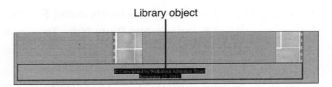

Figure 16.24: The Library object is now centered in the footer area of the page.

21. Save the template. This opens the Update Template Files window, listing all the files in the site that have the template applied. Click **Update** to update these files.

22. When the update is finished, a summary message displays. Select the **Show Log** option at the bottom left of the window to display a summary log of the files updated. Click **Close** to close the window. The copyright information updates on all pages with the Template applied.

23. Notice that any files you had opened before the template update now display as needing to be saved. In the Document window, each document name in the document tab has an asterisk after it, indicating that it needs to be saved. Click one of these documents, and you'll see that the footer is now centered in the footer area. Choose **File, Save All** to save all opened documents.

The Walkabout Travel site is really coming together. Move on to the next chapter to learn more useful Dreamweaver techniques, functionality, and skills.

The Least You Need to Know

- Templates are a powerful feature for controlling your website's design.
- You can create Editable regions in a template through **Insert, Template Objects, Editable Region** in the menu bar. Editable regions let you edit areas on your page for different page content.
- You can create Repeating regions in a template through **Insert, Template Objects, Repeating Region** in the menu bar. Repeating regions enable the import of XML data.
- You can create Repeating Tables in a template through **Insert, Template Objects, Repeating Table**.

- Use templates to create new web pages by choosing **File, New** and, in the New HTML Document window, selecting the **Page from Template** category and selecting the template you want to use.

- You can apply a template to existing pages in a website by opening the page and then choosing **Modify, Template, Apply Template to Page**.

- You can detach a template from a page by choosing **Modify, Template, Detach from Template**.

Testing and Maintaining Your Site

In This Chapter

- Checking your documents for spelling errors
- Finding and replacing text, code, and attributes in a document
- Organizing your site structure and creating new files and folders
- Cleaning up your document's HTML
- Managing and maintaining your site via the Results panel group
- Examining code while working in Design view
- Testing your pages and site on multiple browsers across platforms

Dreamweaver offers numerous tools for you to use to test and maintain your site. And although you can preview your site in different browsers as you develop it to check the layout and design, sometimes you'll need to dig a little deeper to uncover the source of a problem. Fortunately, Dreamweaver offers tools—such as the Code Inspector—that help with this troubleshooting process. And once your site is up and running, maintaining your site is a cinch, thanks to yet more Dreamweaver tools, such as those found in the Results panel group.

Site Maintenance

Maintaining a site is an important part of web design. After you've developed your site, you might need to find and replace word(s) in your site or spell-check the content in each page. You also might need to reorganize the structure of your site or check an HTML document for errors in the code.

Spell Checking Your Site

Dreamweaver's Check Spelling command works just like spell checkers in other applications, such as Microsoft Word.

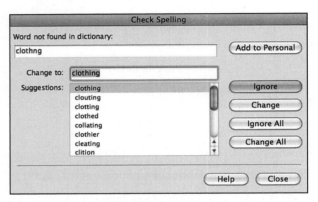

Figure 17.1: The Dreamweaver Check Spelling feature is based on the U.S. English dictionary.

Choose **Commands, Check Spelling** from the menu bar to open the Check Spelling window (see Figure 17.1). It works only on the current document, and it focuses only on the content of your page—it ignores code and tags. The spell checker works on HTML document and other web page types, like PHP or ASP; however, it doesn't work with XML.

DREAMWEAVER TIP

You can change the default dictionary through Dreamweaver's Preferences. Click the **General** category and, in the Spelling Dictionary pop-out menu, select the dictionary that you want to use.

Typical of other spell checkers, when you initiate this feature, it goes through your document looking for words that aren't in the dictionary. When the spell checker finds a word it doesn't recognize, it displays the word in the **Word Not Found in the Dictionary** field. In the **Change To** field, it offers its best suggestion for the correct spelling. If the suggestion in the **Change To** field isn't correct, look in the **Suggestions** field, which displays a list of other possible words. Select the correct spelling or word and then click either **Change** to change that occurrence of the misspelling or **Change All** to change all occurrences of the word. You can ignore the word and move on with the spell check by clicking **Ignore**. If you want to ignore all occurrences of the word throughout the document, click **Ignore All**.

If the word that Check Spelling found is a word that you want to include in the dictionary, click **Add to Personal** to add it to the default dictionary.

Find and Replace

Dreamweaver's Find and Replace feature functions like Find and Replace in other applications. You can use it to search the current document for text, tags, or attributes of a tag. Unlike the Check Spelling feature, the code is searchable. You can also search multiple documents or even the entire site.

You can find the Find and Replace command in the menu bar by choosing **Edit, Find and Replace**. This opens the Find and Replace window (see Figure 17.2).

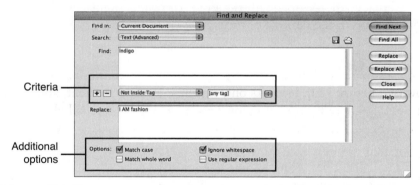

Figure 17.2: You can create a focused search using the Find and Replace feature.

In the **Find In** option, you designate where to search. You can focus your search on the current document or broaden your search to other documents, folders, and even the entire site. Choose your search file(s) by clicking the pop-out menu and choosing the file type from the list.

The **Search** pop-out menu establishes the type of search. You have the following choices:

- **Source Code**—Searches the source code for tags and attributes
- **Text**—Searches only text
- **Text (Advanced)**—Searches for text in specific tags
- **Specific Tag**—Searches for specific tags

You can set multiple criteria for the search by clicking the **Plus** or **Minus** buttons to add multiple search criteria.

In the **Replace** field, type the replacement text or tags based on your search criteria. You can further focus your search by setting the additional options under the Options section of this window.

With your criteria set, use the buttons on the right to perform the search. Choose from the following search options:

- **Find Next**—Moves on to the next incidence of the search criteria without replacing the current incidence.

- **Find All**—Locates all incidences of the search criteria in all documents set for the search.

- **Replace**—Replaces an individual item as dictated in the found results.

- **Replace All**—Works with the Find All results. Replaces all occurrences of the term in the defined document.

DREAMWEAVER TIP

If you perform a search on a group of documents, the found results from all documents display in the Search panel, which is part of the Results panel group. This topic is covered later in this chapter.

File Organization

The Files panel is an excellent tool for reorganizing the file and folder structure of your site. It even maintains the links between the relocated document and any linking documents and images. Because it maintains the links among documents, you should always use the Files panel to move a file to or from a folder in your site. To move a file or folder, simply drag it to a new location. If the document has any links to other files, the Update Files window displays (see Figure 17.3).

DREAMWEAVER DON'T

Don't change your site structure through the operating system's Finder (Mac) or Windows Explorer (PC). You'll break any of the links in the relocated document to other files. If you do change the site structure outside the Files panel, you'll need to manually re-establish the path of all links in the relocated document.

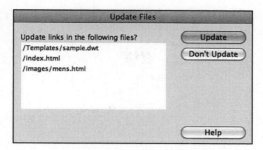

Figure 17.3: You can use the two buttons on the right of the Update Files panel to update the link, or you can leave it as is.

Click **Update** to update the links. Dreamweaver automatically changes these links to reflect the path to the new location of the document.

Creating New Folders and Files

You can also use the Files panel to create a new folder or file. Right-click in a blank area in the Files panel and choose **New Folder** or **New File**. You can set up as many folders as you need to organize your site. You can also create a new document through the Files panel.

To create a new file, right-click in a blank space in the File panel, which displays a pop-out menu (see Figure 17.4). Choose **New Folder** to create a new folder, or choose **New File** to create a new file. Give the folder or file a name that follows naming conventions for a web page or folder.

DREAMWEAVER TIP

You can find many of the commands listed in the right-click pop-out menu in the **Options** menu in the upper-right corner of the Files panel.

Figure 17.4: *You can also use this menu to put or get files from your local site or the hosting server.*

Managing Files

You can use the Files panel to cut, copy, delete, rename, and duplicate any of the files of your site. Again, right-click in a blank area of the Files panel and, in the pop-out menu, choose **Edit** (see Figure 17.5). This displays a submenu that lists other file-management commands. You need to select a file first to focus Dreamweaver on this file; then right-click.

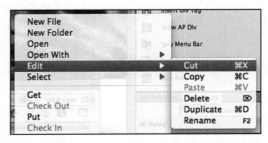

Figure 17.5: *If you cut or copy a file, you can choose Paste to paste the file into a new site or to a different location in your site's root folder.*

Cleaning Up HTML

Dreamweaver offers a command for cleaning up the basic structure of an HTML document. This command is useful for condensing repetitive tags and deleting non-Dreamweaver code from an HTML page. Chapter 4 covered the **Clean Up Word HTML** command, which you can use to strip any unnecessary and noncompliant code that Microsoft Word generates when it creates an HTML document. You can also clean up a regular HTML document. To do this, open the document that you want to work with and choose **Command, Clean Up XHTML** from the menu bar (see Figure 17.6).

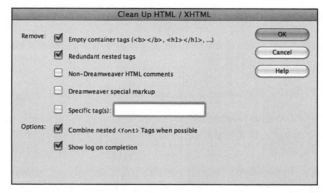

Figure 17.6: You can target a specific tag to be removed by listing it in the Specific tag(s) field.

Dreamweaver cleans up the document and then displays a window that summarizes all the code that was deleted or condensed (see Figure 17.7). If your document is clean, Dreamweaver lets you know that nothing needed to be cleaned up.

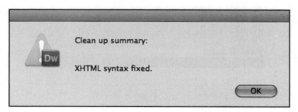

Figure 17.7: If Dreamweaver cleaned up a document, this window displays a list of all tags that were removed or combined.

Helpful Panels

Other Dreamweaver panels are helpful for maintaining your website. These panels display in the Results panel group, which you can access by choosing **Window, Results** from the menu bar (see Figure 17.8).

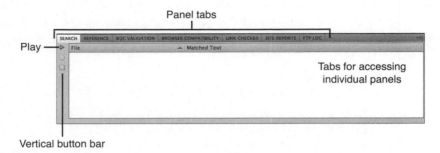

Panel tabs

Play

Tabs for accessing individual panels

Vertical button bar

Figure 17.8: Click a tab to access a new panel in the Results panel group.

Search

The Search panel displays the search results from a multipage search that you initiate through the **Find and Replace** command (see Figure 17.9).

Find and Replace command

Stop Find and Replace

Save Report

Figure 17.9: The three buttons for controlling the Find and Replace results are on the left side of this panel.

If you want to refine your Find and Replace operation, click the **Find and Replace** button on the left side of the panel. This opens the Find and Replace window, where you can adjust your search criteria. To stop a Find and Replace process, click the **Stop** button. To save a report of your results, click the **Save Report** button.

Reference

The Reference panel is another useful panel for understanding and learning HTML and CSS (see Figure 17.10). This panel incorporates the O'Reilly CSS reference guide, which is a standard for both HTML and CSS code. To reference a tag, attribute, or keyword, right-click it in Code view of Dreamweaver. In the pop-out menu, choose **Reference**. This displays the entire Results panel group, with the Reference tab active.

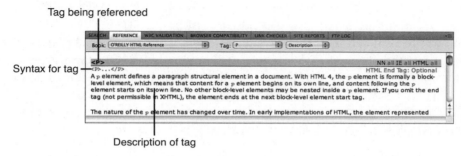

Figure 17.10: The Reference panel lets you research HTML tags and CSS code to correctly use it in your web page.

DREAMWEAVER TIP

You can also access the Reference panel by inserting your cursor into a tag, attribute, or keyword and pressing **Shift+F1**.

W3C Validation

Dreamweaver has a built-in feature—the W3C Validation panel—that validates your HTML document to ensure that it's compliant with current standards. This feature lets you validate the current document or files posted on a live server.

To check your document for compliance with W3C standards, choose **Window, Results, W3C Validation**. This opens the Results panel group with the W3C Validations panel displayed (see Figure 17.11).

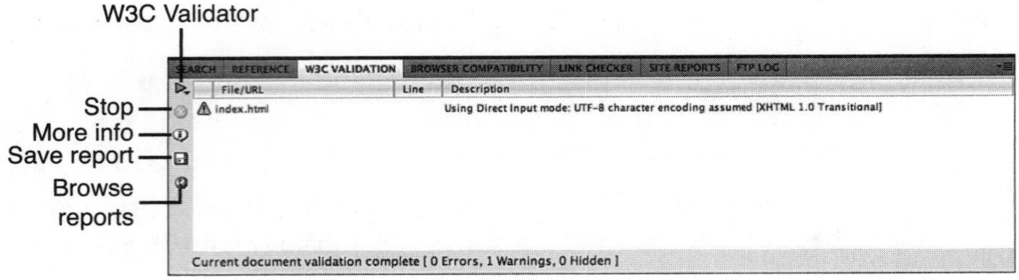

W3C Validator

Stop

More info

Save report

Browse
reports

Figure 17.11: Use the buttons on the left to control the W3C Validation panel.

To activate a validation of the current document, click the **W3C Validation** button on the left and choose **Validate Current Document (W3C)** from the pop-out menu. This displays a message that Dreamweaver has sent your document to the validation service. Click **OK** to send your document to the W3C for validation. A few seconds later, the W3C Validation panel displays the results. To get more information on an error, double-click it. The accompanying code is highlighted in Code view.

Browser Compatibility

The Browser Compatibility Check (BCC) is a great feature for checking compatibility issues that a browser might have with certain combinations of HTML and CSS. You can access this panel through the menu bar command of **File, Check Page, Browser Compatibility** (see Figure 17.12).

Check Browser Compatibility

Compatibility issue information

Stop

More info

Save reports

Browse
reports

Likelihood of occurrence

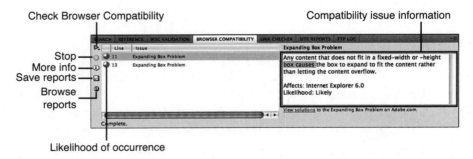

Figure 17.12: The Likelihood of Occurrence icon lets you know the odds of this compatibility issue occurring.

To check the current document for browser compatibility, click the **Check Browser Compatibility** button on the left and select **Check Browser Compatibility** from the pop-out menu. Dreamweaver checks for compatibility and lists any errors. Click an error to get more information on the right.

DREAMWEAVER TIP

A link in the description of the compatibility issue takes you directly to Adobe CSS Advisor, a website that provides details on common browser rendering issues and bugs.

Link Checker

The Link Checker checks the links in your site to make sure they all work. This feature finds broken, *orphaned*, and *external* links. You can check the current document, a group of documents, or all documents on your site (see Figure 17.13).

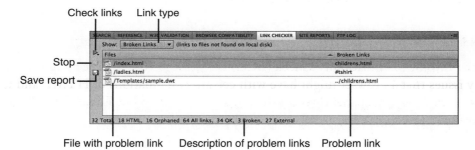

Figure 17.13: The Link Type menu lets you set the type of link you're looking for. You can choose to search for broken or external links and orphaned files.

DREAMWEAVER DEFINITION

An **external link** is a link to a document that resides outside the site. This could be a document on the company intranet or a document on another website.

Orphaned files are files that exist in a site but aren't linked to any other pages.

To check your site for problems with links, first choose the document(s) to check in the Files panel. You can choose to check the current document or multiple documents. Open the Link Checker by choosing **File, Check Page, Link** from the menu bar (see Figure 17.13). Determine the link type you're looking for by clicking the **Link Type** pop-out menu. The default setting is **Broken Links**, but you can also check for orphaned files or external links. Click the **Check Links** button on the left. Dreamweaver displays a list of all links found, based on the link type. Look at the bottom of the window for a description of the link check.

You can fix these links using either of the following methods:.

- Double-click the file name from the list of problem links. This takes you to the document with the problem and even highlights the problem link in the document. If that document isn't already open, Dreamweaver opens it for you. You can change the link directly in the document through this process.

- Click on the link path in the Link Checker panel and simply type the new link path or click the **Browse** button that displays to the right of the link path and browse to the document you want to link to (see Figure 17.14).

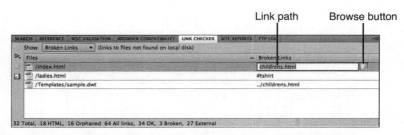

Figure 17.14: Click the Browse button to set a new path to a linked document.

Site Reports

The Site Reports panel runs reports on your site and documents. You can run reports on the HTML code or the workflow of your site. You can even use the Site Reports panel to check for links.

Workflow reports help designers manage the web design process when multiple designers are working on a site. These reports let you know who has checked out a file, what pages have been modified and when, and what pages have Design Notes attached.

HTML reports contain information about HTML attributes, font tags, empty tags, missing Alt text, and redundant and nested tags. You can even identify documents that don't have a title, which is necessary for accessibility.

To run a site report, follow these steps:

1. Open the Site Reports panel by choosing **Site, Reports** from the menu bar (see Figure 17.15).

*Figure 17.15: You can save a report by clicking the **Save Report** button.*

2. Click the **Reports** button on the left. This opens the Reports window (see Figure 17.16).

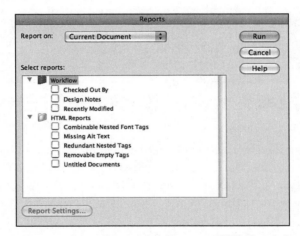

Figure 17.16: Run reports on the site workflow or on HTML code by selecting the options that you want to check.

3. In the Reports window, set the options you want to run the report on. Then click **Run**. The Site Reports window displays your report results.

> **DREAMWEAVER TIP**
>
> The Adobe Dreamweaver Exchange website has other reports that you can download and add to your Site Reports panel, including a font usage report or a meta data report. Open the Adobe Dreamweaver Exchange by choosing **Help, Dreamweaver Exchange**.

FTP Log

Every time you connect, put files to your FTP site, or get files from your FTP site (see Chapter 18), Dreamweaver generates a log of the activity between the server and your local site. You can see this activity in the FTP Log panel. To open this panel, choose **Site, Advanced, FTP Log** from the menu bar. This opens the FTP Log panel (see Figure 17.17).

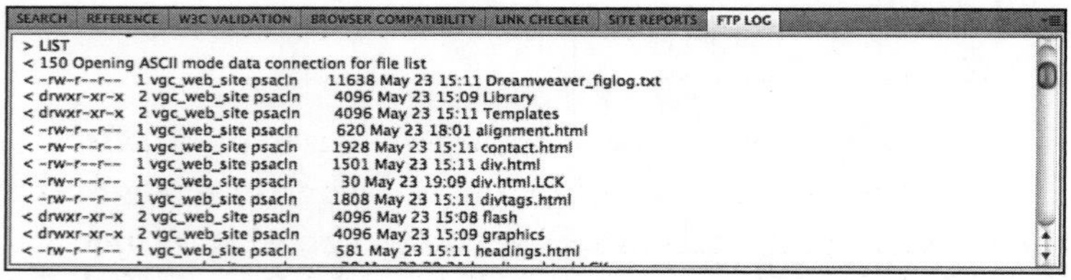

Figure 17.17: If you have errors with a file transfer or FTP connection, this panel lists them.

The log displays a line-by-line list of standard codes and commands. Code numbers identify problems. A description of the activity further explains these codes. Some include links to Adobe TechNotes, which offer more information about the code and suggestions on how to fix them.

Code Inspector

The Dreamweaver Code Inspector lists code for the current document. It works just like Code view, but because it's in a panel, you can work with the full screen of Design view and simply open the Code Inspector panel when you need it to view your code.

Open the Code Inspector panel by choosing **Window, Code Inspector** from the menu bar (see Figure 17.18).

Figure 17.18: *The Code Inspector functions just like Code view but is in its own panel.*

Adobe BrowserLab

Adobe BrowserLab helps you preview your website based on a defined set of browsers (see Chapter 4). It creates a screen shot of how a document in your site will look in a specified browser. You can access BrowserLab by choosing **Window, Extensions, Adobe BrowserLab** from the menu or by clicking the **BrowserLab Integration** button on the Welcome Screen (see Figure 17.19). You need to have a document opened in your Document window to focus Dreamweaver on this document. This opens the Adobe BrowserLab panel (see Figure 17.20).

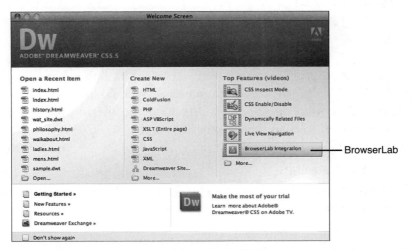

Figure 17.19: *BrowserLab is part of the Adobe CS Services suite of software and is accessible on Adobe's website.*

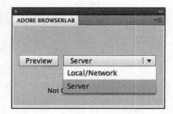

Figure 17.20: You can preview documents on your local site or on the hosting server.

Click the **Preview** button to activate the BrowserLab services. You need to have an Adobe Live ID set up to use BrowserLab; if you don't, you're prompted to set one up or to log in with an existing ID. This takes you to Adobe BrowserLab site (see Figure 17.21).

Browser 1 preview   Browser 2 preview

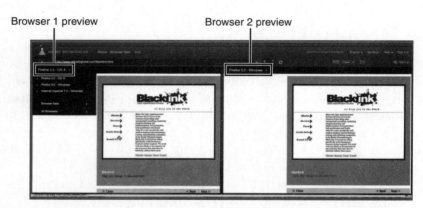

Figure 17.21: You can set your target browser and the number of screen shots of your page to display in the targeted browsers.

BrowserLab is very useful for testing your web pages in multiple browsers across platforms. You don't need to test a page in each individual browser; BrowserLab does this for you in a one-page display. This display is an image, so none of the buttons or site functionality will work in the BrowserLab display.

DREAMWEAVER TIP

Adobe BrowserLab was introduced in Dreamweaver CS5. You must have version 11.0.3 or higher of CS5 to use Adobe BrowserLab.

Tutorial: Checking Your Travel Site

Let's check the Walkabout Travel site for spelling errors, link errors, and HTML code errors:

1. Define the **Chapter17** folder in the **Tutorial** folder as a new site root folder. You'll use this defined site for the tutorial.

2. Open the history.html page and open the Check Spelling window by choosing **Commands, Check Spelling** from the menu bar. Work through the spell-check by fixing any spelling errors on the page.

3. Next, let's check the links in our Walkabout site. Open the Link Checker in the Results panel group by choosing **Window, Results, Link Checker** from the menu bar.

4. Click the **Check Links** button on the left and choose **Check Links for Entire Current Local Site**. This checks the entire Walkabout site for problem links and orphaned files.

5. You'll see that there are a few. These are all the links you set up in Chapter 15 for the side menu of tours. If you have a broken link, click the Browse button to the right of the link path and navigate to the linked document to re-establish this link.

6. To validate the HTML code for compliance with W3C standards, click the **W3C Validation** tab in the Results panel group, then open **walkabout.html**.

7. Click the **W3C Validate** button and choose **Validate Current Document (W3C)** to validate the **walkabout.html** document. The W3C Validator Notification window displays, asking if you want to send your document to the W3C. Click **OK** to allow this.

8. In the W3C Validation window, check the validation results. The two results shown in Figure 17.22 aren't really errors with the code and don't need to be fixed.

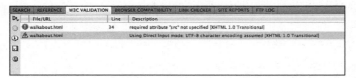

Figure 17.22: The W3C Validation window. These two references are not really errors with the code and do not need to be fixed.

9. If you have any other errors, research the correct code by referencing the W3C panel to find out what is wrong. Next, double-click the error to jump to the problem on the page and fix your code.

10. Save your page by choosing **File, Save** from the menu bar and move on to the next chapter.

The Least You Need to Know

- Spell-check your documents using the Dreamweaver Spell Check feature.
- Use Find and Replace to find text, code, and attributes in a document.
- Use the File panel to organize your site structure and create new files and folders.
- You can clean up HTML for your documents using the W3C Validation tab in the Results panel group.
- The Results panel group offers panels to help manage and maintain your site.
- The Code Inspector is a helpful panel for examining code while working in Design view.
- Adobe BrowserLab helps you test your pages and site on multiple browsers across platforms while working in Dreamweaver.

Posting Your Site to the Internet

In This Chapter

- Using FTP to connect to a remote hosting server
- Posting your website to your hosting server and making the website visible over the Internet
- Cloaking certain file types from being uploaded to a hosting server
- Adding Design Notes to a web page

For the world to see your website, it must be hosted on a remote server. You must upload, or post, the files, folders, and source code documents of your website to the hosting server. This requires establishing a connection to the server. Various technologies enable you to connect to your hosting server. You can use FTP, which is one of the most popular methods for posting files to your site. Another connection type is a company network server. This chapter covers the posting process using Dreamweaver.

Overview of the Posting Process

Posting a website involves putting copies of your website and all its files, folders, and structure on your hosting server. The hosting server then has a mirrored replica of your website (see Figure 18.1).

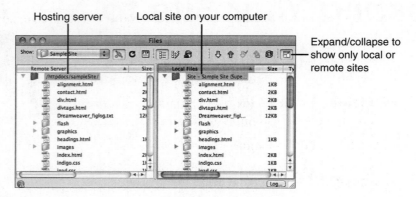

Figure 18.1: You can extend the Files panel to show the defined hosting server for managing posts and downloads.

The Dreamweaver command for posting files to your hosting server is the **Put** command. You use the **Get** command to download files from the server to your computer. Dreamweaver also synchronizes files on the server with the files on your computer. When you modify, add, or delete web pages on your local site, you can synchronize your site with the server. Dreamweaver puts the updated files on the hosting server, which keeps the server and your local website in sync.

DREAMWEAVER TIP

Your hosting server is associated with your domain name. Your website is accessed through your domain name represented in a URL, like **www.mywebsite.com**. When the visitor types this in a browser, the server displays, or serves up, your website.

Connecting Server Technologies

The first step in the process is to define the connection to the hosting server. You can find different types of remote servers and different server connection technologies. In Dreamweaver, when you define your site (see Chapter 3), you can also define the remote hosting server and establish a connection to this server. Choose from the following list of server connection technologies for the various types of hosting servers:

• **FTP**—Short for File Transfer Protocol, a popular connecting server technology.

- **SFTP**—Short for Secure File Transfer Protocol, a secure version of an FTP site.

- **FTP over SSL/TLS (implicit encryption)**—Secures FTP access, but encrypts only the commands that are transmitted to the site.

- **FTP over SSL/TLS (explicit encryption)**—Secures FTP access and encrypts the user's login, user ID, and password.

- **Local/Network**—Connection technology for a local network, or intranet.

- **WebDAV**—Short for web-based Distributed Authoring and Versioning. This connecting technology is an extension of the HyperText Transfer Protocol (HTTP) and allows multiple users to edit and manage files on the remote server.

- **RDS**—Short for Remote Development Services. This is a ColdFusion posting method. ColdFusion is another product from Adobe, and RDS is a security component of ColdFusion Server that permits access to files and databases through a remote HTTP connection.

Connecting with FTP

FTP is the most commonly used connection, and the rest of this chapter focuses on FTP connection technology. You create an FTP connection in the Site Setup window, which is the same window you use to define your site. Follow these steps to set up an FTP connection to a hosting server:

DREAMWEAVER TIP

If you don't know the type of hosting server you're hosted with, or what type server connection you need to use, contact your server administrator.

1. From the menu bar, choose **Manage, Site**. This opens the Manage Site window (see Figure 18.2).

DREAMWEAVER TIP

The **Manage Sites** command is also found in the **Site** pop-out menu located at the top of the Files panel (see Chapter 3). This opens the Manage Sites window. Click the site you want to set as the server connection and click **Edit**. This opens the Site Setup window.

Figure 18.2: Double-click a site from the list in the Manage Site window to manage the site setup.

2. Select the site you want to work with from the list on the left, and click the **Edit** button on the right. This opens the Site Setup window.

3. To define a server connection, click the **Servers** category of the Site Setup window. This displays the **Servers** category options for setting up a connection to a remote server (see Figure 18.3).

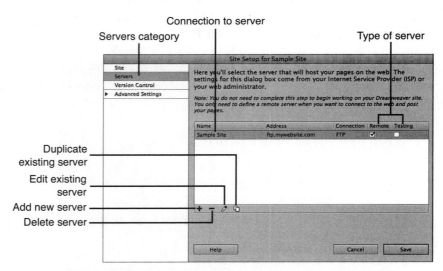

Figure 18.3: The Servers category lets you set up any of the previously discussed server connections.

4. To define a server connection, click the **Add New Server** button, represented by the **+** sign at the bottom of the window. This opens the Server Connection window (see Figure 18.4).

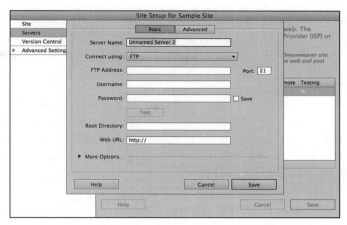

Figure 18.4: *The Site Setup window has a Basic tab and an Advanced tab for defining a new server.*

5. In the **Server Name** field, type a name for your server. This name can be anything you want, with no restrictions on naming convention.

6. Click the **Connect Using** pop-out menu and choose the server connection type you want to use for connecting to your hosting server (see Figure 18.5). For an FTP connection, choose **FTP**.

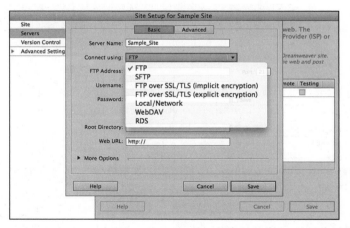

Figure 18.5: *The connection type you choose is based on the type of hosting server to which you are connecting.*

7. Type in your FTP login details, including the user name and password. If you don't know your login information, contact your server administrator.

DREAMWEAVER TIP

As soon as you type in your login information, Dreamweaver automatically puts a check in the Save check box. This saves your login information with your site setup.

8. Before you click the **Test** button that tests your connection, you may need to define the final two fields. The **Root Directory** field provides a way to target a folder for your site files. Type a path to a folder in this field. In the **Web URL** field, establish the connection to your site's domain by typing its URL into the field (see Figure 18.6).

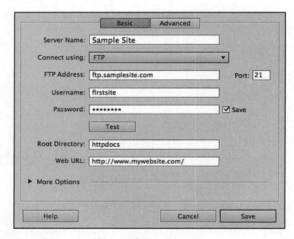

Figure 18.6: A configuration for an FTP connection.

9. Click the **Test** button to test your server connection. If all settings are correct, Dreamweaver connects to your server and the Connection Successful window displays (see Figure 18.7). Click **OK**. (If you have trouble with your connection, contact your server administrator.)

10. In the Site Setup window for the server connection, a remote server is listed, as shown in Figure 18.3.

11. Save your configuration by clicking **Save**. If you're modifying an existing site, click **Done** in the Manage Site window to close it.

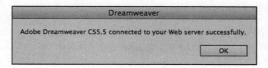

Figure 18.7: The Connection Successful window displays when Dreamweaver successfully connects to your server.

You've established your connection type to your hosting server. You can now post your website to your hosting server.

Advanced Tab

The **Advanced** tab of the Server category in the Site Setup window lets you further customize your connection to the hosting server (see Figure 18.8).

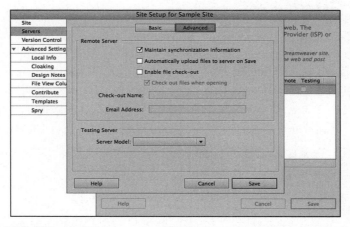

Figure 18.8: This window lets you establish a server connection to a testing server.

Here's an overview of each advanced setting:

- **Maintain Synchronization Information**—Sets your site to automatically maintain synchronization between your local site and the hosting server.

- **Automatically Upload Files to Server on Save**—Uploads a file to the server when you save the file locally.

> **DREAMWEAVER DON'T**
>
> If you set the **Automatically Upload Files to Server on Save** option, anytime
> you save a file, it becomes live on the server. If you're still in the development
> process, it's probably better not to have your site visible until it's finalized and
> tested. Simply turn off this option. This particular setting is nice to have when a
> site is finalized so that Dreamweaver automatically uploads to the hosting server
> any quick changes to pages and files.

- **Enable File Check-out**—Sets up users for check-in and check-out functionality (see Chapter 3). Use this feature if you're collaborating with other web
  designers and developers.

- **Testing Server**—Establishes the testing server model to be used.

Posting Files

When you've set your server connection, you're ready to post your site to the hosting
server. The Files panel makes this process effortless. You can expand the Files panel
so that it also displays your hosting server. Click the **Expand to Show Local and
Remote Sites** button, thus expanding the Files panel (see Figure 18.9).

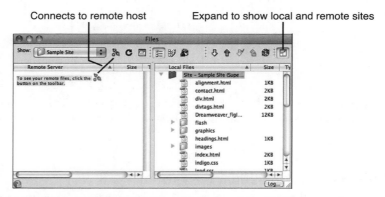

*Figure 18.9: Dreamweaver displays a message indicating that you need to connect
to your hosting server.*

Click the **Connects to Remote Host** button to connect to your hosting server. All
files on the server displayed side by side along with your local website (see Figure
18.10).

DREAMWEAVER TIP

The **Connects to Remote Host** button is a toggle button. To disconnect from your server, select this button again. Click the **Refresh** button to refresh your view of the hosting server.

Files Panel Expanded

When you expand the files panel, it shows access to more buttons and tools to manage your files.

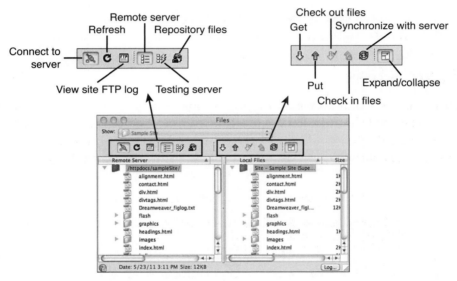

Figure 18.10: *These buttons and tools help you manage your hosting server and assist in testing the server with your local website.*

Put Command

To post your site to the remote server, you use the **Put** command. In the Files panel, you'll see a **Put** button. To post only one file to the server, select the file in the Files panel and then click **Put**. To post the entire site, select the root folder for your site and then click **Put**.

To post multiple files, select them all first by using the Shift-click method to select multiple adjacent files, or **Cmd**(Mac)/**Ctrl**(PC)**-click** to select nonadjacent files listed in the Files panel. Then click **Put**.

This displays the Background File Activity window for the active site (see Figure 18.11).

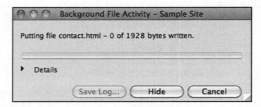

Figure 18.11: *You can see the files being posted in real time in the Background File Activity window.*

If you're posting a web page with inserted dependent files, like images or CSS external style sheets, Dreamweaver displays a window asking if you want the dependent files to be uploaded as well (see Figure 18.12).

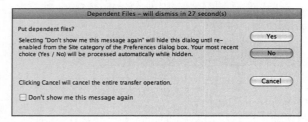

Figure 18.12: *This window asks if you want to upload dependent files associated with your website, such as images or CSS external style sheets.*

The message is common because almost every page posted will have images and other files attached to it. To upload all other files that support the page, click **Yes**. If you've already posted this page with all the supporting files, click **No**. If you click **Cancel**, you cancel the entire Put operation.

If you don't want to see this message again, check the **Don't Show Me This Message Again** option.

DREAMWEAVER TIP

You can post and download the active web document in the Document window to or from your hosting server using the Document toolbar and the File Management button. The Put and Get functionality listed in this menu works only for the active document.

Getting Files from the Web Server

Sometimes you need to download a file from your posted site to your local website. You accomplish this task with the **Get** command. The process for getting files is similar to the process for putting files, but you work in the server area of the extended Files panel. Click the file that you want to download and click the **Get** button. Dreamweaver downloads the file to your local website, replacing the local file.

Synchronizing Your Website

When you modify your website, create new site files, or delete files, you need to synchronize your local site and the server files. Click the **Synchronize with Site** button in the Files panel. This opens the Synchronize Files window (see Figure 18.13).

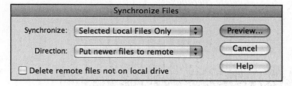

Figure 18.13: Use this window to synchronize your files.

This window provides Put and Get options. From the **Synchronize** pop-out menu, you can choose to synchronize only local files or to synchronize the entire site. From the **Direction** pop-out menu, you can choose whether to put and/or get newer files for posting to, or downloading from, the server.

If you don't click the **Delete Remote Files Not on Server** option, any file that was deleted from the local website remains on the hosting server. When you've established your settings for the synchronization of your files, click **Preview**.

Cloaking Files

Cloaking is a feature that lets you identify certain file types that you don't want included in Dreamweaver processes, such as Put and Get. Cloaking is a subcategory in the Advanced category of the Site Setup window (see Chapter 3). If you include a graphics folder containing all original art for the web images in your website, you can cloak these files to exclude them from all Put and Get operations. These file types are usually Photoshop, Illustrator, or Fireworks files. You can list the file types you don't want Dreamweaver to post to the server by identifying the extension of these file types (see Figure 18.14).

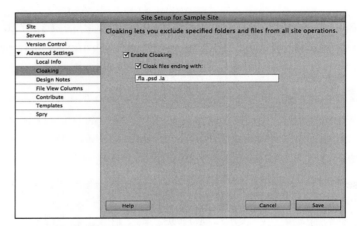

Figure 18.14: Click the Enable Cloaking option first to enable the Cloaking Files Ending With field.

Using Design Notes

Dreamweaver's Design Notes is a particularly useful feature when you're working with a group of people to develop a website. You can use it to add notes to files in your site, which helps keep everyone up to speed concerning the pertinent information of each file. You enable Design Notes through the Site Setup window (see Figure 18.15).

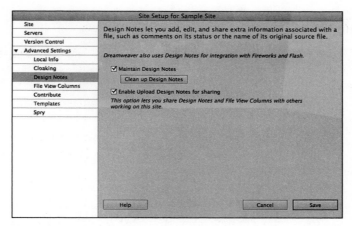

Figure 18.15: *You enable Design Notes when you select the Maintain Design Notes option.*

Turn on this feature by clicking the **Maintain Design Notes** option. You must enable Design Notes functionality to insert a Design Note in a web page.

Inserting Design Notes

You can insert a Design Note on a Macintosh using either of the following techniques; if you are using a PC, you must use the second method:

- From the menu bar, choose **File, Design Notes** to insert a Design Note into the active document in the Document window (Mac only method).

- In the Files panel, right-click a file and choose **Design Notes** from the menu (both Mac and PC method).

Both techniques open the Design Notes window (see Figure 18.16).

Insert date

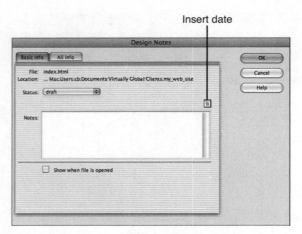

Figure 18.16: *This window has two tabs: Basic Info and All Info.*

On the Basic Info tab, set the status for the document from the Status menu. To insert the current date, click the **Insert Date** button. Type your note in the Notes area. If you want the note to display when the file opens, select **Show When File Is Opened**.

The All Info tab provides full information for all Design Notes inserted into a page. From this tab, you can view the full information on all Design Notes that have been inserted on a page, create new Design Notes, and edit or delete existing notes.

Design Notes are stored in their own document with an .mno extension. This document type is a special format that integrates with XML. Dreamweaver creates a *hidden folder* named _Notes in the Files panel (see Figure 18.17). You can display all *hidden files* and folders from the Options menu in the Files panel. Choose **View, Show Hidden Files** from the pop-out menu.

DEFINITION

Hidden folders and **hidden files** are hidden from normal viewing methods. Names of hidden files and folders are preceded by an underscore (_), distinguishing them as hidden.

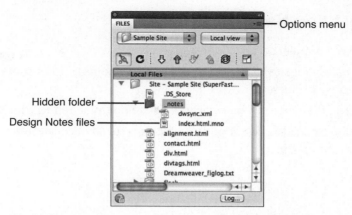

Figure 18.17: All Design Notes documents are located in the hidden _Notes folder.

The Design Notes file is named the same as the document the Design Note is inserted into. For instance, if you insert a Design Note into the index.html file, the accompanying Design Note document is named **index.html.mno** in the _**Notes** folder, located in the Files panel.

Viewing Design Notes

When you open a page that has a Design Note, the Design Note does not immediately display. To see all Design Notes, choose **View, Design Notes** from the menu bar. This displays the Design Notes window and all the notes associated with the page.

DREAMWEAVER TIP

When you're trying to view a Design Note associated with a page that resides on the hosting server, you need to check it out with the check-out process before you can view the note.

This chapter has no tutorial, but if you have a hosting server established, you can set up an FTP connection to practice this process. You can upload the Walkabout site to test the Put and Get technology.

The Least You Need to Know

- FTP is a popular server connection technology.
- To make your site visible over the Internet, you need to post your site to the remote web server.
- Certain file types can be cloaked from being uploaded to your hosting server.
- Design Notes can be added to web pages to aid in collaboration among other team members.

Powerful Friends for Interactivity

This part takes the web design process one step further by introducing other web technologies and walking you through the process of integrating them with Dreamweaver. Interactivity is essential for a website today. Adding clickable tabs that contain focused information, flyout menus, forms, and other interactive features enhances the web experience, allowing your visitors to have more control over their interaction with your website.

Among the interactive tools covered are forms for two-way communication on your website; Spry widgets for adding menu bars, panels, and Tool Tips; third-party widgets and extensions that expand Dreamweaver's functionality; and Adobe Flash movies and videos. Using these tools makes a website come alive and really communicate the information and message to your site visitors.

Interactivity Through Forms

In This Chapter

- Creating forms for two-way communication
- Adding text fields, radio buttons, and menus
- Add common buttons to your form
- Adding Spry Validation form objects

Forms are a great feature to add to your website for gathering information from your visitors. Forms have many uses in web design. You can use them to gather basic information or help a visitor purchase the latest gadget over the Internet. Forms enable two-way communication—between you and your visitors—on your website.

Overview of Forms

A web form is created through the HTML `<form>` tag. This tag wraps around all the form objects, like text boxes, buttons, and checkboxes. Figure 19.1 shows an example of a basic form for collecting a visitor's name and e-mail address.

Label   Text field label Text field

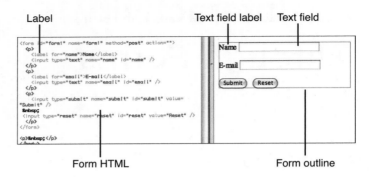

Form HTML   Form outline

Figure 19.1: Each form has its own ID, which is set by default to form1 for the first form you use in a page, form2 for the second, and so on.

Every form contains form objects that enable the visitor to communicate with you. These can be text fields that capture text data, or Select lists or Select menus from which the visitor chooses preset options. These elements help gather the information you need to run your business and transform your website into a two-way communication tool.

Form items have two features: a name and a value. The name is the label or descriptive information used to communicate what the visitor is to input. The value is the visitor's input. These two features organize and capture the visitor information.

DREAMWEAVER TIP

Other common buttons for a form are the Submit button and the Reset button. The Submit button transfers the form data back to you and the Reset button lets users reset the form and start over if they make mistakes.

This data is grouped in pairs of name/value, such as addess/102 Main Street. This gives the structure that can be processed.

A back-end engine or server-side program processes the visitor's input. The engine can either e-mail the results to you or do more complex tasks, such as process a credit card. Form-processing programs include CGI, Perl, VBScript, Java, and PHP, to name a few.

Form-processing programs are frequently processed through a CGI (common gateway interface), which is the link between the programming code that defines the data output from the form and the server that displays the form. Some of the programs have their own scripts for this task, but CGI is still the most commonly used. The program you use depends on what program your hosting server has installed on the server. If you don't know which program your hosting server uses, talk with your server administrator.

All forms have some type of **Submit** button that transmits or sends the visitor input to the back-end engine processing application. In addition, many forms have a **Reset** button, which clears a form of any inputs.

Creating a Form

The first step in creating a form is to insert it into your page. Choose **Insert, Form, Form**, or, from the Insert panel, choose the **Form category** and click the **Form** button. This creates a rectangle outlined by a red border on your page in Design view of Dreamweaver (see Figure 19.2).

Figure 19.2: The boundary area of the form displays in Design view.

The red outline is a visual indicator of the boundary area of the form. This outline displays if you have **View, Visual Aids, Invisible Elements** turned on. The outline doesn't display in Live view. The Property Inspector displays the form settings and options (see Figure 19.3).

Figure 19.3: By default, your form is named form1 in the ID field of the Property Inspector.

DREAMWEAVER TIP

To create a border around your form, you need to set it with CSS and the **Border** category.

These settings and options apply important values to the form that the back-end processing application needs to understand the form. Following is an overview of the settings.

- **ID**—Applies a name to the form. Dreamweaver generically names your form when you create it.

- **Action**—Type a URL or browse to set the processing application to set the form action. (You need to get the URL from your hosting server or back-end application programmer.)

- **Target**—Although most of the options for the **Target** field don't apply to forms, you can use the **_blank** option to have the form results display in a new window.

- **Class**—Applies a Class style rule to the form and form objects (see Chapter 7).

- **Method**—Determines the form-processing method. There are two types, POST and GET. POST is the more common method, though Dreamweaver by default sets this field to GET.

- **Enctype**—Sets the encoding type. Rarely used in forms; this option is usually left blank.

DEFINITION

POST is a form-processing method that transmits form data through the HTML header, making it invisible to the user. This is a more secure way to transmit data.

GET is a form-processing method that transmits form data sent on a URL query string, as in www.my_site.com/actions.cgi?name=Dave&email=dave@my_site. com. This processing method isn't as secure as POST.

If you're using a programmer for creating the back-end code or application to process your form data, ask this person how to set the form settings and values as shown in Figure 19.3. If you set them and you don't really know what you're doing, it can cause the back-end code to fail, which means the form fails. Some programmers will give you a list, while others ask you to use the generic settings that they change as needed.

Using Form Objects

Form objects are inserted inside the form, so they're enclosed in the `<form>` tag in Code view. Here's an overview of various form objects:

- **Text field**—Creates a single-line input field that accepts text data.

- **Text area**—Creates a multiple-line text area with a scrollbar that accepts text data.

- **Radio button**—Creates a button represented by a circle that users can select or leave blank. A group of radio buttons makes a radio group.

- **Checkbox**—A square that users can select or leave blank. A group of checkboxes makes a checkbox group.

- **Select list/menu**—Creates a pop-out menu, or a list of predefined values.

- **File field**—Creates a field that lets a visitor upload a file to the server.

- **Image field**—Sets an image to be used as a button in your form.

- **Hidden field**—An invisible field that can be set to transfer values to the processing server.

- **Jump menu**—A pop-out menu listing preset options.

- **Button**—A button for submitting or resetting a form.

Inserting Form Objects

To insert a form object, follow these steps:

DREAMWEAVER TIP

If you insert a form object before creating the form, Dreamweaver automatically creates a form around the form object. If you're in Design view, a prompt displays asking if you want to add the object to the form tag. Click **Yes** if you want Dreamweaver to create a form around the object.

1. Click inside the form and set your cursor where you want your form object to be located.

2. From the menu bar, choose **Insert, Form, Text Field**, or, in the Insert panel, in the **Forms** category, click the **Form Object** button you want to use. Either method opens the Input Tag Accessibility Attributes window (see Figure 19.4).

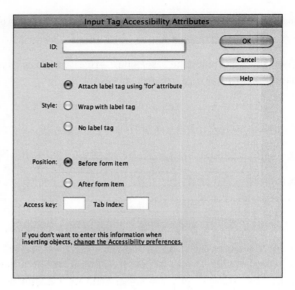

Figure 19.4: You can create both your form label and the input field in the Input Tag Accessibility Attributes window.

Here's an overview of the settings on the window:

- **ID**—Determines the ID name of the text field. This needs to be a unique one-word name, with no special characters except for the underscore (_).

- **Label**—Sets the display label for the field. This name is used by the form-processing application and is coupled with a value, which is the data the visitor inputs.

DREAMWEAVER TIP

Typically you set the ID and Label values to the same name. This helps to clarify the values from what is gathered in the form and what is transmitted to the back-end processing application.

- **Style**—The Style for a form object determines how the label and the form object are represented in HTML. You have a choice of **Attach label tag using "for" attribute**, **Wrap with label tag**, or **No label tag**. These Style options are discussed in the following section.

- **Position**—Sets the visual display for the position for the label, either before or after the field.

- **Access Key**—Determines an access key or combination of keys (like **Shift+T**) that lets the visitor jump to that field when pressed.

- **Tab Index**—Sets the tab order that lets a visitor press the **Tab** key to move through the various fields in the form.

Setting Input Tag for Accessibility

When you establish the Style option, you set the Label type for the form object. Dreamweaver presents you with three options (as described in the previous section) for Style.

The **Attach label tag using 'for' attribute** is the preferred option for accessibility. Each browser interprets this attribute differently. This option creates the HTML in a way that the label and the form object can be separated from each other, such as by putting the label in a table cell and the form object in the adjacent cell. This method also is best for *assistive technologies,* as it gives the user easier access to the form object. For instance, a checkbox form object is typically created with a checkbox and the object label describing the checkbox. Using the Attach label tag using 'for' attribute lets the user click the description of the checkbox to select the checkbox object, which is a common technique for choosing checkboxes and radio buttons.

> **DEFINITION**
>
> **Assistive technologies** are tools that help people maneuver your form. This could be a screen reader for low-vision individuals or keyboard combinations that users can use to jump to different fields in your form.

The Wrap with label tag option wraps the label tag around both the label and the form object. The label and the form object cannot be separated from each other.

The third option of No Label Tag creates the field without assigning it a label. This option is nice if you want to manually add your labels later in the form development.

The Wrap with Label tag using 'for' attribute is the most accessible option and is used most often in web forms today.

Adding a Text Field

To add a text field, from the menu bar, choose **Insert, Form, Text Field,** or, from the Insert panel, click the **Text Field** button in the **Form** category. Set your options for the Input Tag Accessibility Attributes window and click **OK**. This inserts the text field in your form. To select the text field, click the rectangular box represented in Design view of the Document window. The Property Inspector displays the text field attributes and values (see Figure 19.5).

Figure 19.5: *The Property Inspector displays more information for the field.*

You can set more settings for your text field through the Property Inspector. Here's an overview of those settings:

- **TextField**—Determines the ID name for the field.

- **Char Width**—Establishes a width for the box based on the number of characters.

- **Type**—Determines whether your text field is a single-line, multiline, or password field.

- **Max Char**—Establishes a maximum character value for a text field. It's wise to set a maximum character value, as this prevents spammers from inputting huge amounts of text into your fields.

- **Initial Value**—Establishes default information to display in the field, to prompt the visitor for the required information, as in "Please type your first name."

DEFINITION

The **Password** text field is used to create a password input field. This type of text field represents the user input with dots to hide the word from view. Be aware that this type of password isn't encrypted, meaning that it can be intercepted in the transmission process to the server.

Set these options based on how you want your text field to display in your form.

Adding a Text Area

A **text area** is basically a multiple-line text field that allows the visitor to input more text into a bigger area (you determine the size of the area). To insert this type of field, choose **Insert, Form, Textarea** from the menu bar. Text areas have a scrollbar, which makes it possible for the user to view a lot of data by scrolling through it (see Figure 19.6).

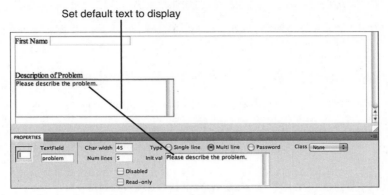

Figure 19.6: Init Value is set to display "Please describe the problem" in the Textarea field.

Adding Radio Buttons and Radio Group

Radio buttons represent a group of options with preset values. Users can select only one of the options in the group by selecting the individual button attached to that option. For instance, this form object is used often for establishing the visitor's gender, Male or Female. Each label has its own radio button and users can only select one. You must use at least two radio buttons for them to be functional. If you use a single button and the user selects it, they can't deselect it.

A radio group is a grouping of radio buttons. Always use Radio Group for creating your list of radio buttons. If you try to add multiple single radio buttons to create your own group, you must hand code them to create a proper group or the form will fail to return legible results. The Radio Group in Dreamweaver gives you a very easy way to create the proper coding in Design View.

To insert a radio button, choose **Insert, Form, Radio Button** from the menu bar (see Figure 19.7). To insert a radio group, choose **Insert, Form, Radio Group**.

Figure 19.7: The Property Inspector shows information on the Male radio button.

DREAMWEAVER TIP

Radio buttons and checkboxes always return consistent values because when the user selects an option, its associated value is also selected. This preset value is returned to the processing server.

Adding Checkboxes and a Checkbox Group

Checkboxes are similar to radio buttons, except that users can select multiple checkbox options in the Checkbox group. This type of form object lets users select multiple preset values for a single field (see Figure 19.8). For instance, you can use checkboxes to present a list of hobbies. You can list various hobbies, such as gardening, running, collecting stamps, and so on—and place a checkbox next to each one. Users can check off more than one hobby. Also, because a checkbox doesn't depend on a toggle in the same way a radio button does, you can have a single checkbox in your form.

To insert a checkbox, choose **Insert, Form, Checkbox** from the menu bar. To insert an entire group of checkboxes, choose **Insert, Form, Checkbox Group**.

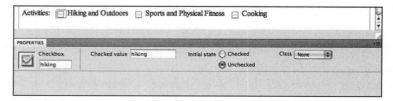

Figure 19.8: Users can select more than one of the checkbox buttons in this checkbox group. The Property Inspector shows information on the Hiking and Outdoors checkbox button.

Adding a Select (List/Menu) Field

Use the **Select (List/Menu)** form object to create a pop-out menu or a list of values. This type of form object is a great way to create a menu or list that has preset options to choose from, like a pop-out menu for establishing what time of day—morning, afternoon, or evening—for contacting the user. To insert a Select (List/Menu) object, choose **Insert, Forms, Select (List/Menu)** from the menu bar (see Figure 19.9).

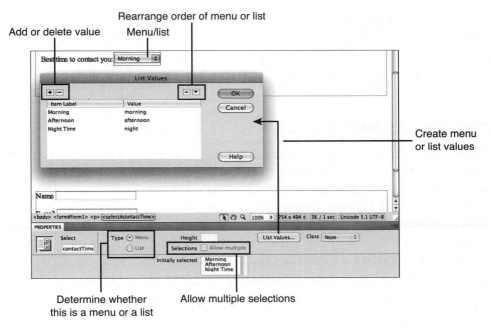

Figure 19.9: *When you insert a Select (List/Menu) object, you can determine its type—either a list or a menu—by selecting the options from the Property Inspector.*

The **Select (List/Menu)** object displays in your form. (If you have set this to a menu, you must use Live view or preview it in a browser to see the menu. However, you must turn off Live view to work again in Design view of Dreamweaver.)

Set the values for the **Select (List/Menu)** object by clicking the List Values button in the Property Inspector. This opens the List Values window (see Figure 19.12). Type your first item label in the active row, and then press **Tab** and type the value. To add a new item to the list or menu, click the **Plus** sign. This creates a new row into which you can type a new label and value. Repeat this process until you've created all your items.

To delete a list/menu item, select it in the List Values window and click the **minus** button.

Adding a Jump Menu

A Jump menu is similar to a **Select (List/Menu)**, but it actually jumps to a linked document. To create a Jump menu, choose **Insert, Form, Jump Menu** from the menu bar. This opens the Insert Jump Menu window (see Figure 19.10). For example, you can use a Jump Menu to help a user understand an acceptance agreement by creating menu options for jumping to different documents that provide more information about the agreement.

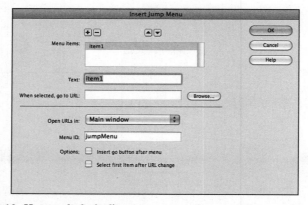

Figure 19.10: You can link the Jump menu to a document in your site or specify a URL to a document on another website.

In the Insert Jump Menu window, first set your options for the Menu items. As with the Select (List/Menu) object, use the **plus** and **minus** keys to add and delete menu items. Use the Text field to label the menu item; then set the URL or path to the document you want to link to in the **When Selected, Go to URL** field. If you want to target a new window or document in a frameset, click **Open URLS** in the menu and select the target.

You can set the Jump menu to have a "go" button to the right of it. That way, the visitor sets a menu choice and then clicks **Go** to jump to the identified linked document. To set this option on your Jump menu, select **Insert Go Button After Menu**.

The **Select First Item After URL Change** option sets the menu to display the first item in the list (see Figure 19.11). This is useful when you need to provide instructions for how to use the menu. For instance, if you have a list of five types of pets, you can create the first item in the list to say "Please select your favorite type of pet." This text automatically displays in the Jump Menu object on the screen, providing instructions to the user for using the menu. The user now knows that they need to select a type of pet from this menu prior to clicking the menu to access the list of options.

DREAMWEAVER TIP

You can change the word on the **Go** button in the Jump menu by using the Property Inspector. Just type the desired word in the **Value** field and **Go** will change to this value.

To see the functionality of the Jump menu, you need to preview it in a browser.

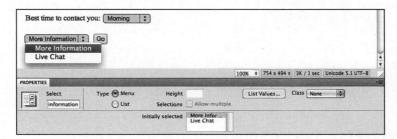

Figure 19.11: The Property Inspector shows information about your Jump menu. You can link your Jump menu to a document in your site or specify a URL to a document on another website.

DREAMWEAVER TIP

You can apply CSS and style rules to a form to format it. You can apply a Tag style rule to format the `<form>` tag, and you can apply Class style rules to format the individual form objects.

Adding Hidden Fields

Hidden fields are fields that are hidden from the user. They store user input such as the user's name. The next time the user visits the site, you can use this field to display his or her name. This type of field is often used for containing a parameter that's gathered from another form object, such as a person's name. You can then use this parameter in a web language like JavaScript to display the person's name with a welcome back message that displays when they visit the site again.

To create a hidden field, choose **Insert, Form, Hidden Field**. This type of field displays with an invisible symbol icon in the Design view (see Figure 19.12).

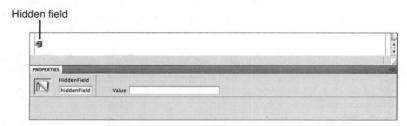

Figure 19.12: A number sign icon displays in Design view of the Document window, indicating the presence of a hidden field. The field's value is shown in the Property Inspector.

Creating Buttons

Every form needs a trigger to transmit the data to the processing application. This trigger is the **Submit** button. Browsers understand two button types that are also commonly used in a form: the **Submit** button and the **Reset** button. To insert a button into your form, choose **Insert, Form, Button** from the menu bar, or, from the Insert panel, click the **Form** category and click **Button**.

This opens the same window for inserting other form objects, the Input Tag Accessibility Attributes window (see Figure 19.13). If you use an ID and label of **Submit** or **Reset,** by default a browser understands the functionality of each type of button. The **Submit** button submits data to the specified server application, and the Reset button clears the form of data.

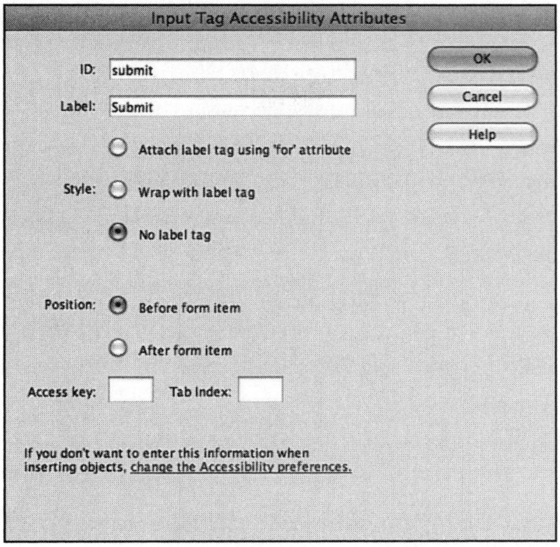

Figure 19.13: Use the values and ID of Submit and Reset to create a Submit or Reset button.

Click the button in the Document window, and notice that the Property Inspector lets you set the button functionality. You have three choices: **Submit**, **Reset**, or **None**. Select the functionality that you want your button to have by clicking the option. You can also modify the button name and value.

Spry Validation Form Objects

A Spry Validation object is part of the Spry Framework (see Chapter 20), which is part of a JavaScript library. This library offers a quick way to access predeveloped functionality and use that functionality in your web page. Web designers often use Spry Validation objects with forms, to validate the user's responses to your form fields. Not only does this ensure consistency in the user input, such as making sure a field contains a valid e-mail address, but it also can help stop spammers from filling your page with nonsense. Based on the Spry Validation object inserted, the validation is displayed either as a certain color indicating correct or incorrect input, or as a visual message to indicate correct or incorrect data.

Dreamweaver offers seven Spry Validation form objects (see Figure 19.14).

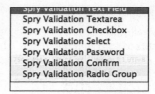

Figure 19.14: These Spry Validation objects create the basic form object but include validation of user input.

To insert a Spry Validation object, choose **Insert, Form, [Spry Validation Object Name]**. This opens the Input Tag Accessibility Attributes window that also displays when a form object is inserted into a page. Set the fields just as you would with a regular form object. Click **OK**, and the Spry Validation object is inserted in the page. To select this object, click the blue tag at the top left of the object (see Figure 19.15).

The Property Inspector lets you configure the validation for the form object. Each Spry Validation object has different validation settings for each object type.

Spry Validation Text Field

The Spry Validation Text Field is probably the most commonly used Spry Validation form object. This object lets you set restrictions on the type of text to be input into a text field. It color-codes correct and incorrect responses. For instance, you can set this to be restricted to accept only an e-mail address; if a user types in a name instead of an e-mail address, the response displays in red, indicating that it's incorrect.

To set validation criteria, click the Spry Validation object in the document. The Property Inspector displays the validation options (see Figure 19.15).

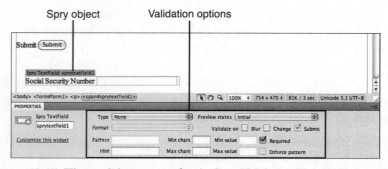

Figure 19.15: These validation types for the Spry Validation Text Field cover the more common uses of validating certain types of text field data.

When you insert a Spry Validation object into your form, Dreamweaver creates a folder labeled **SpryAssets** in your Files panel. This folder holds all the JavaScript and CSS style sheets for creating the functionality and display of the object.

Spry Validation Criteria

Here's an overview of the Spry Validation Text Field options.

- **Type**—Sets the type of object validation. Choose a type of data from the pop-out menu; options include date, time, e-mail address, zip code, and phone number (see Figure 19.16).

DREAMWEAVER DON'T

Don't use a form object for gathering Social Security numbers. The Spry Validation doesn't provide a secure method of inputting/transferring data. None of these Spry Validation form elements are secure as presented. It takes a back-end programmer to provide encrypted data methods to make this data secure.

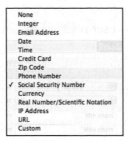

Figure 19.16: These validation types cover the most common uses of validating certain types of text field data.

- **Preview States**—Sets how to indicate an incorrect response.
- **Validate On**—Sets when to validate a field. Blur validates a field when a user moves to the next field, Change validates a field when anything is changed in the field, and Submit validates a field upon submission of the form.

DREAMWEAVER TIP

Validate On works best as Blur for fields that require typing. Blur is a JavaScript term and works hand-in-hand with HTML forms. If you set the validation option to Change for a field that requires typing, the invalid indicator displays after each letter typed because each keystroke is a change in the field.

- **Min/Max Char**—Specifies the minimum or maximum number of characters for a field. If the user types in too few or too many characters, the invalid indicator displays.

- **Min/Max Value**—Specifies a numerical value that must be met. Sets the minimum and maximum value for the field.

Other Spry Validation Form Objects

Each Spry Validation form object has similar validation criteria (see Figure 19.16). Based on the object functionality, the Property Inspector displays the validation criteria options.

Tutorial: Creating a Contact Us Form

All websites can benefit from a form to promote customer communication. The Walkabout Travel site needs a Contact Us form to allow their clients to contact them with issues, questions, and concerns. In Chapter 10 you created the framework through a table for the Contact Us form in the web page contact.html. This tutorial covers the creation of the form and form objects for this page. Follow these steps:

1. Define the **Chapter19** folder in the **Tutorial** folder as a new site root folder. You'll use this defined site for the tutorial.

2. Open **contact.html**, which is the Contact Us page. You're going to create a form for client communication in this page.

3. The first step in creating a form communication is to insert a form in the web page. Click to make the table active on the page by either clicking the table border or by clicking the `<table>` tag in the Tag Selector (see Figure 19.17).

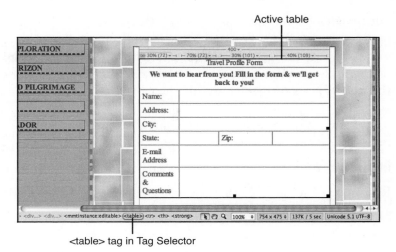

Figure 19.17: This table creates the structure for the form.

4. Press the **Left/Back** arrow key on your keyboard to set your cursor in front of the table. Press **Return** (Mac)/**Enter** (PC) to create a blank line. Position your cursor in the blank line.

5. Insert a form through the Insert panel. Select the **Forms** category and then click the **Form** button. This inserts a form at the top of the table (see Figure 19.18).

Figure 19.18: The red outline indicates the form area.

6. Click the table to make it active, and then cut and paste it into the Form outline by using **Edit, Cut** and **Edit, Paste** from the menu bar. (You can also click the <table> tag in the Tag Selector to select the entire table.) This wraps the form around the table. Delete any blank lines under the table so that the form wraps tighter around the table.

7. Notice that the table already has text that you can use for labels. You need to convert this text to labels to make the form accessible. To do this highlight **Name:**, being sure to include the colon. Now convert this to a label by choosing **Insert, Form, Label** from the menu bar. This converts the text to a label.

8. Repeat step 7 for all the other text you created to be a label in your table.

9. Now let's add the input fields. Click to set your cursor in the second column to the right of the **Name** label. The first input field will go here.

10. Insert a text field by clicking the **Text Field** button from the Insert panel under the **Form** category.

11. This opens the Input Tag Accessibility Attributes window. Set the settings as indicated in Figure 19.19, and then click **OK**. 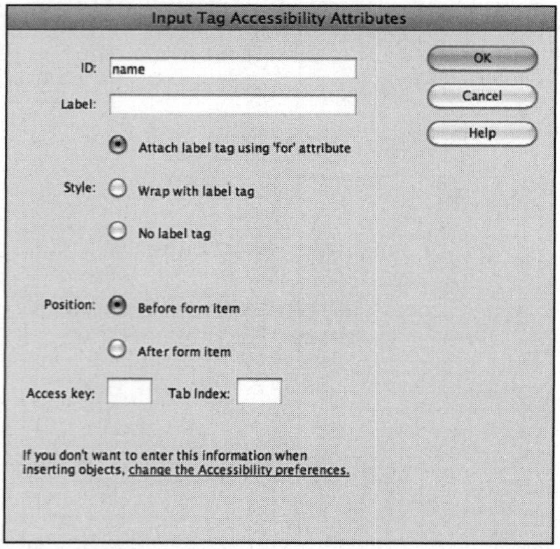

Figure 19.19: The Input Tag Accessibility Attributes window. Since you don't want Dreamweaver to generate a label when it creates the text field, don't set a name in the Label field.

12. A **Text Field** form object displays in the second column next to the **Name** label. Click inside this field to focus Dreamweaver on the field. In the Property Inspector, set the settings as indicated in Figure 19.20.

Figure 19.20: This text field has a display width of 25 characters, but it can hold a maximum of 75 characters. That should be enough for even the longest first and last names.

13. Repeat steps 9 through 11 to create text fields for address, city, and state. Set your ID for each of these input fields to a name that makes sense with the field ("state" for the state field, "address" for the address field, and so on).

14. Now set the Char Width and Max Chars for these new fields. Click in the fields and, in the Property Inspector, set the Char Width and Max Chars to the following:

> Set the Address and City fields to a **Char Width** of **25** and **Max Chars** to **75**.
>
> Set the State field to a **Char Width** of **5** and a **Max Chars** to **25**.

For the **Zip** field, let's create a Spry Validation Text Field that's restricted to only numbers:

1. Click to set your cursor in the cell after the Zip label in the table. Choose **Insert, Form, Spry Validation Text Field**.

2. In the Input Tag Accessibility Attributes window, set the **ID** to zip. Leave the other settings at the default. Click **OK**.

3. This inserts a Spry text field in this cell. Click the tab at the top left of the Spry text field to make it active. In the Property Inspector, set the options to match those in Figure 19.21.

*Figure 19.21: The Zip text field is limited to just numbers by selecting **Zip Code** for **Type**.*

4. Click inside the Zip text field to set your cursor in the field. In the Property Inspector, set the **Char Width** to 10 and the **Max Char** to 10 as well.

5. Save your file by choosing **File, Save** from the menu bar. A message displays indicating that Dreamweaver is going to copy some dependent files to your site's root folder (see Figure 19.22). Click **OK** to copy these files.

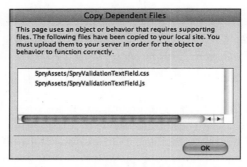

Figure 19.22: To support the Spry Validation text field widget, Dreamweaver creates additional files that are stored in your site's root folder.

6. Now let's test the form by previewing it in Live view. Click the **Live View** button in the Document toolbar to test your form. Test all fields, especially the Zip field. Type a letter instead of numbers in this field. It should display **Invalid Format** when you click in another field or press **Tab** to move to the next field.

7. Exit **Live view** and click in the cell to the right of the **E-mail Address** label.

Now let's insert a Spry Validation Text Field to validate an e-mail address. Follow these steps:

1. In the Insert panel, click the **Spry Validation Text Field** button in the **Form** category. This opens the Input Tag Accessibility window.

2. In the **ID** field type **email** and leave the other fields at the default settings. Click **OK** to close this window and insert the Spry text field.

3. Click the tab at the top left of the Spry text field to select it. Set your Property Inspector to match Figure 19.23.

Figure 19.23: *The E-mail Address text field is set to validate e-mail addresses. The user must input the @ sign for validation.*

4. Now set the width of the email Spry text field. Click inside the text field to focus Dreamweaver on this field and, in the Property Inspector, set the **Char Width** to **25** and the **Max Chars** to **100**.

5. Click in the cell to the right of the **Comments & Questions** label. Let's insert a multiple-lined text area field here to collect more information from the client.

6. Insert a text area field by choosing **Insert, Form, Textarea**. In Input Tag Accessibility Attributes, set **ID** to **questions** and leave the other settings at the default. Click **OK**.

7. A multi-lined text area displays. Click it to make it active. In the Property Inspector, set the options to match Figure 19.24.

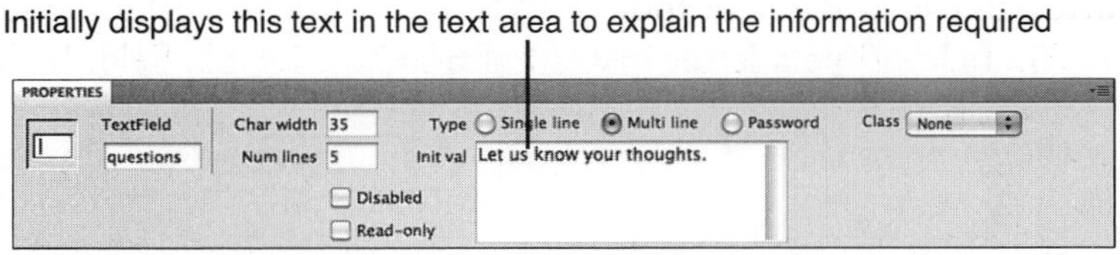

Initially displays this text in the text area to explain the information required

Figure 19.24: *This Questions text field is set to display five lines of text up to 35 characters in width.*

Let's now add a checkbox group to collect information on which tours interest clients. We also need an area for the Submit and Reset buttons. A couple new rows need to be added to the table. Follow these steps:

1. Highlight the **Comments and Questions** row by clicking and dragging the two cells that make this row.

2. Insert two new rows by choosing **Modify, Table, Insert Rows or Columns** from the menu bar.

3. In the Insert Rows or Columns window, set the **Insert** option to **Rows,** set **Number of Rows** to **2,** and set **Where** to **Below the Selection**. Click **OK**. Dreamweaver inserts two rows below the Questions and Comments row.

4. In the first cell of the top new row, click and type **Where Do You Want to Go?**.

5. Now let's add a checkbox group. Click in the cell to the right of this new row, and choose **Insert, Form, Checkbox Group** from the menu bar. This opens the Checkbox Group window (see Figure 19.25).

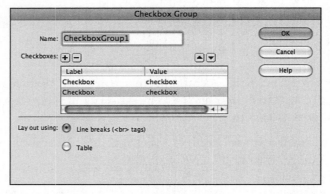

Figure 19.25: Use the plus and minus buttons to create and delete checkboxes.

6. Set the name of the Checkbox group to **Tours** by typing this into the **Name** field.

7. Now create the five tours as checkbox items by the five destinations for Walkabout Tours. In the first field, under **Label**, type **Ireland**. In the **Value** field, type **ireland**. You have just set the ID and value of the checkbox. In the second row, type **British Isles** in the **Label** field and **britishisles** in the **Value** field. Click the **plus** button to add another row. Type **China, china** for the label and value. Click the **plus** again and type **Peru, peru**. Repeat; create one more row and type **Ecuador, ecuador**. Click **OK** to close this window and create the check box group (see Figure 19.26).

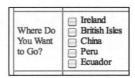

Figure 19.26: Because these are checkboxes, the user can select any or all of them to indicate tour interest.

8. Now it's time to add the buttons. First, let's merge the two cells of the last row in the table. Click and highlight both cells. Then choose **Modify, Table, Merge Cells** from the menu bar. This merges the two cells into one cell.

9. Click to set your cursor in this one-cell row. To create a Submit button, choose **Insert, Form, Button** from the menu bar.

10. In the Input Tag Accessibility Attributes window, set **ID** to **Submit**. Leave the other settings at the default and click **OK**. A Submit button displays in the blank row.

11. Repeat steps 9 through 10 to insert a second button and name this one **Reset** for the **ID**.

12. The second button displays, but it has the same button label as the other button. Select this button by clicking it and, in the Property Inspector, change **Value** to **Reset**. Set **Action** to **Reset form** by clicking this option.

13. Now let's center the two buttons in the row. Click and highlight both buttons. In the Property Inspector, choose **Class, CenterIt** to center the buttons in your form (see Figure 19.27).

14. Click the **Placeholder** image in the display_area Div tag and delete it by pressing the **Delete** key on your keyboard.

15. Save your file by choosing **File, Save** from the menu bar and preview it in a browser. Test your form functionality by filling out all the form fields.

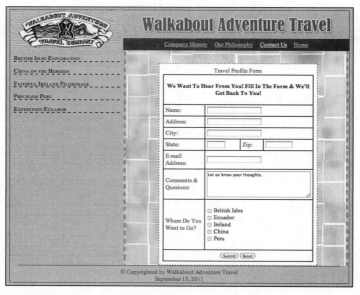

Figure 19.27: Your finished Contact Us page.

DREAMWEAVER TIP

Due to the many different form-processing applications, we can't give instructions for setting the form action. To create the correct form action settings for transmitting form communications, talk with your server administrator.

The Least You Need to Know

- You can use forms to create two-way communication.
- Form objects must be inserted in a form on a web page. If you forget to insert a form first, when you insert the form object, Dreamweaver automatically inserts a form surrounding the form object.
- Form objects include text fields, radio buttons, and menus.
- Use Spry Validation form objects to validate user responses.

The Interactive Spry Widget

In This Chapter

* Using the Spry Framework to create widgets
* Creating a pop-out menu bar with the Spry Menu Bar widget
* Organizing and structuring large amounts of data with the Spry Tabbed Panels or Spry Accordion widgets
* Displaying information based on user interaction with the Spry Collapsible Panel
* Creating ToolTips with the Spry ToolTip widget

In Chapter 19, you learned a little about the Spry Framework of widgets. You learned to use the Spry Validation form objects to create a form. This chapter looks at other Spry widgets preinstalled on Dreamweaver.

Overview of the Spry Framework

The Spry Framework consists of HTML, CSS, and JavaScript. These three languages are used to create widgets. The HTML provides the structure for the widget, the CSS provides the formatting, and the JavaScript provides the functionality. The JavaScript is stored in a library that's accessible to the widget. Widgets open up a huge realm of possibilities for different tools and functionality for web design.

Spry Widgets in Dreamweaver CS5.5

To insert a Dreamweaver Spry widget, choose **Insert, Spry** from the menu bar. This displays the following list of widgets:

- **Spry Menu Bar**—Creates a menu bar with pop-out or pop-up menus
- **Spry Tabbed Panels**—Creates a tabbed panel set for presenting lots of information
- **Spry Accordion**—Creates an accordion-style panel for presenting lots of information
- **Spry Collapsible Panel**—Creates a collapsible panel for presenting lots of information on a web page
- **Spry ToolTip**—Creates a pop-out message providing the name or description of an object you hover your mouse over.

The following sections take a closer look at each of these valuable tools.

Spry Menu Bar

The Spry Menu Bar widget creates menu bars and pop-out menu functionality. To insert a Spry menu bar, choose **Insert, Spry, Spry Menu Bar.** This opens the Spry Menu Bar window (see Figure 20.1).

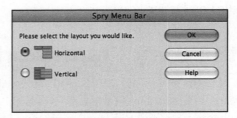

Figure 20.1: The Spray Menu Bar window lets you choose either a vertical or a horizontal layout for your menu bar.

Select either **Horizontal** or **Vertical** for the structure of your menu bar and then click **OK**. Dreamweaver inserts the Spry Menu Bar widget in your page. By default, the menu bar has four menu items, some set up with submenus (see Figure 20.2).

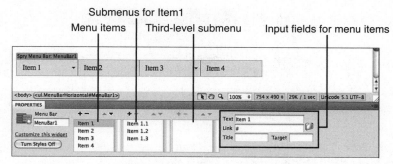

Figure 20.2: *Change the names of the default menu and submenus through the input fields located on the right of the Property Inspector.*

You can modify the Spry widget menu bar by selecting the menu item and then typing the new menu or submenu text, link, title, and target in the input fields on the right of the Property Inspector.

You can also edit a menu item by double-clicking it in the Document window and replacing the highlight text with the text you want to display.

To select an individual menu, click its border in the document window. The Property Inspector reveals other editable properties and attributes that you can change (see Figure 20.3).

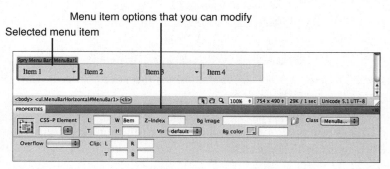

Figure 20.3: *Click on an individual menu to see other editable properties in the Property Inspector.*

This menu item has a Class style rule applied to it, and you can customize the widget through the CSS style rules. When you insert a widget, Dreamweaver automatically adds the external style sheets that control the widget's appearance in the CSS Styles panel (see Figure 20.4).

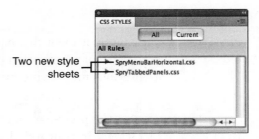

Figure 20.4: *These two style sheets contain all the style rules for formatting the Spry Menu Bar widget and the Spry Tabbed Panels widget.*

When you save a web page that has a Spry widget in it, a message displays letting you know that other documents have been added to your site (see Figure 20.5). These are the external style sheets that support the display of the widget. As the message indicates, these files need to be uploaded to the hosting server when you post your site, to support the display of the inserted widget.

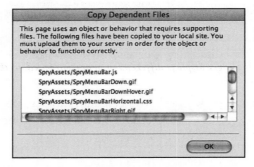

Figure 20.5: *Scroll through the list of additional files to see what was added to your site.*

Click the **Live View** button to test the widget's functionality. Remember to exit Live view to work again in Design view.

DREAMWEAVER TIP

Internet Explorer doesn't automatically allow you to run the JavaScript that makes Spry widgets functional. You'll get a message indicating that the JavaScript is blocked, but you can click a button to allow the blocked content to display.

Spry Tabbed Panels

The Spry Tabbed Panels widget creates a web element that has tabs across the top. You can click each tab to access a new display of information for that tab. This type of functionality is used a lot in other applications for viewing information about options and settings.

This type of widget is great for organizing the presentation of large amounts of information. To insert a Spry Tabbed Panel widget in your web document, choose **Insert, Spry, Spry Tabbed Panels** from the menu bar. Dreamweaver inserts the widget into your page (see Figure 20.6).

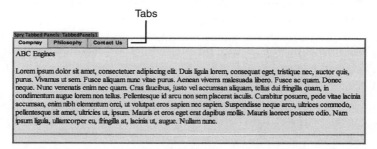

Figure 20.6: *This widget displays different information based on the active tab.*

By default, this widget has two tabs. You can add, modify, and delete the tabs through the Property Inspector. Click anywhere in the widget to select it, and the Property Inspector displays the tab information (see Figure 20.7).

DREAMWEAVER TIP

Sometimes just clicking in a widget in Design View won't bring up the Properties Inspector options. If you move your mouse over the widget, a blue label tab appears; click the blue label tab and the Properties bar displays the widget options.

Active Spry Tabbed Panels widget

Add and delete panels

Rearrange panel order

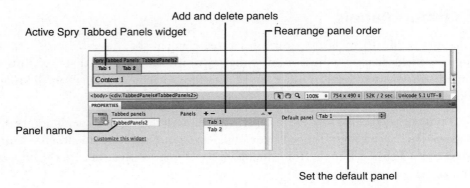

Panel name

Set the default panel

Figure 20.7: Use the plus and minus buttons to add and delete panel tabs. Use the Order buttons to rearrange the order of the panel tabs.

The plus and minus buttons create tabs based on the default naming convention of Tab1, Tab2, and so on. You can edit the name of a tab directly in Design view. Double-click a tab name to highlight it and then type the new name.

DREAMWEAVER TIP

Some widgets allow you to change the displayed name in the Property Inspector; others, like the Spry Tabbed Panels widget, require you to use the Design view and click the tab name to make the changes.

Each panel has its own content area. To add content to the Spry Tabbed Panels widget, you need to be able to access each panel. To do this, hover your mouse over a nonactive tab, and you'll see an eye icon (see Figure 20.8). Click the **Eye icon** to display the associated panel tab.

Eye icon

Nonactive tab

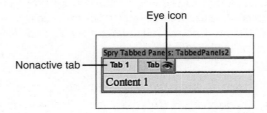

Figure 20.8: The Eye icon lets you switch between tabs to add your panel content.

The panel area presents the information. You can insert any web elements that you need for your information. You're not restricted in what you can add to a panel as long as it's a web element such as text, tables, Div tags, or images.

You can test the panel functionality in Dreamweaver by viewing it in Live view. It's also always a good idea to view it in a browser.

Spry Accordion Panel

The Spry Accordion Panel widget is similar to the Spry Tabbed Panels widget, but with one major difference: it displays information vertically (see Figure 20.9).

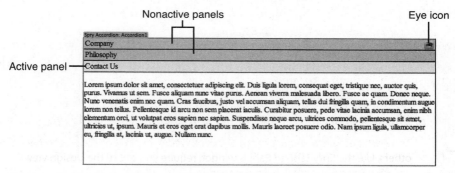

Figure 20.9: *The Eye icon switches between the horizontal tabs to display that associated panel content.*

You can modify this panel using the same techniques you use to modify the Tabbed Panels widget. Select the widget to access the widget options in the Property Inspector. To change the names of your panel, select the names in Design view and type in the new names. To add content, focus Dreamweaver on the panel by clicking the **Eye icon**; then add the desired content.

Spry Collapsible Panel

The Collapsible Panel widget focuses on just one panel area (see Figure 20.10). It's a great feature for displaying information that doesn't necessarily need to be shown in the initial state of the page. The Collapsible Panel can also have all panels open at the same time.

Spry collapsible panel

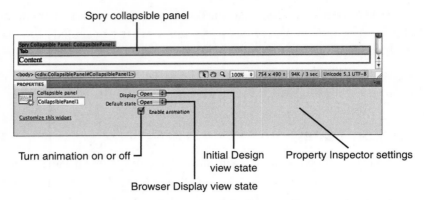

Turn animation on or off ⌐

Initial Design view state

Property Inspector settings

Browser Display view state

*Figure 20.10: A Spry collapsible panel and the Property Inspector showing the panel information. Select the **Enable Animation** option to turn on an animated display of the panel area opening and closing.*

As with other widgets, click anywhere in the **Collapsible Panel** widget to select it. The Property Inspector displays the options for modifying it. You can set the initial state of the widget, which is how it first displays in both Dreamweaver and in a browser. This can be with the panel either collapsed or expanded. For instance, you can set the initial state of the widget to be expanded when viewed in the Design view of Dreamweaver, but you can set the initial state to be collapsed when viewed in the browser.

Collapsible panels are added one at a time. You must insert a new Spry Collapsible Panel widget for each content area you want to display this way.

To edit the tab or content of the panel, click in that area and make your edits directly in Design view.

DREAMWEAVER TIP

Edit the CSS style rules associated with this widget to change its appearance.

Spry ToolTip

The Spry ToolTip widget displays an explanatory message called a ToolTip when a user hovers a mouse over it (see Figure 20.11). You create this functionality through a trigger and a trigger action (see Figure 20.12). The trigger is the text that you create above the ToolTip widget. The trigger action is when the user hovers the mouse over the trigger text.

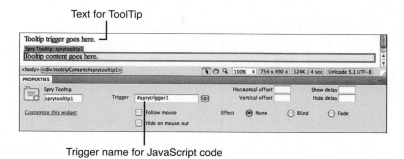

Figure 20.11: A Spry ToolTip widget displays a ToolTip when the user hovers the mouse over the trigger text.

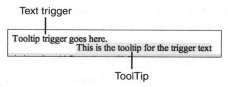

Figure 20.12: You can modify the trigger text and the ToolTip that displays in Design view and the Property Inspector.

You can customize your ToolTip in various ways. Click the widget to make it active; the Property Inspector shows the options that you can set for this widget. Here's an overview of these settings:

- **Trigger**—Names the trigger action. This name is used in the JavaScript code to create the trigger action that displays the ToolTip.

- **Horizontal/Vertical Offset**—Sets how far from the user's mouse the ToolTip displays.

- **Show/Hide Delay**—Sets the number of seconds that it takes for the ToolTip to close after the user moves the mouse from the trigger.

- **Follow Mouse**—Makes the ToolTip follow the user's mouse as it hovers over the ToolTip.

- **Hide on Mouse Out**—Hides the ToolTip when the user moves the mouse outside of the trigger text.

- **Effect**—Creates transition effects for the display of the ToolTip. These transitions are similar to transition effects you can create in Microsoft PowerPoint for slide transitions. You can choose **None**, **Blind**, or **Fade**.

> **DREAMWEAVER TIP**
>
> You can see some of the Spry ToolTip effects and transitions only by previewing the page in a browser. Live view supports many of the displays, but not all of them.

Tutorial: Add a Spry Accordion Widget to Your Website

In this tutorial, you're going to add a Spry Accordion widget to the Walkabout Travel site for displaying information about each of the featured tours of Walkabout Travel. These tours are accessed through the left sidebar menu. Each of the tours has distinct areas of information that need to be communicated. This widget creates an organized presentation of each tour. Let's get started:

1. Define the **Chapter20** folder in the **Tutorial** folder as a new site root folder. Use this defined site for the tutorial.

2. Open the **china.html** file. This is a partially developed page for advertising the China tour.

3. The content for this panel is located in a text file. In the Files panel, double-click the **china.txt** file to open it. Because it is a text file, it opens in Code view. You can click the tabs at the top of the Document window to switch between the two documents.

4. Click the **China.html** tab at the top left of the document window to make it the active document. Click in the **display_area** region on the page, select the placeholder object, and press the **Delete** key.

5. For a Spry widget to work in the **display_area** editable text area, you need to insert a Div tag to hold the widget. Choose **Insert, Layout Objects, Div** tag.

6. In the Insert Div Tag window, keep the **Insert** field set to **At Insertion Point**. You're not going to create any CSS rules for this Div, so click in the **ID** field and type **spryWidget**. Click **OK** to create the Div tag with an **ID** of **spryWidget**.

7. If it's not already highlighted, highlight the default text that's created with the new Div tag and delete it. Now insert a Spry Accordion widget by choosing **Insert, Spry, Spry Accordion** from the menu bar (see Figure 20.13).

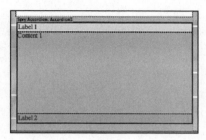

Figure 20.13: By default, Dreamweaver creates two tabs generically named Label1 and Label2.

8. Click the widget tab to make it active. In the Property Inspector, click the **Plus** button twice to add two more tabs, to make the total number of tabs four.

9. Use the **Arrange Order** buttons to list the labels from 1 to 4 in order by selecting the label and then clicking the **up** or **down** order buttons.

10. Let's name the tabs. In Design view of Dreamweaver, double-click the **Label1** text in the widget to highlight it. Replace this text with **Tour Includes** (see Figure 20.14).

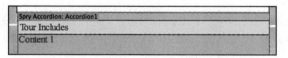

Figure 20.14: You can type whatever you want for the Accordion Label.

11. Repeat Step 11 to create the other tabs. Replace **Label2** with **Tour Does Not Include, Label3** with **Tour Itinerary,** and **Label4** with **Contact Information** (see Figure 20.15).

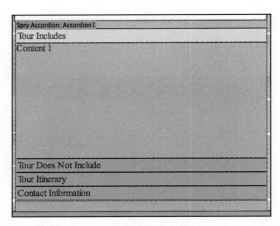

Figure 20.15: You can have as many labels as you need to represent your data.

12. If the "Tour Includes" content area is active (opened), move on to step 14. If this area is closed, make the content area display by hovering your mouse over the label area and clicking the **Eye icon** when it displays. The **Content1** area displays.

13. Access the **china.txt** document by clicking its document tab in the Document window. Highlight the text beginning with **The following services and amenities are included in this tour:,** all the way down to **All hotel, food, & land based taxes** (see Figure 20.16). Copy it by choosing **Edit, Copy** from the menu bar. Return to the **china_tour.html** document by clicking this tab in the Document window.

14. Replace the Content1 text with the copied information by selecting **Content1** in the widget and then pasting the copied information.

15. Format the first line of text, **The following services and amenities are included in this tour:,** with a **Heading 3** tag (see Chapter 6). Highlight the included features below this heading and create a bulleted list of this information by clicking the **Unordered List** button in the Property Inspector (see Chapter 6). Your Spry Accordion should look like Figure 20.17.

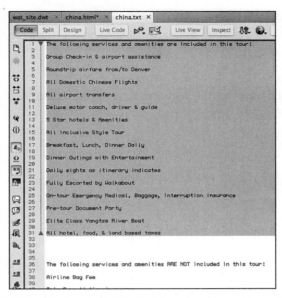

Figure 20.16: *This text document is broken into four content areas. You'll see three blank lines sectioning each content area.*

Figure 20.17: *Format this panel area as you wish to get the look you want.*

16. Repeat steps 13 through 16 to create the other content for development of the panel area. Find the associated text information in the **china.txt** document for each content area.

17. Save your file and then preview it in a browser. You will see a message indicating that the external style sheets need to also be saved. Answer **Yes** to this message to save all supporting files of this document. The page displays in a browser (see Figure 20.18).

Figure 20.18: *The Spry Accordion widget is set up as you need, displaying information based on topic selected.*

Next, let's modify some of the CSS style rules that affect the appearance of this widget:

1. Open the CSS Style panel.

2. Expand the **SpryAccordion.css** style sheet so you can see all the rules that format this widget.

3. Locate the **.AccordionPanelTab** style rule and select it. In the Properties section of the panel, change **Background-color** to **#663300**.

4. Locate the **.AccordionPanelTabHover** style rule and select it. In the Properties section of the panel, change the color to a bright green by clicking the color pallet button and choosing a bright green color from the color pallet.

DREAMWEAVER TIP

When typing a color in hexadecimal format for a property of a style rule, make sure you include the # in front of the six-digit number. Dreamweaver doesn't recognize the hexadecimal number without the preceding #.

5. Locate the Compound style rule of **.AccordionFocused .AccordionPanelTab** and select it. In the Properties section of the panel, change **Background-color** to a **#336600**.

6. Locate the Compound style rule of **.AccordionFocused .AccordionPanelOpen .AccordionPanelTab** and select it. In the Properties section of the panel, change **Background-color** to **#663300**.

7. Now let's add a property to the **.AccordionPanelTab** style rule to change the color of the font in the tab area. Locate the **.AccordionPanelTab** style rule and double-click it to open the CSS Rule Definition window. In the **Type** category, type **#cccc99** in the Color field. Click **OK** to close this window and apply the new color for the font.

8. Finally, let's adjust the color for the display of a panel tab when it is opened. Locate the **.AccordionPanelOpen .AccordionPanelTab** style rule in the CSS Style panel, and in the properties section change the Background-color to **#336600**. Then locate the **.AccordionPanelOpen .AccordionPanelTabHover** style rule and in the properties section change the color to **#ffffff**.

9. Save the document by choosing **File, Save** from the menu bar. If you see a message indicating that other files need to be saved, answer **Yes**. Then preview the page in a browser (see Figure 20.19).

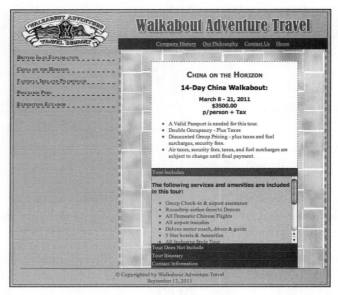

Figure 20.19: Your web page and Spry Accordion widget should look similar to this figure.

The Least You Need to Know

- The Spry Framework offers web designers an easy way to get advanced functionality and programming for a website.
- Use the Spry Menu Bar widget to create a pop-out menu bar.
- Use the Spry Tabbed Panels or Spry Accordion widgets to organize and structure large amounts of data.
- Use the Spry Collapsible Panel widget to display information based on user interaction.
- Use the Spry ToolTip Widget to create ToolTips for trigger text.

Other Widgets and Dreamweaver Extensions

In This Chapter

- Exploring the world of third-party Spry widgets
- Inserting third-party widgets with the Adobe Widget Browser
- Modifying Spry widgets
- Expanding Dreamweaver's functionality with extensions

Chapter 20 introduced you to the five Spry widgets that come preinstalled in Dreamweaver, but many other widgets are available outside the Dreamweaver application. This chapter introduces you to the world of third-party widgets that you can download and insert into your web page to further increase its functionality. Some widgets create cool-looking buttons; others create social networking functionality and links. Still other widgets generate maps, slideshows, zoom functionality, and calendar programs. There's probably a widget for just about anything you can think of. The Adobe Exchange website provides an extensive list of other Spry widgets to extend the functionality of your website.

This chapter also covers the Dreamweaver extension. An extension is a predetermined set of functions that you can add to Dreamweaver to extend its basic functionality. This could be a sitemap generator, a shopping cart, a report extension that modifies the preset reports that Dreamweaver creates, or just about anything else. Just like Spry widgets, if you can think of a function you'd like on your website, there's probably an extension for it.

What Is a Spry Widget?

Spry widgets are predeveloped web objects that perform a set function. Some of them are free; others cost money. You can customize the widgets to create very advanced programming in your website.

The Adobe Exchange website hosts many of these third-party widgets. You can access this site through the **Insert, Widget** menu bar command and then click the **Widget Browser** link in the lower-left corner of the window (see Figure 21.1).

Adobe Exchange link

Figure 21.1: This website is updated often with new widgets.

DREAMWEAVER TIP

You can find other widgets at www.protopage.com or by searching the Internet through the keyword phrase of "third party widgets".

Installing the Adobe Widget Browser

To insert a third-party widget from Adobe's website, you need to install the Widget Browser. When you access the Adobe Exchange site and try to view the available widgets, if you don't have the Widget Browser installed, the site will prompt you to install it. Follow the prompts and install the software.

You can then explore the list of widgets on the Adobe Exchange site.

Inserting Spry Widgets

To insert a Spry widget, you first need to download the widget to your computer. If you're using a Spry widget from the Adobe Exchange site, you'll need to log in to Adobe Exchange.

Click the widget you're interested in. A screen displays with more information about the widget (see Figure 21.2).

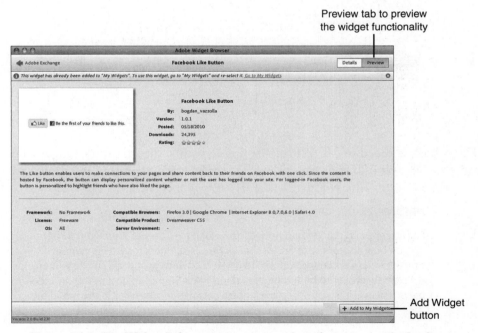

Figure 21.2: The Widget Information screen provides information on the developer, the browsers the widget works with, the cost, and an overall description of the widget's functionality.

Click the **Add to My Widget** button in the lower-right corner to add the widget to your My Widget library. The next screen presents the Widget License screen. Click **Accept** to accept the terms and download the widget to your computer and load it into the My Widget library. A window appears telling you that the widget was successfully downloaded (see Figure 21.3).

> **DREAMWEAVER TIP**
>
> The My Widget library is integrated into Adobe Exchange and stores all downloaded widgets. It's linked to your Adobe ID, and you can access it through Adobe Exchange. When you choose **Insert, Widget** from the Dreamweaver menu bar, you can see all the widgets stored in the **My Widget** library.

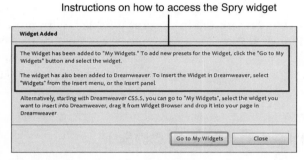

Figure 21.3: This widget is accessible through the Insert menu command or the Insert panel.

The widget is added to My Widgets and is accessible directly in Dreamweaver. You can now insert it into your web pages for more advanced website functionality.

> **DREAMWEAVER TIP**
>
> Pay attention to the "Widget Added" download message, as it provides information on how and where to access the widget. All widgets have their own set process for use and the command to insert them into your page can be in many different locations in the Dreamweaver interface. Some can be a button in a toolbar or the Insert panel; others might be a new menu command in the menu bar.

Modify a Spry Widget

Some widgets don't allow any modifications, but others let you customize them a bit. For example, a slideshow widget might let you add your own photos. You'll find instructions for modifying the widget in the widget instructions (see Figure 21.3). Most modifications are easy to complete. The **Widget Information** window on the Adobe Exchange site also provides information on modifying the widget.

Click the **Spry widget** tab to select the widget. The Property Inspector identifies the editable areas for the widget. Change these options to modify the widget.

Customizing a Spry Widget with CSS

Spry widgets are formatted with CSS. Since you now know a little about CSS (see Chapters 7, 12, and 15 for more), you can look at the style rules that create the look and design of the widget. You can customize the widget by changing any of the style rules and their properties. For example, you might change the border width or adjust the font face, style, and color, or even add background images. By customizing the predeveloped Spry widget, you can better integrate it with your overall website design.

Dreamweaver Extensions

An extension is a predetermined set of functions that you can add to Dreamweaver to have even more functionality. You can see the various extensions that have been created for the Adobe Suite of software by visiting the Adobe Marketplace and Exchange. You can access this site by choosing **Help, Dreamweaver Exchange** (see Figure 21.4).

This site has widgets mixed in with the extensions. You can preview the various widgets and extensions by browsing the site. Many of these extensions are free, but others are for purchase. When you find the one you want, click the **Download** button (if it's free) or the **Purchase** button. You'll be prompted to log in to your Adobe account and, if purchasing the extension, provide payment information.

When you're logged in to your Adobe account, a message displays confirming that you're about to open and download an extension (see Figure 21.5).

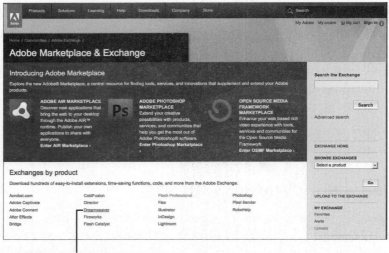

Dreamweaver Exchange

Figure 21.4: Click the Dreamweaver link to see other widgets and extensions that have been created just for Dreamweaver.

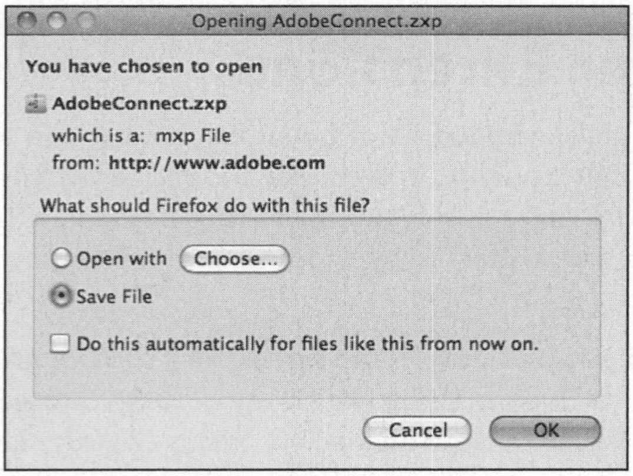

Figure 21.5: You can open the widget directly from Adobe's site or you can save the file to your computer.

You have the choice of either opening the extension or saving the extension to your computer. Choose the option to save the extension to your computer. Click **Save** and then click **OK**. The extension is downloaded to your Downloads folder and is ready to be installed into Dreamweaver.

Adobe Extension Manager

The Adobe Extension Manager is its own software application. You can access it from Dreamweaver by choosing **Help, Manage Extensions** (see Figure 21.6).

Installed Extensions   Install button

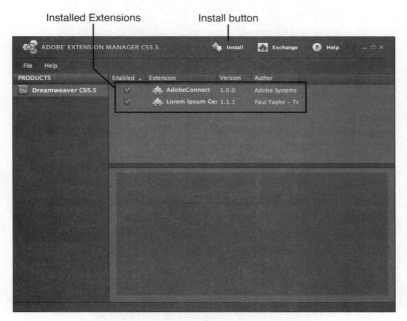

Figure 21.6: The Extension Manager lists all installed extensions for your Dreamweaver software.

Installing Extensions

After you've downloaded the extension that you want to install and launched Adobe Extension Manager, you can install the extension. Click the **Install** button in Adobe Extensions Manager. In the Select Extensions to Install window, navigate to your Downloads folder and locate the extension. Select it and then click **Select**. This displays a window with information about the Extension Disclaimer (see Figure 21.7). Click **Accept** to install the extension or click **Decline** to exit the installation process.

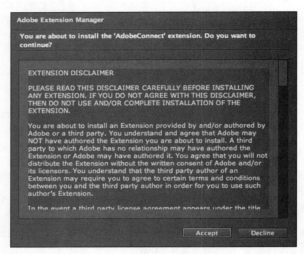

Figure 21.7: *You must accept or decline the extension disclaimer associated with the extension.*

Click the **Accept** button if you accept the licensing terms. This kicks off the install. A confirmation message displays when the download is complete (see Figure 21.8).

Figure 21.8: *To see your new extension, you must restart your Dreamweaver application.*

You need to restart Dreamweaver to complete the installation. Restart Dreamweaver and choose **Help, Manage Extensions** from the menu bar. Your new extension is listed in the Extension Manager.

> **DREAMWEAVER TIP**
>
> If you've upgraded your Dreamweaver application from an older version to the new CS5.5 version and you had extensions installed on the previous version, you can move these extensions to your new version. When you open the Extension Manager, you're prompted to move these extensions to your new version of Dreamweaver. Follow the prompts.

Using Extensions

After downloading an extension, the Extension Manager displays instructions for accessing the extension—it might be located on a menu, on a panel, or in a toolbar of Dreamweaver.

Managing Extensions

Use the Extension Manager to view and manage all your extensions (see Figure 21.9).

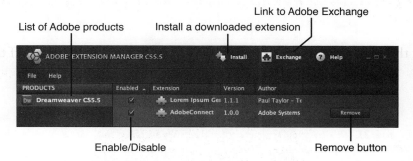

Figure 21.9: The Adobe Extension Manager. To see the Remove button, select an extension.

You can use the Extension Manager to install new extensions that you've downloaded. You can remove an installed extension as well. There's also a direct link to the Adobe Exchange.

Tutorial: Adding a Slideshow

This tutorial guides you through the process of using a freeware widget for creating a slideshow on the home page of the Walkabout Travel site. The widget you're going to use is the Spry Image Slideshow with Filmstrip (1.0), a free widget available on Adobe Exchange. Before proceeding with the tutorial, install the Adobe Widget Browser and create an Adobe account. When you're ready, follow these steps:

1. Define the **Chapter21** folder in the **Tutorial** folder as a new site root folder. Use this defined site for the tutorial.

2. Open the **index.html** web page from the Files panel by double-clicking it. You're going to add the **Spry Image Slideshow with Filmstrip** widget to the page.

3. Download the **Spry Image Slideshow-Basic** from Adobe Exchange. In Dreamweaver, choose **Insert, Widget**. This displays the Widget window (see Figure 21.10).

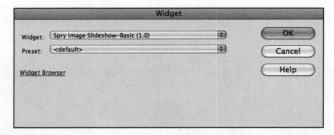

Figure 21.10: Any widgets that you have already installed and placed in your My Widgets library display in the Widget pop-out menu.

4. Click the **Widget Browser** link. This opens Adobe Exchange with your **My Widgets** library active. In the Search box, type **Spry Image Slideshow-Basic** to pull up this widget (see Figure 21.11).

5. Click the widget to select it. This takes you to the Widget Information page (see Figure 21.12).

Search field

Figure 21.11: Use the Search field to find the slideshow widget.

Add to My
Widgets
button

Figure 21.12: Read through the information on this page to learn more about this
freeware widget.

6. **Click the Add to My Widgets** button to add this widget to your My Widgets library. You'll need to sign in to Adobe Exchange at this point. Type your user name (typically your e-mail address) and password and click **Sign In**. The widget downloads.

7. Next you'll see a Widget License window display with copyright information. Click the **Accept** button to accept the copyright terms. When it's done downloading, you'll see the Widget Added window (see Figure 21.13). Click Close to close the window.

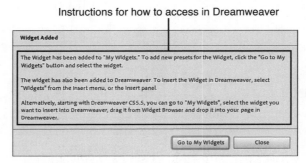

Figure 21.13: The Widgets Added window gives instructions for accessing the widget in Dreamweaver.

8. Return to Dreamweaver and the **index.html** page. Click the **placeholder** graphic and press the **Delete/Backspace** key to delete it from the page.

9. Insert a Div tag in the **display** editable region by choosing **Insert, Layout Objects, Div tag**.

10. In the Insert Div Tag window, set the Insert field to **At Insertion Point**. Click the **New CSS Rule** button and set the **Selector Type** to **ID**. In the **Selector name** field type **slideWidget**. In the Rule Definition field target the **walkabout.css** style sheet. Click **OK**.

11. In the CSS Rule Definition window, click the **Box** category; in the **Cell Padding** area, deselect the **Same for All** option. Set the **Left** field to **15px**. Click **OK** to close this window, and then click **OK** one more time to close the Insert Div tag window. Dreamweaver inserts the Div tag into the editable display region of your template.

12. Delete the default text that's created for a new Div tag.

13. To insert the slideshow widget, access the Insert panel. In the **Common** category, click the **Widget** button. This displays the Widget window (see Figure 21.14).

Figure 21.14: *The Widget pop-out menu in the Widget window displays all widgets that you have downloaded and installed.*

14. Set the Widget pop-out menu to **Spry Image Slideshow-Basic 1.0**, and leave the Preset pop-out menu set to <default>. Click **OK**. Dreamweaver inserts the widget in the **display** editable region (see Figure 21.15).

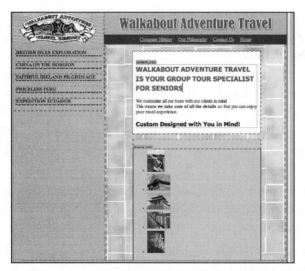

Figure 21.15: *Spry Image Slideshow-Basic 1.0. The photos are JPG files in a bulleted list.*

15. The display of this widget isn't supported in Design view, so click the **Live View** button to see the slideshow display.

16. You need to adjust the width of the slideshow to fit on your page. Exit the Live View by clicking the button again to turn this off. The CSS panel shows style rules for the new widget in both the internal style sheet named <style> and an external style sheet named **SpryImageSlideShow.css**. Expand the internal style sheet <style> by clicking the triangle/**+** beside its name (see Figure 21.16).

Figure 21.16: This widget creates style rules inside the document's internal style sheet and an external style sheet.

17. Select the first style rule, **#ImageSlideShow.ImageSlideShow**. In the Properties section, change **Width** to **390px** and the **Height** to **390px** to narrow the width of the slideshow.

18. To customize this slideshow, you need to add photos from past Walkabout trips. In the Spry Image Slideshow widget, click the first photo to make it active.

19. In the Property Inspector, click the **Browse for File** folder by the **Src** field and change the source file to **slide1.jpg** in the **Slideshow** folder in the **Images** folder. Then delete the link to Adobe's site in the **Link** field.

20. Repeat this step to replace the source and link for the next three slides. Replace these source links to slide2.Jpg, slide3.jpg, and so on in the slideshow folder in the images folder of the root site. Make sure you delete the link to Adobe's site in the **Link** field in the Property Inspector.

21. To preview the new photos in the slideshow, click the **Live View** button near the top of the screen.

22. Save your file. A message appears telling you that you need to copy other dependent files; click **Yes** to save all supporting files. Preview the page in a browser. The Walkabout home page is looking much better (see Figure 21.17)!

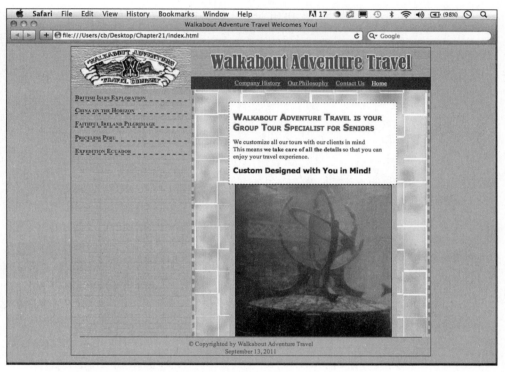

Figure 21.17: The widget introduces great functionality to the page.

The Least You Need to Know

- You can download numerous third-party widgets from the Internet to increase the functionality of your website.
- You can search for third-party widgets with the Adobe Widget Browser.
- Dreamweaver integrates with Adobe Exchange to make downloading and inserting third-party widgets a simple process.
- Dreamweaver extensions increase the functionality of Dreamweaver.

Integrating Adobe Flash

In This Chapter

- Adding Flash SWF to your HTML document
- Adding Flash FLV files to your HTML document
- Creating a Flash Player download message
- Adding ActiveX, plug-ins, and applets to your HTML document

Adobe Flash is part of the Adobe Creative Suite of software and is another powerful tool for web design. You can use it to create fully functioning, dynamic websites. But you can also use it to create small movies that you can insert into an HTML document—whether a banner or an animated advertisement—that fits in a sidebar within your site.

Flash brings animation and advanced functionality to your website. A programming language, ActionScript 3.0, integrated in the application enables you to create very sophisticated code and programs. Combine this with animation and you have a really robust application for web design.

Overview of Flash

Flash offers a powerful design platform capable of motion, interactivity, and visual effects. Flash also has an integrated programming language called ActionScript3.0. ActionScript is an object-oriented programming language that's similar in syntax to JavaScript. It creates all types of functionality and interactivity in a Flash movie. Flashed websites are rich in media with engaging effects, functionality that only a programming language can create.

Flash is also good at compression, including JPG compression. Many designers use Flash to optimize their web graphics. When you publish a Flash movie, it's compressed to a small file format, called *SWF*, or Small Web Format.

Flash and Dreamweaver work well together. When you publish a movie in Flash, it generates an SWF file and the supporting HTML page for viewing it on the web. Dreamweaver offers commands to easily embed an SWF file into a web page.

Inserting Flash SWF

To insert, or embed, Flash SWF files in Dreamweaver, position your cursor in the web page where you want to insert the Flash file. Then choose **Insert, Media, SWF** from the menu bar, or click the **Media** button in the Insert panel and choose **SWF** from the pop-out menu (see Figure 22.1).

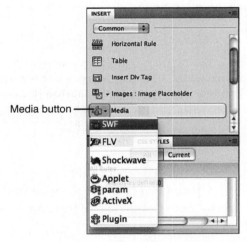

Figure 22.1: You can also insert other types of web media through the Media button of the Insert panel.

This opens the Select SWF window (see Figure 22.2). Navigate to your SWF file. It's a good idea to have the SWF file already copied into your site's root folder.

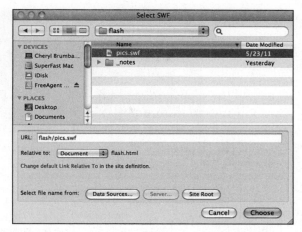

*Figure 22.2: To focus Dreamweaver on the site root folder, click the **Site Root** button.*

DREAMWEAVER TIP

It is a good idea to keep the SWF file in the same folder as the web page that links to it. This is because the Mac operating system and the Windows operating system use a slightly different syntax for the path to a file. Sometimes, if you create a page on a Mac and link to the SWF file in a separate folder, the SWF won't display when viewed on a PC. The PC has trouble finding it due to the slight differences in the path syntax. It doesn't happen all the time, but this is a good practice to follow.

Click **Choose** to select the file. This opens the Object Tag Accessibility Attributes window. To make this Flash movie accessible, type a title in the **Title** field and then click **OK**.

An SWF file placeholder displays in your web document (see Figure 22.3).

Dreamweaver uses the SWF file placeholder instead of the actual SWF file to keep the refresh time down as you develop your site. If you want to see the actual SWF file in the web page, click the placeholder to make it active and, in the Property Inspector, click the **Play** button (see Figure 22.4).

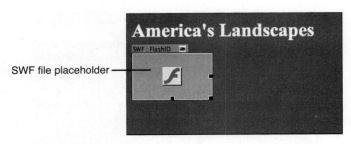

Figure 22.3: The SWF File Placeholder is the same size and dimension as an SWF file.

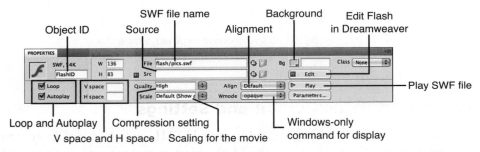

*Figure 22.4: Click the **Play** button in the Property Inspector to see your SWF file play in Dreamweaver.*

Object Tag

Take a look at the HTML code that Dreamweaver created on the fly. There's quite a bit of code, and it begins with the <object> tag of HTML (see Figure 22.5). You use this tag to embed or insert objects into HTML.

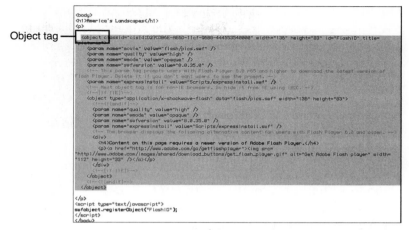

Object tag —

Figure 22.5: Notice that the Object tag is generic until you start setting the parameters to identify the object.

Customizing SWF File Format and Settings

When you have an SWF file embedded in your HTML code, you can apply formatting directly to the SWF file. Click the Flash object to make it active. Then in the Property Inspector, set the following options (see Figure 22.4):

- **Object ID**—Establishes an ID for the SWF file. This ID name must be unique for other object IDs.

- **Loop**—Causes the SWF file to loop back to the beginning when it reaches the end.

- **Autoplay**—Sets the SWF to automatically start playing when the page loads in a browser.

- **V Space/H Space**—Establishes the vertical and horizontal spacing around the SWF file in relation to adjacent web content.

- **File**—File path to the source SWF file.

- **Src**—Establishes the file path to the Flash FLA file for the SWF. The FLA file is the authoring file for Flash. To edit the SWF file, you must edit the FLA file and then publish the FLA to an SWF. You can set Dreamweaver to establish the link to the FLA file so if you need to edit the SWF, you can open Flash and the FLA file while in Dreamweaver.

- **Quality**—Sets the playback quality and sets the amount of anti-aliasing of SWF movie playback. Anti-aliasing is the process of smoothing out the edges and cleaning up distortion artifacts (like black and white noise or pixels) that occur in digital images. Low settings focus on movie playback time and sacrifice playback quality. High settings improve the SWF file playback quality but require a higher-speed processor for the end user's computer.

- **Scale**—Determines how the SWF movie fits into the dimensions set in the width (W) and height (H) fields.

- **Align**—Sets how the SFW file is aligned on the web page.

- **Wmode**—Eliminates conflicts with *DHTML elements*. The Opaque setting enables DHTML elements, like a Spry widget, to display on top of the SWF file(s) when viewed in a browser.

> **DEFINITION**
>
> **DHTML** is a version of HTML that integrates multiple web technologies to create interactivity and animation in websites. DHTML combines HTML, JavaScript, CSS, and the Document Object Model.

- **Edit**—Click this button to edit the SWF file right from Dreamweaver. You must have the FLA source file identified in the **Src** field for this to work.

- **Play**—Play your movie right in Dreamweaver.

- **Parameters**—If your movie is designed to accept parameters passed through code, you can enter these additional parameters here.

All these settings help your Flash file display the way you want it to in the web page.

> **DREAMWEAVER TIP**
>
> Flash SWF files are vector based, which means that they are created based on math. This is a big advantage in web design because they are scalable—that is, they can resize based on the size of the end user's browser.

Inserting Flash Videos

You can also use Flash to create Flash Video (FLV) files. An FLV file is a small compressed movie file that can be played on the web. YouTube uses this format and compression for all its movies. When you upload a movie to YouTube, it's compressed into an FLV file.

Just like an SWF file, the FLV must be embedded into the web page. To do this, use the menu command of **Insert, Media, FLV,** or choose **FLV** from the **Media** button's pop-out menu in the Insert panel. This opens the Insert FLV window (see Figure 22.6).

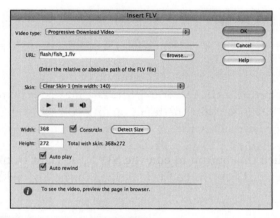

Figure 22.6: You can set the control display for the movie by choosing different Skin options.

This window lets you set many display and functionality elements for the FLV file. You can even set a Skin for the FLV display. A *Skin* is the framework and display for the control buttons that you need to play and stop an FLV file. Here's an overview of the options in the Insert FLV window:

- **Video type**—Choose the video type, either progressive download or streaming. The key difference between streaming and progressive download is how the file is downloaded to the end user's machine. Progressive downloads download the file to the Temporary folder on the end user's machine, whereas streaming downloads stream the download to the end user's machine but the file remains on the streaming server.

- **URL**—Type or browse to the FLV file to set the URL path.

- **Skin**—Choose the type of control display that you want for your FLV movie. The control displays are all similar to a DVD's controls.

- **Width/Height**—Set the dimension of the display of your FLV movie. If you want to use the default setting, click the **Detect Size** button.

- **Autoplay/Autorewind**—Click to set your FLV movie to automatically play when the web page loads and to automatically rewind when finished playing.

Click **OK** when you've finished setting your options. Dreamweaver embeds your FLV movie in the web page.

DREAMWEAVER TIP

Use the Property Inspector's Flash options to set the display of an FLV file, just like you did with an SWF file.

When you embed an FLV file in a web page, Dreamweaver sometimes needs to create additional SWF files to support the functionality you set in the Insert FLV window. If you chose **Progressive Download Video** for the Video type, Dreamweaver creates a new SWF file called **FLVPlayer_Progressive.swf.** Each **Skin** option also requires a supporting SWF for its functionality. You'll find both of these SWF files in the Files panel (see Figure 22.7).

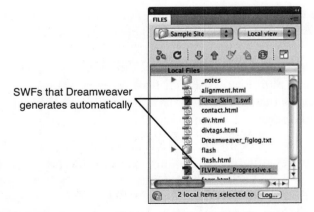

Figure 22.7: When you apply a Skin to an SWF or FLV file, Dreamweaver adds a supporting SWF file to the Files panel.

DREAMWEAVER TIP

Dreamweaver doesn't support the newer F4V, which is a common format for Flash video. This file format is used extensively on the web because of its high quality but smaller file size. Dreamweaver can only embed FLV files; you need to use the Adobe Media Encoder application to translate F4V files to FLV format for use in a Dreamweaver web page.

Creating a Flash Player Download Message

Have you ever got the message when visiting a website that you need to download the latest Flash Player to view the site content? This is because, with each release of Flash, the Flash Player must support the generated SWF file. For every new release of Flash, there's a supporting release of the Flash Player plug-in. For Flash CS5 and CS5.5, this is the Flash Player 10 release. If you try to view a CS5 Flash movie in a version of the Flash Player that's older than the Flash Player 10 release, you won't see any of the cool CS5 or CS5.5 features; the Flash Player skips that functionality because it doesn't understand it. Adobe developed a download message to alert visitors that they need to download the latest version of the Flash player to see your site.

Dreamweaver automatically creates the code for this download message when you save for the first time a web page with an embedded SWF. When you save a web page with an SWF file, you'll see a window letting you know that Dreamweaver is going to create a message to notify the visitor of the Flash Player download (see Figure 22.8).

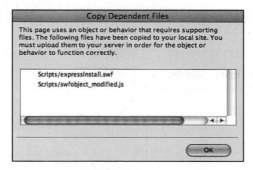

Figure 22.8: *Dreamweaver automatically creates new files to support features of your web page.*

Click **OK**. Dreamweaver creates a new folder in your site root folder called **Scripts**. In this folder, Dreamweaver creates two more files, **expressinstall.swf** and **swfobject_modified.js**. These two files together create the download message and download functionality. The **Scripts** folder and files are now listed in your Files panel (see Figure 22.9).

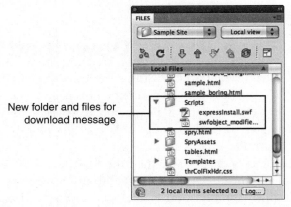

New folder and files for download message

Figure 22.9: Dreamweaver generates a new folder called Scripts and creates two new files in the folder.

DREAMWEAVER TIP

When you upload your site to the remote host, you must include any automatically generated Dreamweaver files and folders. They support Dreamweaver CS5.5 functionality that you've added to your web page.

Inserting Other Web Media

You can insert other types of web media into your web page using the **Insert, Media** menu command (see Figure 22.10).

Figure 22.10: You gain lots of web functionality and interactivity through these other types of web media.

The following web media choices are available:

- **Shockwave**—Compressed file generated from Adobe Director.

- **Applet**—A program that adds new functionality and interactivity to an HTML document.

- **ActiveX**—Small programs that run over the Internet. These are sometimes called add-ons.

- **Plug-in**—Similar to ActiveX, a plug-in is a group of software components that add more functionality to a software application.

To install any of the other web media types, select the option you want from the **Insert, Media** menu. Navigate to the media and insert it into your web page. You can also use the Property Inspector to further format and configure the media.

Through Flash and other web media, you can really extend the interactivity and functionality of your websites. You can create rich, interactive websites when you use Flash and Dreamweaver together.

The Least You Need to Know

- You can insert Flash SWF or FLV files in a web page through the Insert, Media, SWF or FLV menu command.

- When you insert a Flash SWF or FLV file, you can apply a Skin to the movie to create a control panel for playing the movie.

- You can create a Flash Player download message that displays on the visitor's computer if they don't have the version of the Flash player required to support the functionality of the SWF or FLV file.

- You can add other types of media to your web page such as Shockwave files, applets, ActiveX, or other plug-ins.

Glossary

absolute path   The complete address to a document or linked file.

Adobe Contribute   A web publishing and site-management tool that enables others to access, edit, and author website content.

anti-aliasing   The process of smoothing out the edges and cleaning up distortion artifacts (like black and white noise or pixels) that occur in digital images.

AP element   Stands for an absolute positioning element; it is a `<div>` tag that's positioned in a fixed X and Y coordinate. It can contain text, images, and other HTML objects.

assistive technologies   Tools that help people maneuver your form. These include screen readers for low-vision users or keyboard key combinations that allow users to jump to different fields in your form.

bitmap image   An image created through a pixel-by-pixel representation of the image.

browser   An application developed to interpret HTML code and display the information when requested over the Internet.

camelCase   A naming convention that puts two words together with lowercase characters for both words except the starting character of the second word, which is in uppercase; for example *slideShow*.

Cascading Style Sheet   A style sheet language similar to HTML that lets you format web page information. It's used to separate web page content from the format or layout of that content.

checkbox   An HTML form object that allows the end user to select an option. Checkboxes are grouped in a checkbox group and allow for multiple selections.

cloaking   A setting that allows you to designate certain files or file types that you want Dreamweaver to exclude from certain operations.

contextual access   Access to information that changes based on selection.

CS Live services   A free service from Adobe that integrates five online services. These services integrate and further streamline the creative and development process of the entire suite of CS5 products.

CSS box model   The visual model used for the rectangular boxes that hold or contain web page elements.

CSS style rule   A set of formatting that's applied to a document element.

delimiter   A character or sequence of characters used to determine the boundary between text data. For example, if you export Microsoft Excel spreadsheet data to a tab delimited file, the data has tabs that are delimiters between each column of data in each row, separating these individual cells of data.

Device font   An operating system level font, which is either serif or sans-serif. Device fonts are part of the operating system of all computers.

DHTML   A version of HTML that integrates multiple web technologies to create interactivity and animation in websites. DHTML combines HTML, JavaScript, CSS, and the Document Object Model

Div tag   The division tag of HTML, which is represented by `<div>`. This tag creates divisions, or box areas, for web page layout.

DMG file   A binary file type used often on the Macintosh computers to compress files for a quicker download.

document-relative path   A simple and focused way to link a document. You basically leave out the part of an absolute path that doesn't change from one page to another in your site.

domain names   Names associated with IP addresses. These are used in URLs to identify websites.

external graphics editor   An application you can instruct Dreamweaver to use for editing any of your page graphics when you use Roundtrip Editing.

external link   A link to a document that resides outside the site. This can be a document on the company intranet or a document on another website.

fixed layout   A layout structured to have a set width that doesn't change. Fixed layouts give the web designer more control over how a page appears in web browsers.

FLA file   The authoring file for Flash. This file is the one you work with while authoring your Flash movie. You compress this file to an SWF for web use.

float   A property of the Box category in CSS that situates elements left or right of each other on a page.

font-family   A group of fonts that have similar displays. The font-family dictates which font to use, based on the visitor's computer and fonts installed.

frame   A web element you can use to divide a browser window into multiple areas.

frameset   The overall container for multiple frames. A frameset groups frames together in a single window.

FTP   File Transfer Protocol; a standard network protocol for transferring files between remote hosting servers over the Internet.

get   To download files to your computer

heading tag   An HTML code that divides the text content on your page into headlines.

hexadecimal   A six-digit number that's associated with a color for display on a screen.

hidden files/folders   Documents and folders that are hidden from normal viewing methods. The document name of these file and folders is preceded by an underscore.

hosting server   A computer that's set up to make websites visible on the web.

HTML   HyperText Markup Language, the language of web pages. HTML utilizes tags to represent web page data. A browser interprets the HTML and displays that information graphically.

hyperlink   A file path that links to another document.

image map   A transparent button that you use to create a "hot spot" on a web image. These hot spots are clickable and can be linked to other documents or information.

inheritance   A feature of CSS that involves the passing down, or inheritance, of properties from a parent element to a child element.

Internet   A giant network of networks that connects all computers that access it.

IP address   A unique address required for any computer on the Internet. IP addresses are associated with a specific computer.

jump menu   A HTML menu element that jumps to a linked document.

Library   In Dreamweaver, a storage location for commonly used page assets, called *library items.*

library items   Page assets or elements that might be reused often or updated regularly on your site. They are created and stored in the Dreamweaver Library.

line break   A break in a line of text for a block level element.

line height   Set amount of line space between paragraphs.

liquid layout   A layout that expands or shrinks in its width, based on the display area of the browser window.

lossless compression   A compression format that doesn't lose any of the original image details when compressed.

lossy compression   A compression format in which colors and details are combined during compression, causing a loss of the original file's detail and color quality.

meta tag   A tag that's in the `<head>` tag of an HTML document. The `<head>` tag isn't visible to the visitor but is visible to search engines.

mobile application   A program designed to be accessible through a smart phone or other personal handheld device.

orphaned file   A file that exists in a website but doesn't have any other pages linking to it.

post   The process of uploading your website to a remote hosting server.

PPI   Stands for pixel per inch. Mac monitors have a resolution of 72 PPI, and PC monitors have a PPI resolution of 96.

primary browser   The type of browser you're targeting with your design development.

pseudoclass   A type of CSS style rule Class Selector that's focused on a particular web element, like a link state.

put   To upload files to a server.

radio buttons   Options that are presented in a group. They have preset values that the visitor can select.

registration point   A point or location on an element that adheres to x and y coordinates.

remote server   The hosting server that makes your site visible on the Internet or intranet. The files and assets of the root folder are uploaded or posted to the remote server.

root folder   The folder that holds all your website files and assets. You have a copy of this folder on both your local computer and your remote server.

secondary browser   The browser you use to preview web pages after previewing them in the primary browser.

Select (List/Menu)   A Dreamweaver feature that enables you to create a drop-down menu or a list of values.

site root-relative paths   A form of linking that starts at the site root folder and then shows the path to the document.

Skin   The framework and display of control buttons that are needed to play and stop a FLV file.

Smart Object   An object that remembers its link to the original file. Any changes you make to the original graphic file can be updated to the Smart Object in Dreamweaver, synchronizing the development of the original graphic with the Dreamweaver image.

Spry framework   A JavaScript library that offers a quick way to access predeveloped functionality and use that functionality in your web page.

subversion (SVN)   A form of version-control system that allows multiple users to edit and manage files on a remote web server collaboratively.

SWF   Compressed format of a Flash movie; it is compressed down to a file format of SWF or Small Web Format.

syntax   The arrangement and order required in the construction of a programming language's code.

text area   A multiple-line text field that allows the visitor to input a large amount of text into a form.

tiling   The process of repeating the same image both vertically and horizontally to cover the entire area of a window

URL   Universal resource locator; a path to your domain name and each page.

vector images   Images are created through mathematics and an algorithm of endpoints, lines, and fills. These images display precisely no matter what size or dimension they are resized to.

version control   A system developed to keep track of versions of software or files. This typically is a numbering system that increases as new developments are added to software or files.

W3C   The World Wide Web Consortium; the governing organization that establishes HTML, CSS, Browser, and other standards for the web.

web   Short for the World Wide Web.

web application framework   A software framework that is used to develop mobile applications.

website   A collection of web pages.

WYSIWYG   Stands for "What You See Is What You Get." Used in web design to indicate that you can see what you are creating graphically.

Zip file   A compressed file format for downloading and uploading large files or groups of files.

Resources

This appendix contains a list of resources that I have found useful for learning web design skills and discovering new technologies.

In addition to the sites listed here, local web design user groups can be a great way to network with other professionals in the field, as well as a way to learn new information about topics and techniques for web design. You can find these user groups through an Internet search under the keywords "web design user groups." If you also include a city or state reference in your keyword search, you can narrow down your listed results.

E-mail lists are also great sources of information. When you join a web design e-mail list, you receive daily e-mails with questions and information that others on the list have found beneficial for web design. Again, you can find these user groups through an Internet search under the keywords "web design email lists." If you also include a city or state reference in your keyword search, you can narrow down your listed results.

Adobe.com
www.adobe.com

The Adobe website has numerous tutorials and information about its products. The company also hosts discussion boards that can provide insight into issues and problems that you might run into as you use Adobe products to develop a website.

Dreamweaver Help

You can access help for Dreamweaver by choosing **Help, Dreamweaver Help** from the menu bar. This opens the Help file for Dreamweaver. Type a keyword in the **Search** field to see topics that cover the keywords.

The Complete Idiot's Guide series
www.idiotsguides.com

The Complete Idiot's Guide series offers other books on various topics relating to web design. Search the book offerings online at www.idiotsguides.com for relevant books on other topics that you're interested in learning more about.

CSS Tutorial
www.w3schools.com/css/

This is a great site for learning more about CSS. The site offers tutorials, insights, techniques, and user-proven shortcuts for managing and developing CSS-driven websites.

Wikipedia
www.wikipedia.com

Wikipedia offers technical information about various web design topics. Type your keyword(s) in the **Search** field to see the associated information displayed.

Google's Webmaster Central
www.google.com/support/forum/p/Webmasters?hl=en

Google's help forum for web masters addresses many web design issues. It's searchable and relevant to the web design industry and process.

World Wide Web Consortium (W3C)
www.w3c.org

W3C is the international community that governs the development of HTML, other web design programming languages, browser development, and overall processes in web design. This site is a great way to learn more about HTML and CSS tags and syntax. They also provide information about new tags and depreciated tags as well.

YouTube
www.youtube.com

YouTube is a site that lets users submit short digital videos for others to view. It's a wealth of knowledge for learning just about anything. Many people have contributed movies that demonstrate how to perform many web design skills and techniques. To find what you're looking for, type a keyword in the **Search** field.

Forwebdesigners.com

This site is a user-submitted list of resources about web design and development. Topics covered include CSS, Flash integration, fonts, generators, graphic sources, Photoshop tricks and techniques, stock photos, and inspirations. The site also offers forums on many web design issues and techniques.

Webmonkey.com

This web design resource site has been around for a long time. I've used it for years to learn new techniques and technologies.

Webdesign.about.com

About.com is another great resource for learning more about web design. The site has an entire section related to web design techniques and issues.

Dreamweaver's
Mobile Applications

Mobile devices are the wave of the future, and although using Dreamweaver to build mobile applications goes beyond the primary scope of this book, the topic deserves some discussion.

Dreamweaver's new *web application framework* enables users to create mobile applications for the following popular smart phones:

- Blackberry
- iPhone
- Android (Google)
- Windows Mobile
- HP webOS
- Symbian OS[3]

DEFINITION

A **web application framework** is a software framework used to develop mobile applications. Different varieties of frameworks exist, and each has its own set of programming tools, features, and processes. A web application framework integrates HTML, JavaScript, and CSS. Dreamweaver CS5.5 has standardized on the Apple PhoneGap Framework.

A web application framework uses libraries and templates to bundle functionality and features, to streamline the mobile application development process. These bundles are made up of various buttons, menus, sliders, input fields, and so on to create interactive interfaces for mobile devices. These bundles are stored in the associated library. In Dreamweaver, the library is the jQuery library; the framework links to this library for accessing these bundles. As a developer, this means you can access complex code with a click of a button to create a variety of features and functionality for mobile applications.

DREAMWEAVER TIP

You need to download the PhoneGap Framework from Apple's site to get started using Dreamweaver to create mobile applications. You can find this download at http://developer.apple.com/devcenter/ios/index.action.

To access Dreamweaver's mobile application, choose **Site, Mobile Application** from the menu bar (see Figure C.1).

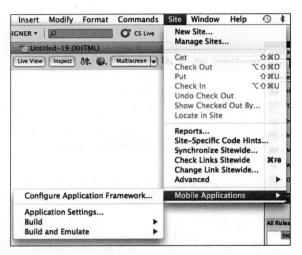

Figure C.1: *Dreamweaver has four menu choices that help you quickly build a mobile application.*

After you've installed the PhoneGap Framework, you can start using the Mobile Application menu and its menu items.

Adobe made it easy to get started with mobile applications by including starter pages, which are generic pre-developed pages you can use to develop your mobile application. To access these starter pages, follow these steps:

1. From the menu bar, choose **File, New** to create a new page (see Figure C.2).

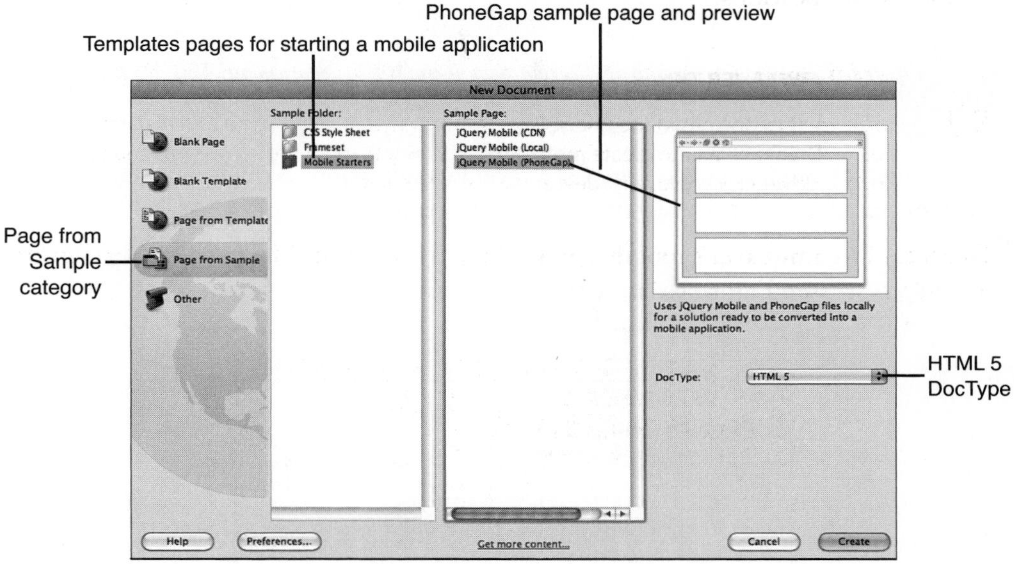

Templates pages for starting a mobile application

PhoneGap sample page and preview

Page from
Sample
category

HTML 5
DocType

*Figure C.2: Choose from among the three sample pages in the Mobile Starters in
the Sample Folder category of the Page from Sample category.*

2. In the New Document window, click the **Page from Sample** category on the
   far left of the window.

3. Click **Mobile Starters** from the Sample Folder category.

4. From the Sample Page category, select **jQuery Mobile (PhoneGap)**. A
   sample of this interface appears in the preview window, and the DocType
   changes to HTML 5 because this version of HTML supports jQuery and
   PhoneGap Framework.

5. Click **Create** to create a sample mobile application page. Dreamweaver generates an HTML page (see Figure C.3).

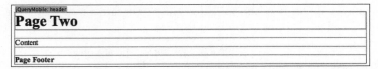

Figure C.3: *The new mobile application page is an HTML document. You can use all the tools, web elements, and functionality of Dreamweaver to develop it.*

You've just created a starter page for a mobile application. Notice the source code that Dreamweaver automatically generates for this page (see Figure C.4).

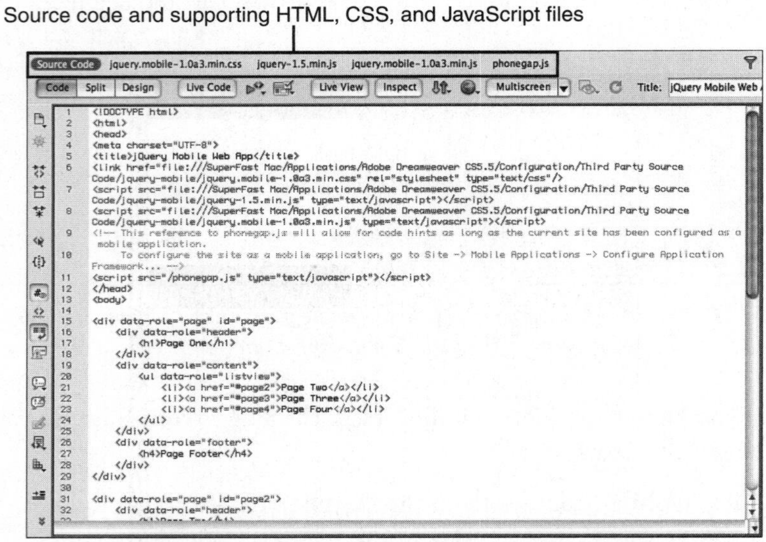

Source code and supporting HTML, CSS, and JavaScript files

Figure C.4: *This code links to both CSS and JavaScript files to support the functionality and format of the page.*

This source code also calls other files that are required to create a mobile application. Dreamweaver displays a series of document tabs in the Document window. Each tab is a document that's called or used in the sample mobile application web page. Click a document tab to view the document, and then switch to Code view to see the file's code. These supporting CSS and JavaScript documents also display in the Files panel (see Figure C.5).

Figure C.5: These Dreamweaver-generated files and folders are stored in your site root folder.

To see how all these files work together, click the **Live View** button in the Document toolbar. This displays a view of your page as a browser would see it (see Figure C.6).

Figure C.6: Live View displays the page by interpreting all the HTML, CSS, and JavaScript code for all linked documents.

In Live View mode, you can click the buttons on Page One through Page Four of the mobile application page and see the linking page.

To customize this mobile application, you can add the content and web elements to each area, all through the Dreamweaver tools and functionality. For instance, you can rename the pages with a descriptive name for the application functionality that you want to include in the mobile application. Click the content area and input the content and web elements that you want to display. You must be in Design view to change your content (see Figure C.7).

Figure C.7: *You can add or delete pages; insert pictures, buttons, and text; and apply other functionality of Dreamweaver and HTML, CSS, and JavaScript.*

You can also create or modify any of the linking CSS and JavaScript files to further customize your mobile application.

With your edits and changes made to customize your mobile application, you can view your page again in Live view and see your page titles and supporting content for each page. View the new application in a smaller window size by choosing the **Multiscreen** pop-up menu, and then choose **320×480 Smart Phone** (see Figure C.8).

Figure C.8: This is how your mobile application will look in a smaller window size display, such as on a smart phone.

To learn more about mobile application, visit Adobe's site; the company periodically releases new tutorials and instructions on how to use the new mobile application feature of Dreamweaver CS5.5.

Search Engine Optimization and Web Design

Dreamweaver is a fantastic tool for designing and creating websites. But when your site is complete and uploaded to your server, you need to find a way to drive visitors to your site. One of the most popular ways people find sites is through search engines such as Google and Yahoo!.

Search engine optimization is a technique for using keywords and keyword phrases on your web pages to make them more visible to search engines. You determine the appropriate keywords and keyword phrases, and then you optimize your website by using these keywords throughout your web pages. For instance, if you have a site for advertising property management of residential properties, you would use keywords and keyword phrases like "residential property management" or just "property management".

What Is Search Engine Optimization (SEO)?

Savvy web developers encode keywords in all their web elements, including metadata (see Chapter 2), heading tags (see Chapter 6), body content (see Chapter 5), page titles (see Chapter 5), and links (see Chapter 9). Based on how you use keywords and keyword phrases in each of these elements, search engines index your pages and rank them accordingly.

SEO comes in two forms, pay-per-click advertising and organic search (see Figure D.1). Pay-per-click advertising is a fee-based service offered through many of the popular search engines, like Google AdWords and Bing's Microsoft adCenter. An organic listing is the ranking and display of your site in the search results by a search engine. This type of listing is attained by strategically placing keywords and keyword phrases throughout a web page.

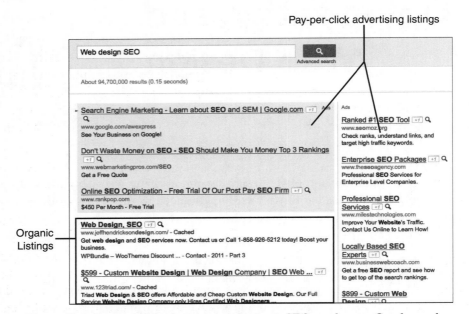

Figure D.1: *Pay-per-click advertising and organic SEO results on a Google search.*

Pay-per-click advertising is a "pay-as-they-click" type of advertising. You create ad campaigns that consist of targeted ads with associated keywords and keyword phrases that you're targeting. Usually no fee is involved in setting up an advertising campaign. In fact, many search engines offer advertising dollars for free to get you started. When you launch your advertising campaign, your ads become immediately visible on the web based on the end user's keyword searches. If the user types in a keyword or keyword phrase that matches your list of keywords, based on your bid amount that you set up in the advertising campaign, your ad displays. The ads are displayed either in the top portion of the search listing page or in a column on the right. If the user clicks your displayed ad, you are charged the fee for that click.

Organic SEO requires more work, because you need to optimize your web pages based on page elements and how the search engine ranks those elements for the relevancy of the search. When you attain a top ranking, this form of SEO can be long-lasting, as search engines have long memories. Based on your SEO efforts for your keyword phrases, your site can be pulled up on the first page results for a keyword search. Because you did all the work yourself to drive visitors to your site, you're not charged a fee when a visitor clicks your organic listing.

How Does SEO Work?

Each search engine has its own set of rules for indexing a site, but these rules are similar among most popular search engines. Typically, search engines rate web pages based on select criteria, like domain name, page title, meta tags, links, and headings. Within each of these criteria, they take into account proximity, or how close to the start of the document or title a keyword or keyword phrase is used, and the number of times a keyword or keyword phrase is used.

Search engines also look at repetition of the keyword or keyword phrase throughout the document and in each criteria area. For instance, a title for a web page that targets residential property management could be "Residential Property Management For Your Property." This would be coded in an HTML `<title>` tag and display in the title bar of a web browser. In this example, the keyword phrase of "Residential Property Management" is listed first in this tag, so it ranks higher when compared to other pages that use the keyword phrase toward the end of their `<title>` tag, like "We provide Residential Property Management". The word "Property" is used twice in this tag, which also reinforces the importance of this word; thus, it ranks higher with search engines than another `<title>` tag that uses the keyword just once.

DREAMWEAVER DON'T

Don't plaster your keywords willy-nilly all over your page or pay link farms (fee-based companies that guarantee a certain number of links) to link to your website in an attempt to get a higher ranking with search engines. This is a red flag to many search engines, and they might ban your site for this type of SEO practice. Once you've been banned, it can be difficult to get listed again with a search engine.

Also, if you use too many keywords, the search engine will truncate, or drop, any past their designated limit. The common limit is 35, although search engines don't publish their exact criteria.

The popularity of your link is also a factor in search engine ranking order. Popularity refers to the number of websites that link to your site.

DREAMWEAVER TIP

Some search engines are case sensitive to your keywords and keyword phrases. This means they distinguish between uppercase and lowercase text. Therefore, it's a good idea to use many forms of your keywords and keyword phrases throughout your page.

Third-Party SEO Applications

SEO isn't rocket science; it's a systematic way to rank keywords and keyword phrases. You can do this on your own or use one of many third-party SEO applications. If you do an Internet search on SEO software, you'll see a listing of many third-party SEO applications. All of them work similarly; they help you optimize your page by offering suggestions and tips to increase your popularity with search engines. Most let you identify a high-ranking competitor site, and you can then optimize your site based on how the competitor site achieves their ranking. This helps you fine-tune your efforts to get that higher ranking. Both free and commercial SEO applications are available. It's a good idea to use an SEO software solution, because they make your job of achieving a high SEO ranking much easier.

Submitting Your Site to Search Engines

After you've optimized your page, it's time to submit it to the popular search engines that accept submissions. Search engines have different processes for submission, and some don't accept submissions at all. Google, for instance, doesn't accept submissions; instead, it searches, or crawls, the web to index sites. On some search engines, like Yahoo!, you'll find a link for submitting your site. Many third-party SEO software packages help you submit your web pages to the major search engines. Some web hosting companies offer features that help you submit your site to search engines; others will do it for you with a click of a button. Check with your hosting company for these features.

Using Frames in Web Design

Frames are a way to present information on a website with multiple documents that are grouped together through a frameset. Although the W3C no longer recommends that web designers use frames and they are becoming outmoded, many web designers continue to find them to be valuable tools in certain contexts. However, mobile devices cannot view websites created with frames.

This appendix walks you through the process of using frames in your site.

Frames and Framesets

A *frameset* is an HTML document that uses the `<frameset>` tag to contain or frame individual HTML documents

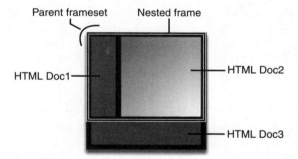

Figure E.1: *The three HTML documents are contained in two framesets, the parent frameset and the nested frameset.*

In Figure E.1, you see three HTML documents: HTML Doc1, HTML Doc2, and HTML Doc3. The parent frameset is the overall container for nested framesets and frames. A nested frameset is a frameset that's nested inside the parent frameset. In

Figure E.1, the parent frameset contains the nested frameset and HTML Doc3. The nested frameset contains HTML Doc1 and Doc2.

Each frameset controls, in physical size and dimension, the display of the HTML documents. In other words, the frameset frames each HTML document to a fixed size and dimension, to create a consistent display of the web page. Figure E.2 shows a sample of frames created from the same frame and frameset setup as in Figure E.1.

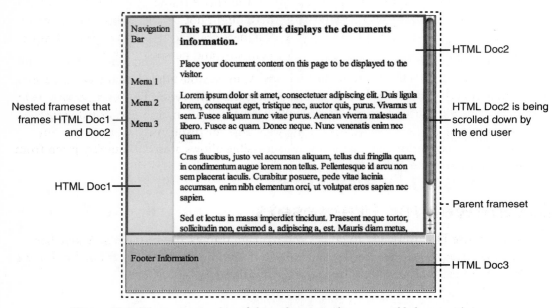

Figure E.2: *The navigation bar of this web page is always accessible because it's in its own frame for display.*

This type of web page allows for consistent displays of the framed HTML documents. For instance, if you want to have a navigation bar that is always accessible even when the user scrolls down the page, you can use frames and a frameset.

The Pros and Cons of Frames

When frames first came out, they were all the rage. All web designers used them to show off their skill using the latest HTML tag and feature. Sites that really didn't need frames were designed using frames for the page layout.

Soon people realized that frames had their own set of drawbacks. The biggest problems developed with the search engines. A search engine indexes only HTML documents. Because a frameset is made up of HTML documents, when the search engine indexes the HTML page contained within the frame, there isn't a way to relate this document back to the parent frameset document. Therefore, when an SEO search pulls up a framed HTML document, it shows the HTML document outside of the frameset structure. Many times, these HTML documents contain just one feature or tidbit of information in relation to the entire frameset layout. Such results do your site absolutely no good, because there might not be any identifying company information on that HTML page. Once designers realized the limitations of frames, they pretty much stopped using them for company and personal websites.

Today frames still have a use in web design. Many online educational tutorials and instructional websites are created through frames. This type of website doesn't really rely on search engines to drive people to a site. In addition, an educational tutorial usually needs to have fixed areas on the web page for displaying information. For instance, a navigation bar that is always accessible allows a user to quickly jump from topic to topic in an online learning course.

Dreamweaver Framesets

You can use Dreamweaver to create and manage frames and framesets. Adobe has included sample frameset pages that you can use to quickly set up a framed web page layout. To create a sample frameset, follow these steps:

1. Open a new document.

2. In the **New Document** window, select **Page from Sample** category.

3. Select **Frameset** from the **Sample Folder** category.

4. Select the frameset layout that you want from the **Sample Page** category. Notice that the **Preview** window reflects a visual of how the selected frameset is laid out.

5. Click **OK** to create your frameset and all contained HTML documents (see Figure E.3).

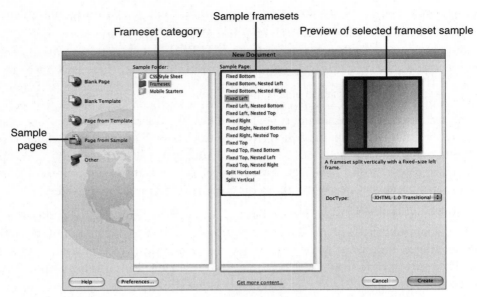

Figure E.3: Dreamweaver offers many different sample frameset layouts for creating a frame web page layout.

Dreamweaver has a Frame panel that makes it easy to select either a frameset or the framed HTML document (see Figure E.4).

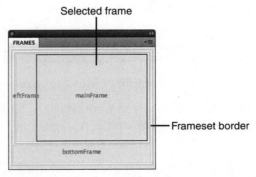

Figure E.4: Click to select a frame or frameset in the panel. This focuses Dreamweaver on that HTML document.

To select a frame, click it. To select a frameset, click the border of the frameset. This focuses Dreamweaver on that HTML document, and the Property Inspector reflects the settings relevant to the selected document.

A frameset is completely customizable. You can set the size and dimension of any of the framed documents through the Property Inspector.

DREAMWEAVER TIP

The `<iframe>` remains a popular tool for opening a new window in e-mail applications. There is no other way to do this without using an `<iframe>`.

Index

I

ID field (Input Tag Accessability), 410

ID names, hyperlinks, 209

ID option (Property Inspector), 177

ID selector type, 146

ID setting (Property Inspector), 408

If-Else statements, 354

Ignore All button (Check Spelling), 117

Ignore button (Check Spelling), 117

Ignore White Space option (Find and Replace), 247

Illustrator, inserting graphics, 172-176

Image command (Insert menu), 167-168, 175

image field form object, 409

image folders, setting default, 55

image links, 196
  creating, 202

Image Map tools (Property Inspector), 212

image maps, 196, 212-214
  creating, 211-214

Image Name field (Insert Rollover Image), 185

Image Placeholder window, 170

Image Preview window, 175

Image Tag Accessibility Attributes window, 168

images
  accessibility, 168-169
  adjusting brightness/ contrast, 181-182

aligning, 179

applying CSS tag style rules, 186-187

bitmap, 166

bordering, 189-190

box model options, 187-188

cropping, 180-181

deleting, 184-185

editing, 177-184

file formats, 166

inserting, 167-171, 190-194
  Fireworks, 176-177
  Illustrator, 173-176
  Photoshop, 172-176
  rollover, 185-186

modifying size, 178

optimizing, 165-166

placeholders, 169-171

resampling, 181

sharpening focus, 182

<img> tag, 168, 323

Import Tabular Data command (File menu), 235

Import Tabular Data window, 236-237

importing
  Excel spreadsheets, 111
  tabular data, 235-237
  Word documents, 111

Inconsistent Region Names window, 358

InContext Editing category (Insert panel), 39

indenting paragraphs, 127-128

inheritance, 266-267

Initial Value setting (Property Inspector), 412

inline elements, 125

inline style sheets, 142

<input> tag, 411

Input Tag Accessibility Attributes window, 410-411

Insert Column Left option (Column Information), 230

Insert Column Right option (Column Information), 230

Insert Div Tag button, 288

Insert panel, 38
  Common category
    Hyperlink button, 201-202
    Named Anchor button, 206-207
  Favorites category, 40-41
  manipulating, 40

Insert Rollover Image window, 185-186

Insert Table command, 223

inserting
  AP Div tags, 311-312
  Design Notes, 399-401
  Div tags, 288-291
  Spry widgets, 449-450
  tables, 231-232

Inspect mode, 12, 245, 254-255

installing
  Dreamweaver, 16-19
  extensions, 453-455

Intel Pentium 4 processors, 16

internal style sheets, 142

Internet versus web, 3

Internet connections, minimum requirements, 17

Invisible Elements category (Preferences), 25

IP (Internet Protocol) addresses, 4-5

CHECK OUT THESE BEST-SELLERS

More than 450 titles available at booksellers and online retailers everywhere!

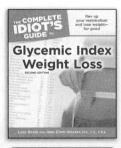
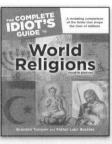

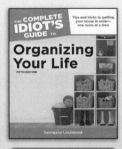

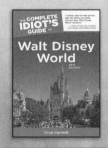

ALPHA

idiotsguides.com

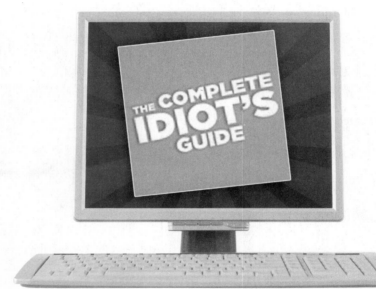